Literary Half-Lives

LITERARY HALF-LIVES

DORIS LESSING, CLANCY SIGAL, AND *ROMAN À CLEF*

Roberta Rubenstein

palgrave
macmillan

LITERARY HALF-LIVES
Copyright © Roberta Rubenstein, 2014.
All rights reserved.

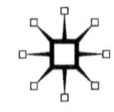

First published in 2014 by
PALGRAVE MACMILLAN®
in the United States—a division of St. Martin's Press LLC,
175 Fifth Avenue, New York, NY 10010.

Where this book is distributed in the UK, Europe and the rest of the world, this is by Palgrave Macmillan, a division of Macmillan Publishers Limited, registered in England, company number 785998, of Houndmills, Basingstoke, Hampshire RG21 6XS.

Palgrave Macmillan is the global academic imprint of the above companies and has companies and representatives throughout the world.

Palgrave® and Macmillan® are registered trademarks in the United States, the United Kingdom, Europe and other countries.

ISBN: 978–1–137–41365–9

Library of Congress Cataloging-in-Publication Data

Rubenstein, Roberta, 1944–
    Literary half-lives : Doris Lessing, Clancy Sigal, and roman à clef / Roberta Rubenstein.
        pages cm.
    Includes bibliographical references.
    ISBN 978–1–137–41365–9 (hardback : alk. paper)
    1. Lessing, Doris, 1919–2013—Criticism and interpretation. 2. Sigal, Clancy—Criticism and interpretation. 3. Romans à clef. I. Title.

PR6023.E833Z86 2014
823'.914—dc23   2013045999

A catalogue record of the book is available from the British Library.

Design by Newgen Knowledge Works (P) Ltd., Chennai, India.

First edition: May 2014

10 9 8 7 6 5 4 3 2 1

For Chuck—
again
and always

Contents

Acknowledgments   ix

Introduction   Where the Story Begins   1
1   Hall of Mirrors   13
2   Truth Values and Mining Claims   53
3   Plays and Power Plays   77
4   Will the Real Saul Green Please Stand Up?   99
5   A Rose by Any Other Name   119
6   Life in the Interior Zone   131
7   Poetic License and Poetic Justice   145
8   Variations on a Theme   165
9   Of Parent and Child   179
Conclusion   His, Hers, Theirs   195

Notes   201
Works Cited   211
Index   221

Acknowledgments

I am grateful to many people who supported me during the writing of this book. First and foremost, I thank—but cannot sufficiently thank—my husband, Charles R. Larson, without whose love, encouragement, patience, good humor, and unstinting support at every step of this project and in every way—including editorial and, not least, gastronomical—I could not have brought the book to fruition.

Without the generous cooperation of Clancy Sigal, this book would not have been possible. I am especially grateful for his permission to quote from unpublished materials in the Clancy Sigal Archive at the Harry Ransom Center, the University of Texas at Austin, and for his answers to questions concerning several details in his archive. Thanks also to Ernest Rodker for permission to quote from unpublished material in the Joan Rodker Archive at the Harry Ransom Center.

Thanks to Brigitte Shull, my editor at Palgrave Macmillan, who was enthusiastic about this project from the beginning and continued to encourage me during its path to publication. I am especially grateful to Alice Ridout, who read the manuscript incisively and with exceptional care under difficult circumstances and whose judicious suggestions have made this a far better book than it otherwise would have been. I thank Paul Schlueter, fellow scholar of Doris Lessing and friend over the years, who has enthusiastically supported my scholarship and who generously provided pertinent materials from his own library for my use. William Roger Lewis, professor of English History and Culture at the University of Texas at Austin, invited me to speak on Doris Lessing's *The Golden Notebook* at the British Colloquium, an occasion that fortuitously opened the door to this project. Thanks to Phyllis Perrakis and Debrah Raschke for their collegial support of the project at an early stage and to Bernth and Judy Lindfors for their hospitality while I was in Austin. Ryan Jenkins, editorial assistant at Palgrave, was unfailingly helpful during the production phase of the manuscript.

Acknowledgments

I am grateful to the Harry Ransom Center, the University of Texas at Austin, for permission to quote from unpublished materials in the archives named above, for supporting my research with a travel stipend, and for offering such a hospitable environment for scholarly pursuits. Richard Oram, head librarian at the Ransom Center, offered wise guidance during my research visits and afterwards; Gabriela Redwine, digital archivist, went beyond the call of duty to enable my access to archival materials; Rick Watson, head of reference services, efficiently managed permission details. Thanks to the College of Arts and Sciences, American University, for supporting my research with a travel grant and other research funds. I acknowledge the *Northwest Review* for permission to quote from Clancy Sigal's story, "Lunch with Rose," and the Estate of Nelson Algren for permission to quote from an unpublished letter from Algren to Clancy Sigal.

INTRODUCTION

WHERE THE STORY BEGINS

"What's true for you isn't necessarily true for me." Doris Lessing
(Walking in the Shade)

As Virginia Woolf famously observed, "Fiction must stick to facts, and the truer the facts the better the fiction—so we are told" (*A Room of One's Own* 16). It is commonplace that writers of fiction draw in myriad ways on the facts of their personal experiences and may at times base their characters to a greater or lesser degree on actual people. However, it is decidedly uncommon—though not unprecedented—for two writers to draw reciprocally on their intimate relationship to create fictionalized or dramatic versions of their overlapping but not identical versions of events and experiences. For four years, beginning in 1957, Doris Lessing, British writer by way of what is now Iran (where she was born), and Zimbabwe (where she grew up), and recipient of the 2007 Nobel Prize for Literature, and Clancy Sigal, American novelist and film-script writer, whose first novel, *Going Away: A Report, a Memoir*, was a finalist for the 1963 National Book Award, were deeply involved in a complex intimate relationship that fundamentally affected both of them and continued to influence their writing, particularly Sigal's, long after their liaison ended. Creating characters in their imaginative writings that are significantly and at times quite transparently based on each other, each writer also drew on events, circumstances, and conversations they had shared to construct imaginative—and differently imagined—versions of their overlapping experiences.

Before the two met in 1957, Clancy Sigal worked in Hollywood, at Columbia Pictures and as a film agent at the Jaffe Agency. When his socialist political affiliations resulted in his blacklisting from Hollywood during the McCarthy era of the 1950s,[1] he left the United States, living for a time in France and then London, where, at the age of 30, he met and began to live with Doris Lessing, then 37. At that time, Lessing was already a successful writer, while Sigal was an aspiring but unpublished writer. With the support of a Houghton Mifflin Fellowship, he struggled—impeded by a writer's block—to complete the manuscript of what began as his first published novel but ultimately became his second, *Going Away: A Report, a Memoir* (1961).[2] Concurrently, Lessing wrote a successfully staged play, *Play with a Tiger* (composed in 1958 but not produced until 1962), and her now-classic novel, *The Golden Notebook* (1962). As I demonstrate in the chapters that follow, both the play and the novel drew directly and often quite transparently on her tempestuous relationship with Clancy Sigal. Over time, Sigal returned the favor, so to speak: characters that closely resemble and at times suggest caricatures of Doris Lessing and Sigal himself appear prominently in his published fiction as well as in a number of unpublished stories, sketches, and plays drafted early in his career.

What makes such transformation of the "raw material" of actual experience into imaginative literature worthy of analysis is that, almost from the beginning of their writing careers, both Lessing and Sigal positioned their writing on the porous boundary between fact and fiction. Moreover, both published not only novels, plays, and short stories, but also autobiographical accounts and memoirs that render more directly the facts of their lives. Up to a certain point in her life, Lessing resisted nonfictional self-revelation by choosing not to collaborate with would-be biographers or to write her autobiography. Ultimately, when she learned that no fewer than five American biographers were working on unauthorized versions of her life, she reversed her position because she wanted to tell her life story her way (Innes, "A Life of Doing it Her Way"). Accordingly, during the 1990s, when she was in her seventies, she published two volumes of autobiography: *Under My Skin* (1994) and *Walking in the Shade* (1997). She chose not to write a third volume because, as she stated in a prefatory note to her novel of the 1960s, *The Sweetest Dream*, she was concerned about "possible hurt to vulnerable people. Which does not mean I have novelised autobiography. There are no parallels here to actual people, except for one, a very minor character." As she elaborated in an interview, "I spent much of the 1960s as a kind of house mother for a lot of deeply troubled teenagers. Now they're all middle-aged, and it wouldn't be fair to expose them" (Interview with Jonah Raskin, June 1999). In 2006, at the age of 80, Clancy Sigal published a memoir of his mother, *A Woman of Uncertain Character: The Amorous and Radical Adventures of My Mother Jennie* (2006) that necessarily depends on details from his own life and observations. At the age of 89, Doris

Lessing published what she called—and what indeed turned out to be—her final book, *Alfred and Emily* (2008), which features two versions of her parents' lives, one based on fact, the other on invention.

Regarding the distinctions between autobiography and literary invention, Lessing stressed on more than one occasion that "there is no doubt fiction makes a better job of the truth" (*Under My Skin* 314). Autobiography, which initially may seem more transparent, poses its own challenges to the truth because, in her judgment, memory is "a careless and lazy organ, not only a self-flattering one" (13). She suggested that, even with the best of intentions to tell the story of one's life without embellishment or distortion, "we make up our pasts." However, in her own case, she qualified that observation with a countervailing one: "[T]here are moments, incidents, real memory, I do trust. This is partly because I spent a good part of my childhood 'fixing' moments in my mind.... Pressure had been put on me to admit that what I knew was true was not so. Why else my preoccupation that went on for years: *this* is the truth, *this* is what happened, hold on to it, don't let them talk you out of it" (*Skin* 13–4, Lessing's italics).

Following the publication of the two volumes of her autobiography, Lessing was reminded by an interviewer, Jonah Raskin, that she had once maintained "the old-fashioned idea that a writer's life is his or her property, until we die," to which she replied,

> There are certain things I don't talk about. I have kept diaries, of course, but they can't be read for quite a long time. What will emerge when people read them? I can't imagine that anything will emerge that can't be deduced from reading any of my books now. This is why I'm always curious about people who are fascinated by writers' lives. It seems to me that we're always in our books, quite nakedly. I wonder, too, does the private life really matter? Who cares what is known about you and what isn't? Even when you make public something that's been private, most people don't get it—not unless they're the same generation and have gone through more or less the same experiences. (*The Progressive*)

Lessing conceded that her imaginative writing contains many autobiographical elements, particularly as reflected in the experiences of her first alter ego, Martha Quest, in the five-volume series, *Children of Violence*. When an interviewer observed that the first volume of the series, *Martha Quest*, had "the shape and feel...of autobiography" and asked her pointedly, "Is there much of you there?" Lessing replied, "Yes, this pugnacious intolerant character, yes absolutely, of course, that's me. But this whole series gets less autobiographical as it goes on.... [H]alfway through the series I wrote *The Golden Notebook*, which completely changed me..." ("Writing as Time Runs Out" 89). Regarding other characters in her novels and short fiction, she acknowledged that "some people I write about come out of my life. Some, well, I don't know where they come from" (interview with Roy Newquist, ed. Schlueter 48) and admitted that she "mined" actual people, relationships, and experiences for her fictional purposes (*Walking in the Shade* 336). Rather surprisingly, given her distaste for readers' fascination with the actual sources of her imaginative writing, in the autobiographical account of her life she readily provides links between specific stories and their autobiographical sources, including real people upon whom she modeled several of her characters. For example, of a visit to Germany with her Czech lover during the early 1950s, she writes, "I went on a trip with Jack to southern Germany. It is recorded in 'The Eye of God in Paradise'" (*Walking* 56). Of one of her friends during the same time period, the actor Miles Malleson, she comments, "I put him in a story called 'The Habit of Loving'" (*Walking* 236).

Yet Lessing seemed to want to have it both ways, for she also reproached her readers for what she regarded as their almost voyeuristic interest in determining the autobiographical sources of her imaginative writing, a curiosity that she found entirely reductive. As she phrased it in the first volume of her autobiography, "Readers like to think that a story is 'true.' 'Is it autobiographical?' is the demand. Partly it is, and partly it is not, comes the author's reply, often enough in an irritated voice, because the question seems irrelevant: what she has tried to do is to take the story out of the personal into the general" (*Skin* 160). However, the "manners and mores of the time" that she includes in *Martha Quest* are "'true', well, more or less—the atmosphere yes, taste and texture and flavour, yes, but sometimes several people have been put together to make one, and of course the story has been tidied up. Every novel is a story, but a life isn't one, more of a sprawl of incidents" (*Skin* 201–2). The third volume of *Children of Violence*, titled *A Ripple from the Storm* (1958) and based on her involvement with Marxism and Communism in southern Africa in 1943–4, is, Lessing indicated, the most "directly autobiographical" of all of her fiction, after which, she claimed, she "left autobiography behind" (*Skin* 267, 298).

Before she did so, however, she wrote *The Golden Notebook*, in which the relationship between fact and fiction is a fundamental concern of the narrative itself. The novel draws significantly and at times quite transparently on Lessing's political, aesthetic, and romantic experiences during the 1950s, including aspects of her long-term intimate relationships with two men, one of whom was Clancy Sigal. Yet she protested rather disingenuously in her autobiography, "[I]f I were to write an obituary about me and *The Golden Notebook* it would consist of me saying very tartly indeed [...] the words written in a balloon over my head: 'Strange as it may seem, I made it up...'" (*Walking* 344, Lessing's ellipses unless bracketed). That her assertion deserves close scrutiny is a central premise of this study.

* * *

Like Doris Lessing, Clancy Sigal, from the beginning of his literary career, drew closely on his own personal experiences and acquaintances for his fiction. Even his first published book, *Weekend in Dinlock*, which one reviewer described as "fictionalized documentary" (Lejeune 45), blends journalistic and imaginative writing, "mining" his conversations and experiences and creating an aesthetic form for his insights concerning a community of Yorkshire miners. Throughout his fiction, transformed versions of actual people—not least, himself—and events appear, sometimes only thinly disguised. His novel, *Zone of the Interior*, which features the character Dr. Willie Last as a clearly recognizable version of the controversial British anti-psychiatrist R. D. Laing, could not be published in England until nearly 30 years after its American publication because of libel concerns.[3] Sigal's literary aim is more often satirical or comedic than is Lessing's; moreover, unlike Lessing, Sigal has not chided his readers for recognizing correspondences between fact and fiction. Indeed, one can imagine his amusement at the traditional publishing disclaimer that appears in the frontispiece of *Zone of the Interior*: "This is fiction, a work of the imagination. Although set in Greater London of the 1960s, all characters and incidents, except for obviously public figures and places, are invented.... *Any similarity to persons living or dead is purely accidental*" (my italics). Similarly, the frontispiece for *The Secret Defector* reads, "This novel is entirely a work of fiction. Though it contains references to historical events, real people, and actual locales, these references are used solely to lend the fiction an appropriate historical context. All other names, characters, and incidents portrayed in this book are fictitious, and *any resemblance to actual persons or events is entirely coincidental*" (my italics).

Concerning such literary disclaimers, Sean Latham observes that "the closer a novel comes to containing some element of historical or biographical truth, the more prominent such disclaimers become, their heightened visibility ironically reassuring the reader that there may indeed be some outrageously scandalous facts for a well-trained social detective to extract" (*Art of Scandal* 70). Or, as William Amos instructively comments, "When an author denies his characters have real-life originals, don't believe him.... Fiction, after all, is licensed lie-telling" (*The Originals* xiii, xviii).

Writing about *romans à clef* and narratives that feature fictionalized versions of actual people and events, Eric Alterman offers the cautionary reminder that readers "should always tread lightly when assigning factual identities to fictional characters, since writers invariably insist that their creations are just that" ("Inspiring Eggheads"). But should one trust the teller or the tale? In an observation that may be applied to several of Lessing's novels as well, David L. Ulin remarks that Sigal's work "has always danced the fine line between memoir and fiction in a uniquely elusive way" ("Reflections in the Fragments").

Leaving aside for a moment the question of *should*, *can* the raw material of a person's life ever be accurately captured in imaginative literature? Strictly speaking, no, since the very act of giving it literary expression and aesthetic form necessarily transforms it into something else—indeed, into fiction (or drama, as the case may be). The novel form called *roman à clef* necessarily pushes the limits of such categories, revealing that the boundary line between fact and fiction is a contested one that has been unstable since the emergence of the novel form in the late seventeenth century. Sean Latham usefully traces the overlapping and intersecting histories of the novel and *roman à clef*, noting that the latter form,

> [f]rom the French for "novel with a key,"... is a reviled and disruptive literary form, thriving as it does on duplicity and an appetite for scandal. Almost always published and marketed as works of pure fiction, such narratives actually encode salacious gossip about a particular clique or coterie. To unlock these delicious secrets, a key is required, one that matches the names of characters to the real-life figures upon whom they are based. (7)

Moreover, *roman à clef* is not simply an "aberration" in the history of the novel. Rather, it is intimately related to the form, having "shadowed the novel from the very moment of its invention and played a crucial role in the new genre's founding attempt to distinguish itself from both romance and history" (Latham 9). Scholars of the history of the novel use terms such as "conditional fictionality" (Genette, cited by Latham 15) and "factual fictions" (Davis, cited by Latham 29) to underscore the fact that, with regard to *roman à clef*, different readers may have different experiences in response to the same novel. While those in possession of the "key" may deduce the actual people who inhabit the pages of the novel in various degrees of fictional disguise, those in ignorance of such information will regard the same characters as purely imaginative creations of the author. Even those who presume to possess the key that unlocks the real-life identities of characters represented as fictitious ones may not be able to establish in the details any clear boundary between fact and invention. *Roman à clef* is distinguished by its narrative "duplicity": "neither quite fiction nor nonfiction, it tests the self-sufficiency of these categories..." (Latham 9). Furthermore, *roman à clef* "occupies an ambiguous critical space by seeming to insist on itself as fiction while encoding scandalous and often disturbing facts about real people and events" (Latham 13).

In this study of *roman à clef* as the form and disguised biography as the method of several imaginative works by Doris Lessing and a number by Clancy Sigal, I focus closely on the ways in which autobiographical and biographical details and events are, one might say, appropriated: transformed—in Sigal's case, repeatedly—for imaginative purposes in the two writers' cross-referenced works, both published and unpublished: Lessing's *Play with a Tiger* and *The Golden Notebook*; Sigal's *Zone of the Interior* and *The Secret Defector*, as well as several of his published stories, a BBC radio play titled "A Visit with Rose," and drafts of unpublished stories, plays, and sketches. I also consider the aesthetic and ethical implications of such repeated literary cross-borrowings in the two writers' works.

Just what is the "truth"—and according to whom? As Lessing has more generally reminded her readers, "What's true for you isn't necessarily true for me" (*Walking* 172). Multiple references to the intersecting "stories" of the intimate liaison between her and Clancy Sigal reveal their volatile relationship, further disclosed in unpolished autobiographical "raw materials," particularly Sigal's journals, which served as a source for not only his own but also Doris Lessing's fictional transformations. Inevitably, despite their four-year intimate relationship and their friendly association for a number of years afterward, Lessing and Sigal necessarily perceived differently both the particulars of their liaison and the "rights" to its transformation into imaginative literature. In addition, each came to regard it even more differently through the filters of time and memory. Initially, emotional injury, injured pride, and defensiveness and, later, greater distance and objectivity altered, if not the basic lineaments, the literary representations of their romantic liaison.

* * *

Doris May Tayler, the older of two children of British parents, Alfred and Emily Maude Tayler, was born in Kermanshah, Persia (then Iran), in 1919. Her father lost a leg as a result of the major shrapnel wounds he sustained during the World War I battle of Passchendaele and later married the nurse he met during the year he spent recovering in a British hospital. According to Lessing, her father went into the fighting "active and optimistic, and came out with what they then called shell shock" ("Impertinent Daughters" 55). She later came to understand that both of her parents were in a state of "breakdown" when she was conceived and born in 1919. Her mother continued to agonize over the choice she had been obliged to make between marriage and career—at the time considered virtually mutually exclusive for a woman—and her father suffered acute physical and emotional distress because of his serious war injury (*Skin* 8). Doris was born while her father was a manager for the Imperial Bank of Persia. When she was five years old and her brother Harry was two-and-a-half, the Tayler family relocated to Southern Rhodesia—then a British colony, now Zimbabwe—where Alfred and Emily anticipated a prosperous life as maize farmers. However, their dream did not materialize. Although Alfred Tayler had always wanted to be a farmer, he was simply not cut out for the task, quite apart from the limits imposed by his physical injury and other health complications that later developed. Unsuccessful at bush farming, he was often in debt, while his wife hated life in the African bush. Doris and her younger brother, Harry—her mother's favorite, Doris knew from a very early age[4]—grew up in the bush. Doris was educated in an all-girls convent school in Salisbury, Rhodesia, from age seven through fourteen, after which she attained no further formal education apart from self-education through voracious reading and a lively curiosity. As she later elaborated,

The school was no good. I read, and when I was interested in something, I followed it up. Whenever I met anyone who knew anything, I would bore them stiff until they told me what they knew. I still have these terrible gaps; things that every child learned at age 14 I have to look up in an encyclopedia.... But I'm glad that I was not educated in literature and history and philosophy, which means that I did not have this Euro-centered thing driven into me, which I think is the single biggest hang-up Europe has got. (Hazleton 26)

At the age of 14, Doris left home to escape from her mother's rigid Victorian childrearing methods and other matters of contention between them. Her first remunerative employment was as what would later be called an au pair. During her adolescent years, she began to write poetry and fiction, even selling two of her stories to "smart magazines in South Africa" (*Skin* 181). When she was 18, she moved to Salisbury, where she worked as a telephone operator. One of her two apprentice novels was what she termed "bad social satire"—"a very mannered artificial book about Salisbury [Southern Rhodesia] social life" ("Writing as Time Runs Out" 86). Soon, caught up in the social whirl of the city and the strong social pressure to pair off and marry young, she married Frank Wisdom, a civil servant, when she was 20; he was ten years her elder.

Looking back at that hasty marriage from a considerably later point in her life, Lessing observed that, although she and Wisdom were "well suited," they were not in love with each other, though "such were the intoxications of the time it was easy to think so" (*Skin* 207, 206). She gave birth to a son and a daughter in fairly close succession but quickly concluded that the provincialism of domestic life would absolutely stifle her. Accordingly, after four years of marriage, she left Wisdom and their toddler children and became deeply involved in the activities and theories of the Left Book Club, a group of idealistic young socialists and intellectuals in Southern Rhodesia. Through the club, she met and later married Gottfried Lessing, a pivotal member of the group and an "enemy alien"—a refugee whose partly Jewish family, originally from Russia, had emigrated to Germany and, on the eve of World War II, to England (*Skin* 293). Doris and Gottfried married less out of love than out of political idealism and convenience. They had a child together but divorced amicably in 1949, after which Doris left Africa for England with her young son, Peter, along with the manuscript for what would become her first published novel, *The Grass Is Singing* (1950).

Although Gottfried Lessing lived briefly in London after the divorce, he returned to East Germany, eventually cutting himself off completely from Doris and Peter Lessing. Doris Lessing speculated that, as he rose in the Communist Party, he feared political repercussions if he maintained contact with them. As a single parent, she supported herself—with difficulty at first—through her writing; she later estimated that it took her ten years from the time she arrived in London to earn as much as an average British worker (*Skin* 409). Encouraged by the publication of *The Grass Is Singing*, she began to write what eventually became the five-volume series, *Children of Violence* (1952–69), for which she drew significantly on her own experiences for its protagonist, Martha Quest. Based on the political nature of her writing, Lessing was declared a Prohibited Alien in Southern Rhodesia and South Africa, a fact of which she was entirely unaware until she was denied entry when she tried to visit Southern Rhodesia in 1956.

By the time Doris Lessing met Clancy Sigal in the spring of 1957, she had had several other romantic liaisons, the most significant of which was a four-year relationship with a communist Czech psychiatrist who had left his wife and family behind in Prague. Lessing regarded him—the man to whom she refers by the pseudonym "Jack"—as "the most serious love in [her] life" (*Walking* 155) and was profoundly distraught when their relationship ended in 1956. She fictionalized aspects of their relationship through the characters Jan Brod and Julia Barr in *Retreat to Innocence* (1956)—a book that she later repudiated as a "shallow novel" and an "opportunity lost" (*Walking* 253)—and through Anna Wulf and Michael in *The Golden Notebook*. By that time, she was also well on her way to a successful and prolific writing career. In the seven years between 1950 and 1957, she published an astonishing eight books: four novels (*The Grass Is Singing*, 1950; *Martha Quest*, 1952; *A Proper Marriage*, 1954; and *Retreat to Innocence*, 1956), three volumes of short fiction (*This Was the Old Chief's Country*, 1951; *Five: Short Novels*, 1953; and *The Habit of Loving*, 1957), and a nonfictional account of her visit to Southern Rhodesia in 1956 (*Going Home*, 1957).

Doris Lessing died on November 17, 2013.

* * *

Clarence Sigal, the illegitimate son of Leo and Jennie Persily, was born in Chicago, Illinois, in 1926. When Leo Sigal emigrated from

Russia at the age of 16, he was "already a weapon-carrying radical" (*A Woman of Uncertain Character* 92). Jennie, along with her parents and nine siblings, made their way—although not all at once—to Ellis Island and settled in New York's Lower East Side, where she grew up. The "bohemian" of the family, she became passionately involved with Leo Sigal, a married man and radical union organizer. She was 31 when she gave birth to the son she named Kalman/Clarence. Following Leo to Chicago, she became a union organizer herself, often towing her young son along with her to raucous union meetings. From his mother, Sigal inherited not only political radicalism and complicated attitudes toward women but a passionate love of cinema. He speculates, only partly in jest, that, even during his early years when he accompanied Jennie at political rallies, he "may have been planning a movie career" because he enjoyed turning those meetings into "Hollywood extravaganzas" (*Woman* 38) in his imagination. As he elaborates, "I was born out of Jennie's movie-loving rib. The closest either of us had to a religious life was a shared, almost insane passion for sprocket-hole fantasies" (146).

Jennie Persily raised her only child in a poor, predominantly Jewish neighborhood on Chicago's west side. Looking back at his childhood, Sigal recalls his father's arrivals and disappearances as a kind of mystery. He was "in and out of our lives when the mood was on him according to cosmic laws of motion I never understood" (37). From the son's point of view, his father "came and left us according to laws of his own nature...vanishing without a word or a note and months later reappearing as if he'd just stepped out for a moment to the corner drugstore..." (84). When Sigal was 13, Leo Sigal disappeared permanently from his life. The son blamed himself for his father's disappearance and eventual abandonment of him, for, in child-logic, "[i]f you have admired your father, then you must see his wisdom in ditching you" (182). During his adolescence, Clancy was regarded as academically slow and was "kicked out of high school" (246). He was sent to another high school that, he learned to his chagrin, was a girls' school, from which he later graduated as the only male student in his class. Afterward he obtained his first paid employment as junior mail clerk and part-time stock-boy in a department store (212). At the latter job, his name changed from Clarence to Clancy as a result of a tongue-twisted supervisor's error (217).

Years after Leo Sigal disappeared, Sigal learned to his profound shock that the reason his father was so irregularly present in his early life was that he was married to another woman, with whom he had two children. In 1962, when Sigal was 36, he tracked his father down in New York City. Despite having been abandoned and later disowned by Leo Sigal, Clancy Sigal generously credits his father with passing along to him a "restless spirit, always finding new horizons as a means of escaping from myself in the service of a greater good" (*Woman* 94).

In 1944, Sigal volunteered for the US army and was inducted into the 4th Infantry Division, serving in Germany until 1946. Following his military service, he returned to the United States to attend college, earning a bachelor's degree in English from UCLA in 1950. After working for a year for the United Auto Workers in Detroit, he worked in Hollywood for four years, first as a story analyst for Columbia Pictures and subsequently as an agent for the Jaffe Film Agency. During that time, he began to write a novel, the partial draft of which garnered him a Houghton Mifflin Fellowship in 1956. By then, and in the spirit of his socialist parents, Sigal had become politically radicalized, having joined several organizations whose socialist orientation eventually led to his blacklisting by a Hollywood studio and his decision to leave the country. He went first to Paris in 1956, relocating to London in the spring of 1957. At that point, the paths of Doris Lessing and Clancy Sigal converged. While living with Lessing, Sigal suffered from physical and emotional illnesses as well as a protracted writer's block, which ended in 1958 with the publication of his first journalistic piece in the *New Statesman and Nation*. Within the next four years, he published a documentary novel, *Weekend in Dinlock* (1961) and a novel whose subtitle strongly signals its position on the boundary between fiction and autobiography. Although it was published in England, *Going Away: A Report, a Memoir* (1962) was the book Sigal began to write before leaving the United States for Paris in the fall of 1956.

Chapter 1

Hall of Mirrors

> "I'm going to London tomorrow." Clancy Sigal ("Going Away" Journal, May 15, 1957)
>
> "An American 'ex-red' comes to London. No money, no friends." Doris Lessing (The Golden Notebook)
>
> "Ex-Hollywood Red. Comes to London. No money, no friends." Clancy Sigal (unpublished writing about Doris Lessing)

Preliminaries

Doris Lessing's *The Golden Notebook* has not traditionally been regarded as a *roman à clef*, in part because it has not been viewed as a "novel with a key." At various points, the narrative draws on transformed autobiographical experiences of its author that are not included in this analysis. To understand the disguised autobiographical aspects of portions of the novel that draw directly and at times quite transparently on the vexed intimate relationship between Lessing and Clancy Sigal, it is useful to know several facts: first, Sigal arrived at Lessing's London flat in May, 1957, penniless and seeking to rent the room that was available in her large two-story flat. Soon afterward, the two became involved in a complex intimate liaison that lasted for four years. By the time their lives converged, both had already adopted the technique of "mining" their actual experiences for their fiction. By 1957, Lessing was well along in her writing career, with four novels, three volumes of short fiction, and a memoir to her credit.[1] Sigal was an aspiring but not yet published writer by that date, although he had drafted enough of a first novel to have received a Houghton Mifflin Fellowship to support its completion. The strongly autobiographical first-person narrative, *Going Away*, completed while he was living with Lessing and published by Houghton Mifflin in 1962, traces the literal and interior journeys of an unnamed narrator, who strongly resembles Sigal himself, as he drives his battered 1940 Pontiac sedan across the country from California to New York. At the end of his sojourn, as he departs on a ship bound for Europe, he wonders whether he can write the book "that was to be the sum and total of all that I knew of myself and the worlds in which I had grown up" (*Going Away* 511).

A significant part of the period during which Doris Lessing composed *The Golden Notebook* coincided with the critical first year of her relationship with Clancy Sigal, who began to live with her in the intimate sense soon after he moved into her flat as a lodger in May 1957. As Lessing acknowledges in her autobiography, she was "deep" in the novel in 1957 and 1958 (*Walking in the Shade* 261); she explained to an interviewer that she wrote the novel in one year, presumably the period straddling 1957–8 ("Breaking down These Forms" 115). Considerably more than traces of Sigal and their complicated relationship made their way into the novel in progress. Of additional significance for the matter of the disguised autobiographical and *roman à clef* elements of Lessing's and Sigal's literary works, both writers kept private journals and diaries. Lessing's diaries are not available for scholarly scrutiny. As she explained, "I have kept diaries, of course, but they can't be read for quite a long time" (Interview with Jonah Raskin). However, her fictionalized persona, Anna Wulf in *The Golden Notebook*, is an inveterate journal-writer who divides her experiences among four color-labeled notebooks. Sigal recorded his thoughts and experiences in handwritten journals, the raw material upon which he initially drew extensively to compose versions of his experiences that were disguised, to a greater or lesser degree, for sketches, stories, plays, and novels, both published and unpublished. His maintenance of a private written record of his personal life is important for understanding two decisive developments that occurred quite early in the relationship between Lessing and Sigal.

Doris Lessing/Anna Wulf—I

The Golden Notebook is structured as a series of repeating segments of four different notebooks plus the singular inner golden notebook. Together, they track and reflect Anna Wulf's cumulative emotional and intellectual self-division: her struggle to examine her aesthetic premises and political disillusionments, to stave off emotional pain, to resist (but also to embrace) psychological breakdown, and to resolve her writer's block. Interspersed between each cycle of notebooks are installments of what Lessing later termed a "conventional novel" titled *Free Women*. As she explained, the "envelope" for the notebooks is "an absolutely whole conventional novel, and the rest of the book is the material that went into making it" ("A Talk with Doris Lessing" 81). Moreover, as first-time readers discover only quite late in the novel, Anna Wulf is the author not only of the notebooks but also of *Free Women*. Aesthetically, the cycles of notebook portions, interrupted by segments of *Free Women*, create the novel's structural organization. The four color-labeled notebooks span the years from 1950 to 1956, with several exceptions that encompass earlier dates. The final three notebook segments in the narrative—concluding installments of the yellow and blue notebooks and a newly introduced golden notebook that appears for the first and only time late in the novel—are undated and focus on events that, as can later be determined by internal evidence, were written by Anna Wulf sometime between September 1956 and the summer of 1957. These three notebook segments, in particular, convey the sense that events are happening virtually as Anna records them; the character named Saul Green, who is first introduced by name in the final segment of the blue notebook, figures centrally in these three notebooks.

The Golden Notebook pivots on a narrative irony: the same Anna Wulf who struggles relentlessly to close the gap between language and experience and who protests that she is unable to write another novel following *Frontiers of War* nonetheless writes—indeed writes compulsively and prolifically—in the notebooks that reflect her emotional and intellectual divisions. The black notebook, which appears first in each repeating sequence, focuses on Anna's career as a writer. It also features extended flashbacks to events of her young adulthood in Southern Rhodesia, the acknowledged raw material that went into her first and only novel. The second notebook in each cycle of the series, the red notebook, focuses on Anna's political life, including her conflicted feelings about joining and later leaving the British Communist Party. At several points, in place of journal entries, the black and red notebooks are "taken over by newspaper cuttings" concerning political events in "Europe, the Soviet Union, China, the United States" (*The Golden Notebook* 492^2). By 1956 and 1957, respectively, Anna ends the black and red notebooks with bracketed statements describing "a double black line across the page, marking the end of the notebook" (492, 497). These marks, which are not visually reproduced in the text, signify, as Lessing explains elsewhere, "the need for drawing lines—*finis*"—demarcations that mark the end point for certain kinds of experiences (*Walking* 338, Lessing's italics). The third notebook in the sequence, the yellow notebook, focuses on Anna Wulf's unsatisfying relationships with men. By projecting her experiences into a thinly fictionalized character named Ella, protagonist of a novel in progress titled *The Shadow of the Third*, Anna examines the dynamics of her intimate experiences, including her emotional, sexual, and intellectual responses. In the fourth notebook in the series, the blue notebook, she records her experiences in diary form, endeavoring to articulate them "truthfully," presumably without embellishment or aesthetic shaping.

The final installment of the yellow notebook consists of 19 brief sketches or synopses, nearly all of which describe seeds for possible stories or short novels that Anna Wulf might write, based on a complex intimate relationship between a man and a woman. In turn, the sketches suggest troubling aspects of the relationship between Doris Lessing and her American lodger and lover, Clancy Sigal, which began and continued while she was composing *The Golden Notebook*. The first sketch describes "A woman, starved for love [who] meets a man rather younger than herself, younger perhaps in emotional experience than in years; or perhaps in the depth of his emotional experience. She deludes herself about the nature of the man; for him another love affair merely" (*GN* 497). Sketch 8 describes a kind of emotional parasitism that infects an independent woman artist—"painter, writer, doesn't matter which"—who lives alone but whose "whole life is oriented around an absent man for whom she is waiting. Her flat too big, for instance." Waiting for this man to arrive, she ceases to paint or write, while continuing to regard herself as an artist. Finally, "a man enters her life, some kind of artist, but one who has not yet crystallised as one." However, the intersection of love and aesthetic creativity proves to be destructive rather than productive for the woman but not for the man: "[h]er personality as 'an artist' goes into his, he feeds off it, works from it, as if she were a dynamo that fed energy into him. Finally he emerges, a real artist fulfilled; the artist in her dead. The moment when she is no longer an artist, he leaves her, he needs the woman who has this quality so that he can create" (*GN* 500). These sketches suggest the ways in which Doris Lessing gave fictional form to her own artistic and emotional anxieties as her complicated relationship with Clancy Sigal unfolded.

One anxiety in particular was triggered by the matter of sexual fidelity, as is expressed by Anna in yellow notebook sketches 6, 7, and 12. The first describes "[a] man and a woman, in a love affair. She, for hunger of love, he for refuge" (*GN* 499). Just before an intimate sexual moment between them, they reach an awkward impasse: the man only desires her when she refuses him. She accuses him of having recently been with another woman. Initially, he admits as much—"How did you know?"—but then denies it, attributing the complaint to her imagination. Eventually, he concedes that her assumption is correct but that he "didn't think it would matter. You have to understand, I don't take it seriously." The sketch concludes, "This last remark makes her feel diminished and destroyed, as if she does not exist as a woman" (500). In a variation of this scene, sketch 12 describes a man who unconsciously wants his unfaithfulness to be discovered as a way to assert his sexual and emotional independence. He needs to be able to say to his wife, "I'm not going to belong to you" (502). Sketch 7 describes a man who "happens to land in the house of a woman whom he likes and whom he needs." Soon he realizes that "his need for temporary refuge has trapped him into what he most dreads: a woman saying, I love you." He terminates the relationship, writing in his diary, "Left London. Anna reproachful. She hated me. Well, so be it. And another entry, months later, which could read either: Anna married, good. Or: Anna committed suicide. Pity, a nice woman" (*GN* 500).

Clancy Sigal/Saul Green—I

In what might initially seem the most transparent of Doris Lessing's fictionalized references to Clancy Sigal in *The Golden Notebook*, sketch 9 in the yellow notebook—Anna Wulf's idea for "a short novel"—begins, "An American 'ex-red' comes to London. No money, no friends. Black-listed in the film and television worlds" (*GN* 501). After seven months in Paris in late 1956 and early 1957, Clancy Sigal—an American "ex-red" who was "black-listed in the film and television worlds" during the McCarthy era—arrived in London in May 1957, at the age of 30 with little money, few friends, and no place to stay. At the time, Doris Lessing's good friend, Joan Rodker—whose name was apparently given to Sigal by political friends—recommended that he contact Lessing, whom Rodker knew had a room to let in her large two-story maisonette on Warwick Street. In her autobiography, Lessing, without identifying Rodker by name, recalls that "[s]omeone had telephoned to say that this American was in town, he needed a place to stay, could I let him a room. I said my career as a landlady had not encouraged me to try again" (*Walking* 167).

According to Clancy Sigal's journal and several thinly fictionalized drafts that focus on the initial encounter and first phase of his relationship with Doris Lessing, they first met on May 19, 1957.

Apparently—and rather surprisingly—Sigal did not record that meeting in his journal, although on his last day in France, several days before that fateful day, he did write, "I'm going to London tomorrow" ("Going Away" Journal, May 15, 1957[3]). At some point, he began to draw on the details of their first encounter for his early and thinly disguised autobiographical accounts of the unfolding of their intimate relationship. Some of that material was incorporated into early unpublished typescripts, most pertinently a 14-page typescript fragment titled "The Sexual History of Jake Blue" and a longer untitled and unfinished multi-chapter typescript that apparently takes up his disguised autobiography where his novel/memoir, *Going Away*, leaves off: Sigal's departure from the United States in the fall of 1956 and his seven months' residence in Paris in 1956–57, including his love affair with a married woman, Riva Boren Lanzmann.[4] The heavily edited "Jake Blue" typescript thinly fictionalizes the single day and evening in May 1957 that initiated Clancy Sigal's relationship with Doris Lessing; two chapters of the longer untitled typescript not only encompass that day but extend into the succeeding days and early months of the relationship. In both versions, Sigal created fictional stand-ins for Lessing (Coral Brand) and himself—Jake Blue and the unnamed narrator of the longer typescript—and lightly disguised a number of details based on their first encounter.

Chapters Four and Five of the untitled longer typescript are headed with the address, "58 Warwick Road"—the actual address of Doris Lessing's London flat—which Sigal apparently later crossed out, inserting in longhand the fictitious surname and address, "Brand, 2 Tregunter Rd."; the chapters are further subdivided with headings of dates during the summer and fall of 1957.[5] The pages contain virtually no editorial corrections except for one especially significant change: the name Doris is deleted throughout, apart from several instances that Sigal apparently overlooked. Over the white-out, Sigal printed in longhand block letters his fictional name for Doris Lessing, Coral Brand; for Lessing's son, Peter, he substituted the name David in longhand throughout ("CS writing about DL," Coral typescript). Portions of these chapters overlap with events recounted in the shorter typescript, "The Sexual History of Jake Blue."

In both typescripts, Sigal, rather than composing overt autobiography or memoir, began to disguise and transform the particulars of his early days with Lessing. The title of the shorter piece, "The Sexual History of Jake Blue," obviously plays directly on the name of Saul Green, a major character in *The Golden Notebook*. Significantly, the shorter typescript opens with Jake Blue's statement, "Now it's my turn" ("The Sexual History of Jake Blue" 1)—Sigal's intention to tell his side of the story of their complicated love affair. The two chapters of the longer Coral typescript seem more polished than the "Jake Blue" piece. In them, Sigal's narrative persona not only describes but also reflects on certain events and ponders behaviors on both his and Lessing's part that decisively shaped the course of their relationship. Though it is not possible to date or establish the sequence of the two overlapping typescripts, one may speculate that "The Sexual History of Jake Blue" and the Coral chapters of the longer lightly disguised autobiographical typescript—both narrated in the first-person point of view—were drafted fairly close in time to each other, either just before or soon after Sigal and Lessing separated early in 1960, with the incomplete "Jake Blue" sketch drafted before the Coral chapters that exist as part of a longer semi-autobiographical manuscript. In both versions, the day of the initial encounter between Sigal and Lessing in May 1957 is recounted in extensive detail.

"The Sexual History of Jake Blue" draws on a number of details from the personal histories of both Clancy Sigal and Doris Lessing. Jake Blue arrives in London following half a year in Paris that included a love affair with a French woman—impaired, he jests, by his admittedly imperfect French. On the very evening of the day he takes the room in Coral Brand's flat, their relationship begins to unfold. He and Coral exchange biographical information, describing their respective Leftist political involvements and Coral's—but, significantly, not Jake's—intimate history. Thinly fictionalizing details from Lessing's life, Sigal describes Coral's youth and early adulthood in Southern Rhodesia. Unlike Lessing's real father, whose serious injury during World War I resulted in the amputation of one of his legs and who later settled in Southern Rhodesia, Coral Brand's father was gassed during the war and later settled in South Africa. Coral married a "Bloomfontein tobacco planter" who enlisted in the Royal Air Force [RAF] soon after she gave birth to their son and who was stationed in Egypt for training ("Jake Blue" 9).

Concerning Lessing's own fictionalization of some of the same details of her young adult life in Southern Rhodesia, Anna Wulf explains in the first (black) notebook of *The Golden Notebook* that she was briefly married to a Southern Rhodesian tobacco farmer named Steven; she left the marriage because she "could never stand the life" (*GN* 65) and became a secretary in Salisbury. In Sigal's rendering, the dissatisfied Coral left her first marriage and began to work in a Johannesburg department store. There, she became involved with its manager, a "German-Jewish refugee, a Communist playwright and friend of Brecht" ("Jake Blue" 9), who not only was married but, as it later emerged, was a spy for British intelligence concerning South Africa. When Otto Vogel's wife discovered his affair with Coral Brand, she filed for divorce; because of Otto's prominence in the community, the legal action led to a high-profile scandal (10). Subsequently, Coral left South Africa for London with the by-then divorced Otto, leaving her young son behind with his father as a condition of their divorce. The relationship soon ended when Otto returned to East Germany. These details conflate and fictionalize details concerning Lessing's two marriages, the latter of which was to Gottfried Lessing, an RAF sergeant of German descent and the father of her third child, who ultimately returned to East Germany, leaving Doris and their son, Peter, behind. In Sigal's "Jake Blue" typescript, Coral became pregnant as a result of a brief relationship with one of Otto's cousins and gave birth to a daughter. By the time Jake Blue meets Coral Brand in London in the spring of 1957, her daughter, Trina—whose name becomes Vera later in the "Jake Blue" typescript—is 11 years old. Coral, by now the veteran of several unhappy love affairs, is legitimately wary of men.

The Coral typescript rendering of the decisive first encounter between Clancy Sigal and Doris Lessing commences just before their actual meeting, when—like Saul Green in *The Golden Notebook*—Sigal's unnamed narrator inquires by phone about Coral's room for rent. The typescript provides the date of the unnamed narrator's first meeting with Doris/Coral as May 19, 1957 (Coral typescript 98). After he agrees to take the room for two pounds ten per week, Coral invites him to stay for dinner. As he elaborates, "she could cook, too" (Coral typescript 99). In both fictionalized versions of the initial encounter, Clancy/Jake and Doris/Coral converse at length, comparing their political histories and experiences in the American and British Left. In the Coral typescript, Coral explains that "she'd left the Party last November [1956] over Hungary" and the narrator responds that he had "gotten out before the Korean War..." (Coral typescript 100).

From dinner and conversation in the kitchen, they move to Coral's "bedroom–living room" for coffee, a cigarette, and further conversation. The narrator notices Coral's desk and typewriter in the corner of the room. He learns that she has a 11-year-old son who is currently away visiting a relative during the school holidays; in the "Jake Blue" version, Coral's 11-year-old child is a daughter who is present in the flat when Jake arrives. In both versions of their first encounter, Coral puts on a Billie Holiday record and they relax to the strains of "Lady Day." At some point during the evening, a kiss initiated by Jake leads to lovemaking. When he worries that Coral's daughter might discover them in bed, Coral reassures him that the creaking sounds he hears overhead are merely those made by her other lodger. The unfinished "Jake Blue" typescript ends without proceeding beyond the first day of the meeting between Jake and Coral.

The longer semi-autobiographical Coral typescript carries the narrative beyond the point where the "Jake Blue" fragment leaves off. In the longer version, the next morning—their first morning together—the unnamed narrator and Coral have breakfast together, enjoying Coral's homemade jams and reading the morning newspapers over coffee as if they'd established the routine long before (Coral typescript 102). The narrator settles into his room on the upper floor of Coral's flat. During his first full day there, he and Coral make love several times (102) and continue to share personal details. At this point in the Coral typescript, Sigal began to depart more freely from Lessing's biography, combining several particulars based on her two actual marriages and inventing others through details that differ from those he uses in the "Jake Blue" variant of their first encounter. For example, in the longer version, Coral is the daughter of white Southern Rhodesian settlers; her mother was a nurse. Coral was briefly married to a homosexual RAF pilot, Phillip, in a "marriage of convenience" (103). Although Lessing's mother was indeed a nurse during the Great War, Doris's first husband, Frank Wisdom, was a civil servant, and her second, Gottfried Lessing, was a sergeant in the British Royal Air Force; neither was gay. However, while married to Gottfried, Doris was, in her own words, "romantically in love with" a Royal Air Force pilot—"as much as I have been with anyone—but I except one or two" (*Under My Skin* 317).

In Sigal's longer fictionalization of Lessing's young adult life before they met, Coral had a baby and moved to London with her husband and young son in 1946—not 1949, the year Lessing actually emigrated from Africa. A month after Coral and her child arrived in London, she and her husband separated (Coral typescript 103). A single mother with no source of income, she obtained a job as an ad-copy writer and began to write a novel, which she successfully placed with a publisher. Subsequently, she wrote "another novel and a collection of short stories," after which she received a "really big literary award for 'Empire' writers" (Coral typescript 104)—a direct allusion to the Somerset Maugham Award that Lessing received in 1954 for *Five: Short Novels*.

"And then," Sigal writes, "she spoke about men" (Coral typescript 104). It quickly becomes apparent to the narrator that Coral's intimate history is complicated. In a statement that appears in virtually the same words in both of Sigal's thinly fictionalized versions of their early encounter, Coral cautions Jake/Sigal's unnamed narrator just before they make love for the first time, "I've been treated badly by men.... I don't want to be treated badly any more. Please treat me decently" ("Jake Blue" 13; Coral typescript 104). By way of explanation, Coral offers the fact that she has "been in love twice. The first time was with a young poet, an RAF boy, in Rhodesia who had drunkenly walked into a propeller one night. He was the hero of her second novel" (Coral typescript 104). The circumstances of the man's horrific death duplicate those that tragically end the life of a character in *The Golden Notebook*: Paul Blankenship, Anna Wulf's RAF pilot friend and—briefly—lover:

> Paul was killed the last day before he left the Colony.... That night he drank himself blind.... He went back to camp as the sun was coming up to say good-bye to his friends there. He was standing on the airstrip..., still half-conscious with alcohol, the rising sun in his eyes.... A plane came in to land, and stopped a few paces away. Paul turned, his eyes dazzling with the sunrise, and walked straight into the propeller.... His legs were cut off just below the crutch and he died at once. (*GN* 73–4)

The similarities between the two versions of the RAF pilot's death suggest that Sigal was not above borrowing for his own fictional purposes a vivid incident from his lover's work in progress. The real-life RAF pilot with whom Lessing was romantically involved for several years during the 1940s, John R. M. Whitehorn, did not die in the horrific manner described in *The Golden Notebook*. In fact, he lived to a ripe old age, dying in May 2003 (Lessing, The Whitehorn Letters, 1944–9).

In Sigal's fictionalized version of events, Coral/Doris's most significant intimate relationship was with a married Czech refugee named Vashes, who "worked for the Czech Embassy until the [Communist] show trials of 1952 and then asked for asylum in Britain.... They had lived together, at first in Joan Rodker, her friend's house and for a while he had had a room in her flat. Then he had returned to his wife" (Coral typescript 104). Of note, Sigal does not alter the actual name of Lessing's (and his) good friend, Joan Rodker, upon whom the character Molly Jacobs in *The Golden Notebook* is modeled. Lessing's Czech lover—whom she identifies in her autobiography with the pseudonym, Jack, and fictionalizes in *The Golden Notebook* as Michael—was, in her own estimation, the most serious love relationship of her life (*Walking* 155). In Sigal's thinly fictionalized version of Lessing's biography, Coral has been "desperately unhappy" since Vashes left her (Coral typescript 104). Though she wishes for a man in her life as much for her young son's sake as for her own, she acknowledges that she's "gotten used to being alone and living on [her] own" and that, no matter how lonely she is, she will not compromise her integrity for a man (104).

Of significance for what was to follow between Clancy Sigal and Doris Lessing, the narrator of the Coral chapters indicates that he does not volunteer comparable details concerning his own intimate history. Rather, changing the subject altogether, he comments that he, like Coral, is also working on a novel, his first. Two other significant details about the unnamed narrator who resembles Sigal soon emerge. The first is that he has been and continues to be suffering from some sort of illness that manifests itself both physically and psychologically. He explains—not to Coral but to his implied reader—that a British doctor has prescribed sleeping pills for him and that he often wakes up in the middle of the night "stifling a scream" (Coral typescript 106-7). He names this and other episodes of night terrors "it" (107). Although he is "dying" to tell Coral about it, he realizes that "under no circumstances should [he] mention [his] affliction" (107) to her. Over the days and nights that follow, his night terrors and anxiety attacks begin to affect their sexual intimacy. Once, as he clings to Coral in terror, holding onto her "for fear of dying" (108), Coral understandably mistakes his intense embrace as an expression of passion. The second crucial detail, mentioned later in the Coral typescript, is that Sigal's American passport will soon expire, a circumstance that produces considerable anxiety in him because of his socialist associations in the United States during the McCarthy period. He is distressed that he cannot renew his passport without signing a loyalty oath, which, on principle, he is unwilling to do (Coral typescript 114). Several pages of Chapter Five of the typescript, set in "late spring, early summer, 1957" (110), focus on Sigal's passport crisis and Coral's efforts to help him resolve it through her personal contact in the British Home Office.

In the same chapter, the Sigal-like narrator gets to know Coral's son, David; he is troubled by the boy's proximity in the flat while he and Coral are engaged in lovemaking. Occasionally during such moments, he thinks about his French lover, Riva Lanzmann, whom he has only recently left and whom he does not mention to Coral. In longhand, Sigal substituted the name Mimi for Riva throughout (Coral typescript 110). When letters from Mimi begin to arrive for the narrator, Coral becomes jealous and closes the door to her bedroom; "a moment later I heard her typewriter going furiously. So I went up to my room and tried to use the typewriter" (112). However, the narrator is seriously stalled in his progress on "The Dealmakers," a thinly disguised reference to the unfinished manuscript, then titled "The Romancers," that had earned Sigal a Houghton Mifflin Fellowship and would eventually be published by Houghton Mifflin as *Going Away: A Report, a Memoir* (1961). Instead, he has written a couple of stories: one about himself and Riva and another about "a Hollywood writer, only English (me), and his wife, Gillian (Doris).... She hates his work and thinks she can do better than he as a writer. They have imprisoned each other. I meant it to be a 'tragi-comic' story but can't figure out the end. A lot of it is based on how Coral talks to me about what is happening to us" (113). Sigal's reference to the correlation between the still-incomplete story and "what is happening" to him and Lessing clearly demonstrates Sigal's disguised-autobiographical method in progress. The narrator of the Coral typescript also mentions looking up a London friend of Mimi's, named Brigitte, to whom he refers as his "girl-friend" (116). That detail exposes an issue that was to become a major irritant in the relationship between Clancy Sigal and Doris Lessing: their different assumptions concerning sexual fidelity.

Concurrently, the narrator's psychological malaise, accompanied by such physical symptoms as "stomach pains, head-aches, nausea, feverishness and 'loss of appetite,'" worsen (Coral typescript 117). It should be noted that, according to his journal entries, before he left the United States for France and before he met Doris Lessing, Clancy Sigal was suffering from symptoms of severe emotional distress. Even living in Paris did not dispel his dark mood. In December of that year, he worried over forgetting significant details such as his mother's first name. He commented in his journal, "Perhaps I'll write a book w/ the subtitle 'The Diary of a Nervous Breakdown'" ("Going Away" Journal, December 1, 1956). By March 1957, his symptoms had become so acute that he sought medical advice. The doctor at the American Hospital in Paris who examined him hinted that he was, in Sigal's words, "just a bit well if not nuts then neuro scared" (March 19, 1957).

Five months after he and Lessing became lovers, Sigal recorded in his journal observations that suggest emotional depression: "the past becomes increasing removed; the present intolerable, something to be gotten in under one's belt, so that it becomes the remote past & can be dealt with; the future non-existent, except as animal fantasy. Here, there is a situation I never thought I could be in: in the midst of a prolonged breakdown of the emotions & intellect, living with a woman & her 11-year-old child for whom I have affection & respect..." ("Going Away" Journal, October 28, 1957). In his fictionalization of these developments, the Sigal-like narrator is finally persuaded by Coral Brand to see a psychotherapist. He meets with several, each of whom offers a different diagnosis and prescribes a different remedy. One therapist diagnoses "acute manic-depression" and proposes electro-shock therapy, which the narrator refuses; another recommends hypnosis (Coral typescript 117, 118).

Doris Lessing/Anna Wulf—II

In *The Golden Notebook*, Anna Wulf, following the end of her five-year affair with her lover, Michael, feels herself on the verge of emotional breakdown. Her attempts to master her inner chaos through language, rather than halting the process of breakdown, only succeed in making her more acutely aware of it. Her private anxieties are compounded and reinforced by her distress concerning political and geopolitical developments and the chaotic state of the world in general. The final installment of the blue notebook begins with her remarking that the upstairs room in her flat is empty and that her daughter, Janet, who represents her "normality" (*GN* 508), will soon depart for boarding school. When her friend Molly informs her of "an American in town looking for a room" (508), Anna protests that she doesn't want to let rooms in her flat any more. She writes, "[Molly] said: 'Have a heart, he's an American lefty, he's got no money, he's been black-listed, and there you are in a flat with all those empty rooms.' I said, 'If he's an American on the loose in Europe, he'll be writing the American epic novel and he'll be in psychoanalysis and he'll have one of those awful American marriages and I'll have to listen to his troubles—I mean problems'" (508). Although Anna's observations seem prophetic—written in hindsight not only by Doris Lessing, of course, but (as is ultimately revealed late in the novel) by Anna Wulf herself—she nonetheless agrees to let the American come to see the available room.

Inauspiciously, even before the prospective renter arrives, tensions develop between them. Saul Green, who is first introduced by name at this point (*GN* 511, 513), phones Anna Wulf to postpone by a day his appointment to see the room because, he explains, he has accepted an invitation from a friend named Jane Bond to show him around Soho.[6] Saul's excuse makes Anna "angry" (*GN* 512) because—prophetically, in terms of later events—she feels that this man whom she has not even met has already lied to her. Her impression gathers greater weight as the narrative develops and Anna increasingly believes that Saul prevaricates, in particular about his involvements with other women. When Anna and Saul meet for the first time, their initial conversation is "jarring, discordant" (*GN* 514). Anna is offended by Saul's transparent and rather crude "sexual inspection" (514) of her, which she later describes as his way of "[undressing her] with his eyes" (520). Later Anna unconsciously mirrors the "sexual inspection" that she had found objectionable when directed toward her. Observing Saul discreetly, she registers that, with "his thumbs hitched through his belt, fingers loose, but pointed as it were to his genitals...the he-man's pose" (517), he seems a caricature of Hollywood film studs.

Soon after Saul arrives, a bracketed sentence in the blue notebook signals a development with decisive emotional and narrative implications for the progress of Anna's incipient emotional breakdown: "[From this point on in the diary, or chronicle, Anna had marked certain points in it with asterisks, and numbered the asterisks]" (515, brackets in original). One may understand this bracketed comment—along with others that appear at various points in Anna's notebooks—as information later inserted by her as the invisible editor of *The Golden Notebook*. Readers are invited to connect the asterisks, so to speak, finding direct correspondences between Anna's sketches for short stories or novels described in the final yellow notebook segment and events detailed in the blue notebook that immediately follows it. Of both aesthetic and psychological significance is the fact that, *before* the character Saul Green enters the narrative, readers encounter the fictional sketches concerning a woman and a man very like Anna Wulf and the not-yet-introduced Saul. Anna remarks on her "awful second sight...a kind of intelligence...that is too much painful to use in ordinary life" (*GN* 535). Even earlier in the narrative, she expresses her capacity for foreknowledge through her alter ego,

Ella, who anticipates "[a] man and a woman.... Both at the end of their tether. Both cracking up because of a deliberate attempt to transcend their own limits. And out of the chaos, a new kind of strength. Ella looks inwards, as into a pool, to find this story imaged; but it remains a series of dry sentences in her mind. She waits,... patiently, for the images to form, to take on life" (*GN* 437). The images of that man and woman indeed "form" in the final installment of the yellow notebook and "take on life" in the blue notebook that immediately follows it.

Doris Lessing insisted that she composed *The Golden Notebook* in precisely the chronologically scrambled order in which readers progress through its pages. As she explained in the 1971 introduction to the novel, "keeping the plan of it in my head I wrote it from start to end, consecutively, and it was difficult...[in part] because of what I was learning as I wrote" (*GN* xvi). Since written narratives are necessarily linear for readers, they are limited in the ways they can represent simultaneous events, a fact that is repeatedly tested in the final segments of *The Golden Notebook*. Even before Saul Green is introduced by name late in the novel, readers encounter Anna Wulf's fictional sketches based on her complicated emotional and imaginative responses to either a man very like him or the man who is later revealed to be him. Structurally, these sketches may be understood as foreshadowing: the yellow notebook sketches, which both anticipate and dovetail with characters and events that unfold in the blue notebook segment that follows, are explicitly linked through corresponding numbers and asterisks. One may interpret this purposeful cross-referencing and foreshadowing in several ways that confound traditional narrative chronology: either Anna Wulf uncannily foresees an intimate liaison that will unfold between herself and a man before he actually enters her life; *or* she attempts to distance herself from a relationship that has already begun to consume her emotionally by fictionalizing its destructive dynamics; *or* both. In the last interpretation, one may imagine Anna writing in her yellow and blue notebooks *concurrently*—even though readers necessarily encounter them sequentially—simultaneously narrating from different aesthetic distances and narrative perspectives as she gives both fictional and "factual" form to her developing relationship with Saul Green. Compounding the effect of fluid narrative boundaries in *The Golden Notebook*, the character Saul Green, one of Doris Lessing's most complex literary characters, may thus be understood as existing in the same "reality" as Anna Wulf, as her artistic creation, or both.

Several sketches in Anna's yellow notebook express her ambivalence about the man with whom she falls in love—or will fall in love—despite herself. Sketch 5 focuses on a woman like Anna "who has fallen in love, against her will. She is happy" until the tenor of her intimate encounter with the man shifts from affection to anxiety and fear (*GN* 499). Similarly, the initial phase of the relationship between Anna and Saul, as traced in the blue notebook, oscillates between pleasure and fear. At first, Anna is "so happy, so happy" (*GN* 525), but her mood quickly gives way to anxiety when she deduces that Saul has been "sleeping with another woman" (526). He dismisses her suspicion, even while acknowledging its truth, in his casual response, "it doesn't mean anything, does it?"(526; see also sketch 6, *GN* 499–500). As the lovers become more deeply involved, their clashing expectations concerning emotional and sexual fidelity prompt each to attack the other for "making use" of her/him (527–8). Anna's anxieties are exacerbated by jealousy, an element of their relationship that directly mirrors the relationship between Doris Lessing and Clancy Sigal. Each time Saul leaves the flat, Anna is certain that he has an assignation with Jane Bond or some other woman and is repelled by the fact, as she sees it, that he can make love to her after having just been intimate with another woman.

A noteworthy example of the mirroring of themes and events that is a central literary technique of *The Golden Notebook* as a whole is Anna Wulf's own occasional engagement in a variation of the promiscuous sexual behavior that so distresses her when engaged in by Saul Green and other men she knows. Early in the black notebook, Anna revisits the autobiographical "material" (143) that went into her first novel, *Frontiers of War*. One incident is her sexual indiscretion at Mashopi following the crisis that results in the firing of the Boothbys' black cook, Jackson. Anna, who is not in love with her husband, Willi Rodde, spends the night outdoors with Paul Blankenship, the RAF pilot with whom she is in love. When she returns home at dawn, Willi, who quickly grasps what has taken place, pulls her into bed. Anna recalls "lying there and hating him and wondering why the only time I could remember him making love to me with any conviction was when he knew I had just made love to someone else" (141).

Later in *The Golden Notebook* the gender roles are reversed, with Saul cast as the promiscuous lover and Anna as his jealous partner. That circumstance prompts one of the most decisive narrative and psychological developments in this portion of the narrative. Anna, unpersuaded by Saul's repeated denials that he has recently been with another woman, goes to his room while he is away from the flat, in search of incriminating evidence of his philandering. First, she finds and skims his personal correspondence, which consists of letters from women with whom he was involved before he came to London. She defends her invasion of her lodger/lover's privacy "thinking, without any shock at myself, but as if it were my right, because he lied, that this was the first time in my life I had read another person's letters or private papers. I was angry and sick but very methodical" (*GN* 534). Then, discovering "stacks of diaries," she unashamedly begins to read them. Her first surprised discovery is that Saul's journals run chronologically, "not all split up" like her own (534). She struggles to reconcile her impressions of the Saul Green she thought she knew with the "totally self-pitying, cold, calculating, emotionless" man who inhabits the pages of his journal. What is absent from his writing about himself is "vitality, life, charm" (534). She acknowledges that this may be a product of the diary form itself. As she observes about her own private writing, "something strange happens when one writes about oneself. That is, one's self direct, not one's self projected. The result is cold, pitiless, judging" (534). Though Anna recognizes from her own efforts in the blue notebook that diaries are inherently unreliable, she nonetheless finds enough damning information in Saul's journals to influence her understanding of him.

Anna is curious to know what Saul has written not only about his involvements with other women but about her. She is particularly stung to discover the comment in his journal, "Anna doesn't attract me.... Funny thing, I like Anna better than anyone, but I don't enjoy sleeping with her. Perhaps time to move on?" (*GN* 535) An entry in Clancy Sigal's actual journal, written two months after he and Lessing began to live together, includes the similar observation, "I like her but I am not crazy to sleep w/ her. I like sleeping w/ other women but I don't like them out of bed ½ as much as Doris. Dilemma. I don't wish to hurt Doris. But I don't equally wish to strangle myself" ("Going Away" Journal, July 11, 1957). In *The Golden Notebook*, Anna is deeply injured by the observation—not intended for her eyes—that Saul does not enjoy making love to her. In her words, his candid comment "cut me so deep I couldn't breathe for a few moments. Worse, I didn't understand it" (*GN* 536). The revelation challenges what she has regarded as her most authentic emotional response to a man during lovemaking, the part of herself that she believes "can't be lied to" (536).

Earlier in the novel, in her examination of the phases of her by-then-ended relationship with Michael, Anna describes her responses during lovemaking more explicitly in terms of the connection between the psychological and physiological dimensions of sex. She asserts not only that "sex is essentially emotional for women" (*GN* 200) but also that "there is only one real female orgasm and that is when a man, from the whole of his need and desire, takes a woman and wants all her response. Everything else is a substitute and a fake..." (*GN* 202). In her later shocked reaction to Saul Green's journal entry that he does not enjoy making love to her, readers may recognize the echo of her romanticized view of female sexual response. Anna's sense of injury over this point is further cross-referenced with sketches 15 and 17 in the yellow notebook. Sketch 15 concerns "an American man, English woman" whose "attitudes," including their intimate expectations, clash; each expects to be "possessed and taken" by the other, a circumstance that results in "emotional deadlock" (504). Sketch 17 briefly describes the "ironical concourse" of "two rakes" whose emotional and sexual needs clash, leading each to seek casual sexual involvements with other partners. However, this solution is asymmetrical, stimulating the man's desire for the woman while it "freezes" her desire for him (504).

The matter of sexual fidelity is a persistent bone of contention between Anna Wulf and Saul Green, as it was between Doris Lessing and Clancy Sigal. Saul states matter-of-factly to Anna, "The trouble is, when we took each other on, you took fidelity for granted and I didn't. I've never been faithful to anyone. It didn't arise" (*GN* 538). In a journal entry written early in his relationship with Lessing, Sigal wrote, "<u>I like being here for the most part, & yet the concept of fidelity, about which she is so firm, is foreign to me.... Living w/ a woman who is good to me makes me feel married when I'm w/ another woman</u>" ("Going Away" Journal, July 11, 1957; Sigal's underscoring in pencil). In the novel, Anna, driven by jealousy, distrust, and curiosity, returns to Saul's room when he is away—not once but repeatedly—to peek into his journals, compelled to know not only what he is up to when he is not with her but also what he privately writes about her. At one point, she reads "with cold triumph" his comment, "Anna's jealousy is driving me mad" (*GN* 539). The statement closely echoes one of Sigal's actual journal comments, "Doris' jealousy drives me round the bend & will kill us yet. A postcard from France, a phone call from a girl, & she retreats into a frigid politeness which I'd better learn to ignore" ("Going Away" Journal, September 6, 1957).

If Clancy Sigal's semi-autobiographical fictions can be trusted on this point, Doris Lessing never admitted that she was secretly reading his journal; by contrast, in *The Golden Notebook*, Anna Wulf eventually admits outright to Saul Green the source of her certainty about his sexual dalliances: "I read your diary" (*GN* 542). Saul objects to her jealous and intrusive "spying" on him, insisting, "I haven't touched a woman since I've been here and for a red-blooded American boy like me, that's something" (*GN* 542). Applying her own armchair psychology, Anna accuses Saul of projecting onto her his unresolved feelings about his emotionally dominating mother, a central feature of which is his need to dissemble to Anna. The quarrels between them typically stimulate love-making. As they repeatedly enact the neurotic "cycle of bullying and tenderness" (*GN* 543) in which they are enmeshed, Anna concludes that they are trapped "inside a cocoon of madness" (544). When she reads Saul's diary, she learns that he feels similarly trapped. His entry for that day reads, "Am a prisoner. Am slowly going mad with frustration" (549). The core of Anna's own anxiety is her realization that "this man was repeating over and over again a pattern to which she is disturbingly vulnerable: courting a woman with his intelligence and sympathy, claiming her emotionally; then, when she began to claim in return, running away" (549). The reflection dovetails with several of Anna's sketches in the yellow notebook (sketches 15, 16, and 17, *GN* 504).

In the most fundamental recurring pattern of the "sado-masochistic cycle" (566) in which she and Saul are neurotically entangled, Anna continues to accuse her lover of infidelity and he continues to deny it. However, Saul finally breaks the cycle by moving in a new direction. He challenges Anna, "Instead of making a record of my sins in your diary, why don't you write another novel?" (565). Anna admits—not only to Saul but, for the first time, to herself—that what prevents her from doing so is a "writer's block" (565). Saul is surprised because he regards Anna, the author of a published novel, as a successful writer. Indeed, he envies her artistic superiority, admitting that he much prefers the patriarchal social arrangement in which "women are second-class citizens" (565). But of course this observation, like all of Saul Green's pronouncements, is necessarily rendered through Anna Wulf's/Doris Lessing's perception of men's fear of emotionally and sexually "free women."

Clancy Sigal/Saul Green—II

In the fall of 1957, Clancy Sigal described in his journal his dilemma regarding fidelity. As he expressed it, "How do I keep Doris happy & secure and still have other women. A problem. I guess I stop sleeping w/ other women, which more or less I've done. It will probably kill me" ("Going Away" Journal, October 16, 1957). Though the colloquial use of the verb, "kill," which appears more than once in Sigal's journal entries during this period, would not be remarkable in private jottings of the time, the intense tone of the comments hints at the heightened tensions and points of emotional conflict that Sigal registered early in his relationship with Lessing. This entry was likely written during the same month in which he recorded his discovery that Lessing was secretly reading his journal. The first documentation of that fact appears next to the journal entry dated October 30, 1957. At some point, Sigal appended in the left margin next to that journal the undated comment, "I know by now that she is reading this diary." The note, like a number of other brief marginal notes and occasional pencil underscorings throughout Sigal's journal entries that appear to have been added later, may have been noted as he prepared to transform this discovery and other aspects of his relationship with Lessing for his own fiction, including the thinly disguised "Jake Blue" and Coral typescripts. Describing the evidence of Lessing's snooping into his private writing, the narrator of his thinly fictionalized Coral typescript writes, "I found this out by accident one day, after I left the house for an afternoon walk and carelessly left my notebook on the small sewing machine table I used for a desk. Nobody was in the house but Coral. When I returned I saw that it had been opened because a bottle of ink I had left standing on it was now on the window sill. I didn't know how long her snooping had been going on..." (Coral typescript 119).

Though troubled by Lessing's secret intrusions into his private diary, Sigal decided to turn the development into an opportunity to "talk" to her, expressing feelings that he was unable to communicate to her directly. As he wrote, the narrator of the Coral typescript "enthusiastically fell into the next phase of [their] relationship": "In the old days (as I was beginning to think of them) I had spoken to myself in the journal. Now I was 'eating for two', as pregnant women say. I repeated in my own words our situation, with some special pleading, from the point of view of a man entering insanity" (Coral typescript 119). The unnamed autobiographical narrator explains at length his daily activities and other subjects, including his "views on sex," but "all with a slightly fictional 'twist' now that I fi someone reading me." Moreover, "The person I now was in my journal had shifted over several degrees. I was now more aggressive, probing and—now that I was sure I had an audience—demanding.... The style in which I now wrote my journal was livelier, more animated. One had to please as well as instruct" (119). Sigal was correct that Doris/Coral's "all-consuming curiosity" would insure her continuing unacknowledged sorties into his journal (119). Apparently beginning sometime after October 30, 1957, his private journal evolved into an intentionally shaped record intended not simply for himself but for one particular reader. As he phrased it, "All through the passportless, illegal autumn I wrote to Doris in my diary in the guise of private thoughts, long impassioned 'letters' denying, pleading, explaining, protesting—above everything else, swearing I was not making love to anyone else" ("CS writing about DL" 124).

Several days later, Sigal noted in his journal that his former French girlfriend, Riva Lanzmann, had come to London and, while there, had suffered a miscarriage. In the left margin of the page, he jotted, "Riva—Doris still reading this [journal]" ("Going Away" Journal, November 3, 1957). There is no way to establish the period of time that elapsed between the journal entries themselves and the added marginal notes; however, one can read the entry for November 11, 1957 with reasonable certainty that Sigal was writing self-consciously, and at times self-servingly, for Lessing's eyes: "My feeling now is that I was an utter fool to jeopardize my relationship w/ Doris, but it may turn out to be a good thing.... I've really spent a disproportionate amount of time running down stairs away from hungry women in this town. If only Doris knew how I've trained myself to say no. But what I can I do? There are periods in my life when every dame I meet seems to want to lay hands on me" ("Going Away" Journal, November 11, 1957). Whatever his actual activities were, Sigal's words suggest that he was playing to and attempting to placate his jealous audience of one.

While one must be especially cautious in extracting any "true" version of the relationship between Clancy Sigal and Doris Lessing from the hall of mirrors that reflects their multiple fictional personas, sketch 14 in the final yellow notebook segment of *The Golden Notebook* stands as a vivid and—in view of the autobiographical evidence—particularly noteworthy example of the fuzzy borderline between fact and fiction. Does art imitate life or is it the reverse? The sketch describes two lovers who mutually pry into each other's private diaries. Anna imagines

A man and a woman, married or in a long relationship, secretly read each other's diaries in which (and it is a point of honour with them both) their thoughts about each other are recorded with the utmost frankness. Both know that the other is reading what he/she writes, but for a while objectivity is maintained. Then, slowly, they begin writing falsely, first unconsciously; then consciously, so as to influence the other. The position is reached where each keeps two diaries, one for private use, and locked up; and the second for the other to read. Then one of them makes a slip of the tongue, or a mistake, and the other accuses him/her of having found the secret diary. A terrible quarrel... drives them apart forever, not because of the original diaries—"but we both knew we were reading *those* diaries, that doesn't count, how can you be so dishonest as to read my private diary!" (*GN* 503, italics and exclamation point in original)

This sketch has an interesting, albeit coincidental, parallel in an unexpected place. More than four decades after *The Golden Notebook* was published, Doris Lessing wrote the foreword to a new translation of Sofia Tolstoy's diaries. In it, she mentions that both Sofia and Leo Tolstoy not only kept diaries but that, "When [they] were first married, they read each other's diaries, as a part of their plan to preserve perfect intimacy between them, but later they might easily create two diaries, one for the other to read, one to remain private" (Foreword, *The Diaries of Sofia Tolstoy* vii). Readers of Sofia's diaries learn that, during the first year of the Tolstoys' marriage and diary-sharing, Leo used the diaries as a form of communication with his young wife. On one occasion, he penned an entry in Sofia's diary in which he begged her forgiveness for his recent irritability (*Diaries* 17). Twenty-seven years into the marriage, with the mutual diary-writing process still quite active, Sofia, puzzled because Leo had "broken off all [intimate] relations" with her, secretly searched his diary for an explanation of his change of feelings. In her own diary, she wrote, "I secretly read his diaries...in the hope of discovering how I could help him, and myself, understand how we might be reunited. But these diaries have reduced me to even greater despair; and he must have discovered I was reading them, for he has started hiding them away. He hasn't mentioned it though" (*Diaries* 75). Nor does Lessing mention the eavesdropping detail in her own Foreword to Sofia Tolstoy's diaries. What interesting parallels she might have drawn had she been disposed to do so.

According to sketch 14 in *The Golden Notebook* (quoted above), Lessing knew that Sigal knew she was reading his journal and that he was tailoring his entries for her eyes. One must wonder: did she read his revealing marginal notes as well or did Sigal add them only after he had removed his journals from her further inspection—by which time both writers had already begun to fictionalize aspects of their relationship for their respective literary purposes? Sigal subsequently described several different versions of his new strategy of communicating with Lessing through his journal. By that time, he had grasped two benefits that followed from Lessing's eavesdropping: not only the calculated opportunity to "talk" to his lover through his private journal but a development with literary benefits for himself as well.

Beginning with Chapter Five of his Coral typescript, Sigal no longer replaced Doris's name. Moreover, the typescript contains an increasing degree of authorial analysis and self-reflection on the part of its autobiographical narrator. In one draft version, he writes,

> Psychologically, I was prying apart a mental log-jam, constructing what I hoped would be a more serviceable "other" me.... The new me as journal keeper was a combination of the actual human being I was myself and including me as I would like to be (and thought I was), the Jed of my manuscript, the unfaithful and neurotic American Doris constantly talked about, and a kind of omnipotent politician of love and life who knew for a fact that it would all turn out for the best in the end.
>
> I was preparing myself for my second book. ("CS writing about DL" 122)

The most telling version of this shift in strategy and purpose appears in a variant of the passage just cited, in which Sigal directly acknowledges the value for his own writing of his discovery of Lessing's secret prying: "I assumed she somehow did her work in her imagination, on another planet, or from historical researches in the library. *It simply never occurred to me at first that she worked directly from her own experience, as I was to do later*" ("CS writing about DL," 123, my italics). The observation is revealing but also somewhat puzzling since, with his draft of *Going Away*—the novel/memoir he had begun before he and Lessing met—Sigal had, not "later" but already, begun to "[work] directly from [his] own experience." One may speculate that his discovery of Lessing's literary technique reinforced his own fledgling writing strategy, in effect authorizing his method—like hers—of appropriating and sometimes only lightly fictionalizing autobiographical details for literary purposes.[7] Indeed, "working directly from experience" has remained the signature aspect of his fictional method throughout his literary career.

In the continuation beyond Chapter Five of his early autobiographical typescript, in which Doris Lessing's name is not replaced, Sigal elaborates further on the cat-and-mouse game he enjoyed playing with his lover by way of his journal:

> Once I had unconsciously established the woman's interest in me it became child's play to set up the system of one-way communication.... I put the journal far back inside a drawer in the bureau, and shut it and tied a tiny silken thread between the right-hand knob of the second drawer and left-hand knob of the fourth (or first and third, just to change locations) to ensure detection. My "radar" warning system told me Doris scanned my journal, every day I was not home, from sometime in September of 1957 until the spring of 1958, when I summarily removed the journal to the safekeeping of my locked suitcase on publication of my first article in England. ("CS writing about DL" 123; Sigal's strikethrough)

As suggested by the multiple fictional permutations of this critical development in their relationship, Sigal apparently varied his detective strategy for verifying Lessing's unacknowledged perusal of his journal entries—or, equally plausibly, varied his fictionalization of it—virtually mythologizing the original, apparently "true," event. The later iterations increasingly highlight Sigal's ambivalent view of his writing as raw material for Lessing's: "She sneaked up to my room, when I was at the store or in the bathroom, and went through its [his journal] pages. I placed a tiny piece of thread on the first page of the diary. It was never there when I got back. *She was transferring my pages to her pages*" (undated typed fragment p. 10, my italics). In what is probably a somewhat later fictionalized iteration, he commented, "She never let on she was reading my journal.... I never, not once, asked her to cease poring over my journal—I was genuinely getting interested in her work methods—which I now used almost exclusively to supply data for her novel" ("How to live with a Lady Writer" 11–12).

In the curious life/art exchanges that transpired between Clancy Sigal and Doris Lessing while they lived together during the period that overlapped with Lessing's composition of *The Golden Notebook*, another event occurred concurrently that was considerably more unsettling for Sigal. He learned that Lessing, in addition to secretly reading his private journal, was modeling a major character in her novel in progress on him, drawing quite transparently not only on characteristics of his behavior and personality but also on details of their intimate relationship. In late October 1957, Sigal first describes with shock and surprise his discovery of what might be regarded as a kind of literary identity theft:

> Yesterday... I came back & in the kitchen found (was it out there for me to see?) Doris' notebook and a typescript "profile" of Clancy.... I read only the 1st few lines, by reflex, & left off. It gives me the dam creeps, knowing she is keeping this mucking dossier on me.... I think what hurts is that she should peg me so definitely as a nut. I am rather ashamed of this and sorry I ever began leveling with her. She demands the truth & when she gets it becomes so hurt that she must call it a lie. ("Going Away" Journal, October 30, 1957, Sigal's added underscoring)

In the margin next to this entry written in ink, he apparently later wrote in pencil, "I find Doris's ms." In a case of art imitating life imitating art—with no clear chronology—Sigal's own thinly fictionalized iterations of that discovery contain sentences and phrases that are virtually identical to language in *The Golden Notebook*. Who borrowed from whom? In Sigal's version, and from his point of view, the damning evidence, visibly displayed on a page in Lessing's typewriter on the kitchen table, is headed, "The case of C...S" ("CS writing about DL" 124, Sigal's ellipsis). It continues,

> "Ex-Hollywood Red. Comes to London. No money, no friends. A wandering man, happens to land in the house of a woman whom he likes and whom he needs. He is a man with a long experience of women needing love. He makes love to her, but realizes that his need for temporary refuge has trapped him. Aggressive; hostile to women...." And then followed a curious, pithy short story or rather an outline for a short story.
> [...] I went up to my room in a state of shock. (124, Sigal's ellipses unless bracketed)

In *The Golden Notebook*, Anna Wulf's sketch 9 begins, "An American 'ex-red' comes to London. No money, no friends. Black-listed in the film and television worlds" (*GN* 501) and proceeds to describe a series of events that may or may not correspond with the actual circumstances of Clancy Sigal's radical political life, including ostracism by the black-listed man's political peers. The sketch concludes with the man's suicide. Of note, the "theme" of suicide appears at several other points in *The Golden Notebook*, most explicitly in Molly's son Tommy's unsuccessful attempt to end his life by shooting himself.

Additionally, in the first segment of the yellow notebook, Anna describes the novel-in-progress of her alter ego, Ella—*The Shadow of the Third*—which focuses on "[t]he death of a young man who had not known he was going to commit suicide until the moment of death, when he understood that he had in fact been preparing for it...for months" (*GN* 162). Anna wonders whether she has "made a secret decision to commit suicide that [she knows] nothing about? (But she did not believe this to be true)" (163).

A sketch in the final segment of the yellow notebook returns to the subject of suicide, imagining it as one possible outcome for Anna Wulf herself. Sketch 7, which also suggests several psychological and emotional parallels between Clancy Sigal and Saul Green, reads in its entirety,

> *A wandering man happens to land in the house of a woman whom he likes and whom he needs. He is a man, with a long experience of women needing love.* Usually he limits himself. But this time, the words he uses, the emotions he allows himself, are ambiguous, because he needs her kindness for a time. *He makes love to her,* but for him the sex is no worse or better than what he has experienced a hundred times before. He *realizes that his need for temporary refuge has trapped him* into what he most dreads: a woman saying, I love you. He cuts it. Says good-bye, formally, on the level of a friendship ending. Goes. Writes in his diary: Left London. Anna reproachful. She hated me. Well, so be it. And another entry, months later, which could read either: Anna married, good. Or: Anna committed suicide. Pity, a nice woman. (*GN* 500; words and phrases that are identical to those in Sigal's "CS writing about DL" 124, qtd. above, are italicized)

There is no way to establish which of these overlapping passages came first. One may speculate that its first author was Doris Lessing, via Anna Wulf, and that Clancy Sigal borrowed it for his own writing as evidence of Lessing's overzealous appropriation of details concerning his character and personality. Less critically, he later wrote that he found it exciting "to know I was even halfway involved in the creation of something when I was so badly blocked. Nothing surprised me more than to realize years later that [Doris] too had been 'blocked'" ("CS writing about DL" fragment beginning "The widespread purge of dissidents..." 15). On this point, Lessing insisted that she did not suffer from a writer's block; rather, she claimed that she was curious about the sources of such a condition. In a 1994 interview, Francois-Olivier Rousseau asked her whether Anna Wulf's writer's block reflected her creator's experience. Lessing replied, "No, but the idea seemed interesting to me. For a time I was analyzed by a psychoanalyst specializing in artists suffering from 'blocks.' She would have loved to see me 'blocked.' I always disappointed her about it. What I wanted to discover was the origin of this blockage" ("The Habit of Observing," February 1985, 149). One case study that she had ample opportunity to observe, closely and at firsthand, was the writer's block suffered by her intimate companion, Clancy Sigal.

Doris Lessing's unauthorized literary appropriations ultimately benefited both writers: she moved forward on her composition of *The Golden Notebook*, drafting some of her most intense and psychologically probing explorations of a multifaceted intimate relationship between a man and a woman, while Sigal, initially shocked, soon felt unexpectedly released by his discovery of Lessing's writing about him. He began to write extensively in his journal, leaving it around by design when he was not in the flat, and to draft his own fictional transformations of their relationship. In a later iteration of the discovery that initially unnerved but ultimately released him from his writer's block, Sigal further burnished the details for humorous effect, writing that Lessing "[left] chapters of what later became *The Golden Notebook* around the house for me to stumble on, read and dash upstairs to scribble responses in my journal which she'd then creep up to examine (I always knew when, because the thin black thread I tied between my bureau drawers would be broken) and translate, sometimes verbatim, to her novel, which I'd then discreetly read as the manuscript gathered height next to her typewriter and rush upstairs to..." (fragment beginning, "The widespread purge of dissidents..." 6, ellipsis in original).

Clancy Sigal's fictionalizations of the literary equivalent of the "primal scenes" in his relationship with Doris Lessing suggest that he came to enjoy his role as a collaborator for the portion of *The Golden Notebook* in which the invented Saul Green figures so centrally. Perhaps he wished Lessing had given him credit for his role not only as lodger and lover but as in-house editor in the development of the central male character in the last 100 pages of the novel. In effect, Lessing *did* give Sigal credit, albeit slyly and in a kind of literary code: the sentence that, late in the novel, Saul Green gives Anna Wulf as the opening sentence for her novel became the first sentence of *The Golden Notebook*.

In one of the most provocative reflections in the infinite regress of mirror images that extends between the lives and fictions of

Clancy Sigal and Doris Lessing, Sigal virtually took another page out of Lessing's book—or was it the other way around?—recording in his journal the synopsis for a story or short novel that would pivot on the same kind of symbiotic and emotionally sadomasochistic relationship that Anna Wulf repeatedly sketches in the final segment of the yellow notebook:

> Two writers, male & female, create character in b[rea]kfast table disputes, a character based almost totally on her fears, desires & compulsions. The male writer (starved for characters) then goes off & does his novel or screenplay using this imaginary protagonist (imaginary to all but the wife) which comes off so real that the wife becomes more convinced than ever that she is right. This has been so successful [that] husband realizes that wife is an unconscious gold mine of characters. By placing subtle psychological clues around the house, he "clues" her off every time he needs a new one. She responds unfailingly because of kaleidoscopic vulnerabilities. (1958 Journal, March 3, 1958)

At this point, Sigal does not yet see how the story might end. He continues to develop the sketch to the surprising moment when the male character realizes that the tables have entirely turned and that

> the wholly unrecognizable, horrid person wife is "making up" from the clues is really him.... [He realizes] that he has fallen into his own trap, that the wife[,] whom he had turned into a literary machine, has found him out. He is shattered, possibly also realizes this is what he wanted all the time. He commits suicide. She smiles. For she had intended it; she had devilishly trumped his ace by, a long time ago, maneuvering him into a position where he wouldn't leave her because she was his literary factory & when she tired of him, she destroyed him. A Gothic tale of, or for, our time. (March 3, 1958; Sigal's underscoring)

Indeed, the sketch captures what had by then deteriorated into a neurotic dynamic between lovers who need each other emotionally even as they feed on and compete with each other artistically. Sigal, clearly writing for Lessing's eyes—even as he imagines the fictional possibilities of their increasingly fraught relationship—complains in his journal that Lessing "has become so hardened & rigid in her fears, in her own conviction of Clancy as monster rake, that she is well past the boundary of rational analysis." Moreover, he is determined not to let her call the shots; he also sees in their confrontations interesting seeds for his own fiction. He advises himself, perhaps for Lessing's edification,

I will try to handle this w/ humor.... (*Could short story be used centrally in short novel about England, made comic?*) I think at this point I should go out & do exactly what she says I've been doing these past months. No, that is silly.... This is ludicrous, not going out to lunch w/ women because Doris likes to twist a knife in her own heart.... For all I know this may be an unconscious attempt on her part to drive me—by now, something of a neurotic bore—out of the house. (*Another idea for story.*) (1958 Journal, March 3, 1958; Sigal's parentheses and added underscoring in pencil; my italics)

Ironically, there was an unintended consequence of Sigal's calculated strategy of what might now be termed "tweaking" his private journal entries for Lessing's benefit. In the draft of an unfinished novel titled "Ceiling Spike," apparently written sometime after he drafted the thinly disguised autobiographical Coral typescript and still closely based on details in his journals, Sigal has his fictional alter ego realize with chagrin that he can no longer trust his diary as an unmediated record of his thoughts and experiences; by his own choice, it had become, at least in part, fiction. As he writes, "For several nights I stayed awake, sitting on the bed, studying my diaries. But they were unreliable: entries for the past year had been written 'for her'" ("Ceiling Spike" 128).

During the next several months of 1958, the tensions between Lessing and Sigal escalated, with Sigal fretting about her jealousy and feeling increasingly "caged" by their relationship. The tone of his journal entries—and, implicitly, of Sigal's messages to Lessing—is one of irritation and outright castigation, not only of her but also of himself. Unsettled when "Doris gets a lover" (April 10, 1958), he retaliates with casual dalliances of his own. The flat "explodes w/ sheer tension"; Lessing bitterly accuses Sigal of using her. Months later, he remarks in his journal, "I am caged in this house.... I must get out of here.... And yet I know I could really appreciate her if only I didn't have to live w/ her day in & out. I am ready to explode" (November 5, 1958; Sigal's added underscoring in pencil). By January 1959, the further deterioration of the relationship was manifested in Sigal's accelerating symptoms of acute physical and emotional distress. He describes having been "sick for several weeks" with what became bronchitis and mentions falling down the stairs of their flat. He and Lessing both fled the flat on Warwick Street, Lessing to a friend in the West End, Sigal to friends in Hampstead (January 21, 1959). On the one hand, Sigal wrote in his journal, "Life w/o Doris has lost much of its point. Yet what point was there? the sex thing was missing." On the other hand, "She is the only woman who came near making me feel content: and yet there was never total commitment. Probably it is true: I am not capable" (1958–9 Journal, January 21, 1959). Several months later, Sigal and Lessing mutually concluded that their differences were irreconcilable. Sigal wrote in his journal that he "would never love another as I did [Doris], and yet... I could simply not bear to live with her. And not only not live with her, but there were periods during which we self-consciously lived apart when I literally could not stand the sight of her. Almost always she interpreted these phases as having their provocation in another woman, and rarely was she correct in this surmise" (1959–60 Journal, July 1959: p. 3 of 4 unnumbered pages).

Doris Lessing/Anna Wulf—III

During the four years that Doris Lessing and Clancy Sigal lived together, Lessing posted frequent letters to her good friend, Joan Rodker, with whom she had shared a flat during her first few years in London; Rodker was also the acknowledged model, in part, for the character Molly Jacobs in *The Golden Notebook*. In her letters, Lessing described her complicated relationship with Sigal, explaining that she was variously happy, distressed, and at times greatly concerned about both his and her own emotional health. According to her comments, Sigal seemed to have half a dozen—even as many as ten—different personalities and she "never [knew] which personality [was] going to emerge."[8] He was by turns loving and pain-giving—"the calm kind friend, the compulsive liar, the cheap lothario, the lover—everything, like a film running and flickering."[9] Imaginative transformations of these observations made their way into *The Golden Notebook*, including Anna Wulf's idea for a story, recorded in the final segment of the yellow notebook, of a man who is a "psychological chameleon" (*GN* 505) and her characterization—concentrated in the final segment of the blue notebook—of her lodger and lover, Saul Green, who manifests a variety of personas, often in rapid succession. Among Saul's multiple roles, one is his function as the "invisible projectionist" (*GN* 577) who appears in the inner golden notebook as the director of film versions of numerous scenes in Anna's life.

Writing to Rodker several months into her relationship with Sigal, Lessing described her life as "so chaotic I can't write sensisbly [*sic*] about it" (letter headed "July" [1957]). She felt that she was "going to crack up altogether" if she and Sigal remained together. Her phrasing anticipates Anna Wulf's emphatic statement on the opening page of *The Golden Notebook*—dated "Summer 1957"—that "as far as I can see, everything's cracking up" (*GN* 3) and her distraught remark to Saul Green in the final segment of the blue notebook, "you'll crack us both up" (*GN* 543). In a letter to Rodker written after she and Clancy Sigal had been living together for fifteen months, Lessing expressed her distressing realization that she had absorbed symptoms of Sigal's emotional illness into herself. As she phrased it, "I knew I had become part of Clancy's sickness.... My stomach tightened up into a fist, and I couldn't move—its [*sic*] Clancy's symptom, not mine...." (letter headed "Friday"). In *The Golden Notebook*, Anna Wulf absorbs Saul Green's illness, "as if a stranger, afflicted with symptoms [she] had never experienced, had taken possession of [her] body..." (*GN* 521). As is also reflected in both Lessing's and Sigal's fictionalized versions of their relationship, Lessing objected to the unchosen roles of mother-figure and therapist.

Writing to Rodker, Lessing expressed her hope she could master the emotional pain that her relationship with Sigal was causing her by transforming it into fiction: "I suppose I ought to put this into a novel and try and get rid of the hurt of it that way, but at the moment I can't write" (letter headed "Friday"). She admitted that she blamed herself in part for having fallen in love with Sigal rather than simply offering him a haven: "He came here for a refuge he needed, and I should have behaved like a solid rock instead of like a woman who needed a man badly."[10] She regarded her lover as a neurotic who lacked in insight into himself, for which reason he could not grasp the emotionally damaging consequences of his behavior. Though in her judgment he urgently needed psychiatric intervention, for quite some time he refused to take her advice on that matter. She repeatedly implored Rodker, who was also a friend of Sigal's, to support her entreaties on this subject if he came to her for solace, as Lessing apparently expected him to do (letter headed "Friday").

In the final segment of the blue notebook, Anna Wulf anatomizes the relationship between herself and Saul Green as both of them reach their extremes, careening from intimacy to antipathy, from affection to aggression, from madness and illness to sanity and back to madness again. The blue notebook concludes with what appears to be a breakthrough for Anna: in a moment of sanity and clarity, she recognizes the underlying connection between her inner division and her writer's block and resolves that she will "pack away the four notebooks. I'll start a new notebook, all of myself in one book"

(GN 568). Yet, although she purchases a golden notebook for that purpose, she cannot proceed without still another struggle with Saul Green, this time for possession of the new notebook itself. Like a spoiled child who is accustomed to having his own way, Saul covets Anna's golden notebook and secretly lays claim to it, inscribing an "old schoolboy curse" that is reported in the final page of the blue notebook and repeated verbatim at the beginning of the new notebook (GN 568, 571). The golden notebook thus begins not—as readers might expect—with Anna's words but with Saul Green's. Moreover, in a pointed irony that gains even greater significance when one knows that Doris Lessing was secretly borrowing and transforming details from Clancy Sigal's journals, Saul's curse is directed toward those who pry into others' private writing:

> Whoever he be who looks in this
> He shall be cursed,
> That is my wish.
> Saul Green, *his* book. (!!!) (571, italics, exclamation points, and parentheses in original)

In light of Lessing's and Sigal's shared method of mining details of their personal experiences for their respective literary purposes, the struggle between Anna Wulf and Saul Green over ownership of the new golden notebook might be read as the fictional analogue of the struggle between Doris Lessing and Clancy Sigal over who owned the raw material of their liaison – contested "property" that both participants claimed and sought to transform into fiction.

Moreover, Saul Green's curse creates confusion for the reader: just whose notebook *is* the golden notebook? Throughout that segment of the novel—the final actual notebook within *The Golden Notebook*—Anna Wulf describes herself as more frequently ill than well. During the periods of illness, she is tormented both by her past and by the destructive patterns in which she and Saul remain stubbornly and painfully trapped in the present. She experiences hallucinatory dreams in which she is invaded by other personalities, including people she has described in earlier notebooks. Yet when she is not experiencing nightmares of self-disintegration, she and Saul quite dispassionately discuss their relationship, their political disillusionment, and the future.

In the inner golden notebook, a new figure enters Anna's struggle to escape from madness and reclaim control of herself—an "invisible projectionist" (*GN* 577) who urges her to revisit her experiences in order to "name" them and thereby, presumably, to master the feelings and circumstances that have so profoundly destabilized her. The subjects of this exercise appear to her as a series of film scenes, all directed by Anna Wulf. Soon Anna recognizes that the invisible projectionist of her dream—"a sort of inner conscience or critic" (580) who has in effect become a part of herself and who is directing her to see her life differently—is Saul Green. Concurrently, she concludes that the only thing that will release the actual Anna and the actual Saul from their toxic emotional struggle is for them to break up. Saul, misunderstanding her conclusion that they must separate for both of their sakes, resents what he sees as Anna's decision to "kick him out" because he has failed to "toe [her] particular line" (580). He stalks around the room "like an animal, a talking animal, his movements violent and charged with energy a hard force that spat out I, Saul, Saul, I, I want" (587). Emphasizing the repeating sequences of multiple "I I I"s—sometimes as many as six in a row that, in Anna's suggestive language, echo "a machine-gun, ejaculating regularly" (587)—Anna identifies Saul as "I I I, the naked ego" (588). Following a particularly intense exchange of angry invectives, she is tempted to examine Saul's journal yet again to learn whether he is speaking "the truth." However, in a sign of her progress toward emotional recovery, she decides that she will not peek into his journal this time or ever again. "All that was finished" (*GN* 591).

Although by this point late in *The Golden Notebook*, Anna Wulf has generated virtually thousands of words in her struggle to corral her insights and experiences into language, she is dismayed to find that the truth eludes not simply her multiple attempts but language itself. Yet—the ultimate paradox of the relationship between the raw material of experience and its aesthetic expression—it is only through words that Anna can express her despair concerning the inadequacy of language. Even if, as she concludes, "the real experience can't be described" (*GN* 592), she never surrenders language as her tool of discovery and self-expression. Rather, late in the inner golden notebook she takes up her most characteristic strategy for maintaining control, sketching her idea for a "comic and ironic" story or novel: a woman, "appalled by her capacity for surrendering herself to a man, determines to free herself" by taking two lovers, "sleeping with them on alternate nights—the moment of freedom being when she would be able to say to herself that she has enjoyed them both equally." Her strategy fails because "[t]he man she is in fact in love with, hurt and appalled, leaves her. She is left with the man she does not love and who does not love her..." (595).

Although the ironic aspect of the proposed story is evident, readers may find it difficult to grasp its comic dimension. This disturbing final sketch in *The Golden Notebook* derives from Doris Lessing's own experience. In 1957, six months into her relationship with Clancy Sigal and exasperated by what she regarded as his philandering and his dissimulations about it, Lessing retaliated by engaging in brief affairs with other men. The strategy was not successful because, as she wrote to Joan Rodker, although she wished she "could have two men at once," she discovered that she was incapable of doing so. "I do think it is sad that women are monogamous, [*sic*] the more I think about it the more I think our lives would be so much easier if we weren't."[11] In *The Golden Notebook*, when Anna describes her story idea to Saul, he urges her to write it as a novel rather than giving another excuse for not doing so. To prompt her, he offers her the opening sentence. Significantly, he shifts the emphasis from the woman in Anna's sketch who chooses involvement with two men to the "two women you are, Anna": he instructs her to write down in the new golden notebook, "The two women were alone in the London flat" (597). Saul oversimplifies: both narratively and psychologically, there are more than two Annas, just as there are more than two Sauls, in Doris Lessing's multi-layered novel. Nonetheless, Saul's observation about the "two women" who are Anna suggests that several figures in the narrative, including Anna's friend Molly, literarily serve double duty, simultaneously functioning as separate characters and as aspects of Anna Wulf herself.[12]

In effect, Anna and Saul serve as midwives for each other's recalcitrant muses; each becomes the source of the other's artistic and emotional breakthroughs. Indeed, *The Golden Notebook* ultimately demonstrates the inseparability of these two dimensions. Anna Wulf cannot create artistically until she can become a "free woman": free from the neurotic, often masochistic, dynamic of her intimate relationships. Even as she and Saul concede that their fraught and flawed neurotic relationship must end, each enables the resolution of the other's writer's block. The sentence that Saul gives Anna precisely duplicates the first sentence of Lessing's *The Golden Notebook*, bringing Lessing's metafictional *tour de force* almost—but not quite—full circle.

Clancy Sigal/Saul Green—III

In friendly return for Saul's fictional prompt for her novel, Anna offers him the first sentence for *his* novel: "On a dry hillside in

Algeria, the soldier watched the moonlight glinting on his rifle" (*GN* 598). Saul insists that Anna write that sentence in the new golden notebook, over whose possession they continue to struggle (*GN* 600). In a bracketed statement, the invisible editor of *The Golden Notebook* advises the reader that Anna's handwriting ends here; "the golden notebook continued in Saul Green's handwriting, a short novel about the Algerian soldier" (600). A synopsis of Saul's novel continues within the brackets, including the statement that the soldier was "captured, tortured by the French, escaped, rejoined the F. L. N., and found himself torturing, under orders to do so, French prisoners" (600). He later died next to the French student who guarded him.[13] The final line of the inner golden notebook is the invisible editor's separately bracketed statement, "[This short novel was later published and did rather well]" (601, brackets in original). Readers may well wonder who wrote this novel, since the actual golden notebook nested within *The Golden Notebook* contains entirely different content from the book that is ostensibly—according to the bracketed synopsis "written by" Saul Green. Since one reads the first line of Saul's novel as part of *The Golden Notebook*—the entirety of which, readers very soon learn, was written by Anna Wulf—it cannot be "in Saul Green's handwriting" (600) unless we understand Saul to be in some sense an aspect of Anna Wulf.[14] In one of the dreams Anna describes in the final segment of the blue notebook, in which she disintegrates and finds herself entering into other people, she experiences herself as "an Algerian soldier... fighting the French" (*GN* 561). As Lessing explained in her 1971 preface to *The Golden Notebook*, "In the inner Golden Notebook, which is written by both of them, you can no longer distinguish between what is Saul and what is Anna, and between them and other people in the book" (*GN* xiv).

Unlike the opening sentence that Saul suggests for Anna's novel—which doubles as the opening sentence of *The Golden Notebook*—the opening sentence for Saul's novel that Anna pens in the contested inner golden notebook bears no resemblance to the first (or any) sentence of any novel that Clancy Sigal actually published. However, his first book, like the fictitious Saul Green's first book, indeed did "rather well." In *Weekend in Dinlock*, published in 1960 and dedicated to Doris Lessing, Sigal records his observations as a sympathetic observer of the Yorkshire colliery village of Thurlock, England, fictionalized as Dinlock. Befriending the miners and their wives, he observes their hand-to-mouth existence and the men's dedication to coal mining despite the hardships and risks they face underground each day.

As an outsider who gained the trust of the miners and, through it, access to their world, he documents the complicated social interactions of a highly socially stratified community, illustrated not only through their verbal interactions but through such manifestations of their social arrangements as the pubs where they socialize in separate cliques. Two sly cross-references in *The Golden Notebook* allude to Clancy Sigal's actual work in progress at the time and to that of his fictitious stand-in, Saul Green. In the final blue notebook segment, Anna learns from Molly that her son, Tommy, filled with revolutionary fervor, has "signed up to do a series of lectures all over the country about the life of the coal-miner, you know, the Life of the Coal-miner." Tommy also speaks of "going to fight with either the F.L.N. in Algeria or in Cuba" (*GN* 560), a detail that resonates with Saul Green's "short novel about the Algerian soldier" who joins the FLN (600).

Clancy Sigal's actual documentary novel garnered favorable reviews in both British and American venues. Anthony Lejeune, reviewing it for the *Times Literary Supplement*, regarded the book—for which he borrowed a term then used to describe a television genre, "fictionalized documentary"—as a "remarkable achievement. It has an atmosphere as thick and authentic as the coal-dust in the mine" ("Reluctant Young Louts"). The reviewer for the *New Yorker*, Whitney Balliett, pairing *Weekend in Dinlock* with Sigal's second novel, *Going Away*, judged the first book "brilliant" and the second "good." In his estimation, both books, "though labeled 'novels' by their publishers, are a nearly unique cross between reportage and autobiographical fiction, in which the nameless narrator—in contrast to the shadowy observer-catalyst in most reportage—is shaped and changed by the distilled facts he records." Speaking of *Weekend in Dinlock* in particular, he praises Sigal for his "finished" prose, "solid" characters, and "unfailing" taste and humor. Further,

> Sigal—the tactful, resilient narrator—emerges as a tough, quick, ingratiating man whose psychological insights are sometimes breathcatching. He has made himself acceptable in a village where all non-residents—British or not—are regarded as foreigners.... But he has not cheapened his success by making noble savages of the Dinlockers, nor has he sociologically dismembered them. They *are*—we know again and again—precisely what Sigal says they are. (185, Balliett's italics)

Years later in her autobiography, Lessing herself praised Sigal's "capacity for minute acute social observation" in *Weekend in Dinlock* (*Walking* 258). Given the passage of time, she may be forgiven for referring throughout her discussion of his book to the fictitious Yorkshire village of "Dimlock" (258–9).

Although in *The Golden Notebook* Anna Wulf and Saul Green assist each other in resolving their parallel writer's blocks, their exchange of first sentences is not the conclusion of the novel. Rather, it remains for Anna to write—or to complete—the novel-within-the-novel titled *Free Women*. By that point late in the narrative, virtually everything that readers have assumed about the aesthetic form and the reliability of details in *The Golden Notebook* is revealed to be false: the portions that are articulated by an ostensibly omniscient narrator who describes with apparent authority the lives of Anna Wulf, Molly Jacobs, and others, are as fictitious as everything else in the novel: *all* are the work, and words, of Anna Wulf herself. That realization gives particular ironic weight to Anna's treatment of the character Saul Green in the final portion of *Free Women*. In this segment—titled, in parody of the descriptive chapter titles of many traditional nineteenth-century novels, "Molly gets married and Anna has an affair" (605)—Anna condenses, reduces, alters, and rings changes on issues and events that she has so exhaustively detailed, particularly those recorded in the emotionally intense final segments of the yellow and blue notebooks and the inner golden notebook. Her most transformative "illumination" (*GN* 610) about the meaning of her experiences and the limits of language to express it *precedes* the introduction of a 30-year-old "American left-winger" named Milt who comes to stay in her flat for five days (611)—analogous to the earlier yellow notebook sketches that structurally precede and narratively foreshadow Saul Green in the blue notebook.

As Lessing's nested Matroushka doll structure opens to reveal one last iteration of that man, Milt (no surname) is to Saul Green as Saul Green is to Clancy Sigal: the *Free Women* version of his character both resembles and diverges from his model. Prior to Milt's arrival, Anna quite consciously determines that "the remedy for her condition was a man. She prescribed this for herself like a medicine" (*GN* 606). Saul Green's counterpart in this version is not single but on the verge of divorce. More cynical than Saul, Milt is also considerably less complex—neither the combative and philandering lover nor the helpful "invisible projectionist" (577). Nor does he keep a journal. Among other noteworthy differences, Milt stays with Anna for less than a week, not several weeks. However, like Saul Green, he is an emotionally distressed man "in extremity" (614); though he "can't sleep alone" (614), he also "can't sleep with women [he likes]" (618).

Before he and Anna make love for the first time, Milt observes the chaos of her bedroom, which is "billowing with newspapers and journals; the walls were papered with cuttings..." (612), and intervenes by painstakingly removing the disorganized clutter that is the visual correlative of the chaos of Anna's life. His intervention is a variation on Saul Green's role as the "projectionist" who directs Anna Wulf's return to sanity. However, with Milt, the process is both psychologically oversimplified and narratively flattened: neither is it reciprocal nor does it concern Anna's artistic persona, including the resolution of her writer's block. Anna's account of the five days Milt spends with her is a surgically pared-down, oversimplified reprise of her emotionally oversaturated involvement with Saul Green. The narrative of their brief relationship reduces the complexity, and compresses the elapsed time, of the sexual battle and emotional logjam between Anna and Saul that she has so microscopically detailed in the preceding three notebooks. Anna, by now known to the novel's readers as the author of this final segment of *Free Women*—and, thus, of the four segments that precede it—exaggerates to the point of parody her neurotic emotional neediness. As if quoting from a script, she begs Milt to stay with her longer, knowing that her request is precisely the cue for his departure. Milt, as both mirror and caricature of other important men in Anna's life who flee from intimate attachments, indeed promptly departs.

Later, Anna and Molly chat in Molly's kitchen, as they do in earlier segments of *Free Women*. In another example of the recurring mirror technique of the narrative, their observations about Milt reprise in a different key a conversation that Anna had earlier imagined having with Molly—but which did not actually occur at that point—concerning Saul Green. In the inner golden notebook, Anna tells Saul that she plans to ring her friend Molly, who, she can predict, will ask her about her recently arrived American lodger. As she explains, she will reply, "I'm having an affair with him," to which Molly will comment, "That's not the most sensible thing you ever did in your life?" and Anna will answer "no" (584). When Anna actually rings Molly, her friend doesn't answer. Instead, their conversation—whose subject is now, ironically, Anna's American lodger named Milt, not Saul—occurs face to face and virtually verbatim in the section of *Free Women* that concludes the novel (622).

The final sentence of *The Golden Notebook*—"The two women kissed and separated" (623)—is the bookend, both literally and figuratively, to the opening sentence suggested by Saul Green, "The two women were alone in the London flat" (*GN* 3, 597). One might almost say that everything in the novel happens as if bracketed by these enclosing sentences that signify connection and separation. By the end of the narrative, readers understand that Anna Wulf wrote not only both sentences but also everything in between. Or, more accurately, neither Anna Wulf nor Saul Green is the source of the many sentences that comprise *The Golden Notebook*—except through the typewriter of Anna's creator, Doris Lessing.

In fairness to both Lessing and Sigal, it must be said that the fictitious Anna Wulf and Saul Green are ultimately something other than the literary doubles of Doris Lessing and Clancy Sigal. Saul Green is a larger-than-life character, a complex invention that serves multiple functions—both constructive and destructive—in Anna Wulf's struggle for artistic, political, and emotional authenticity and in the resolution of her profound inner divisions. In the 100-plus pages of the novel in which he figures so centrally, he also serves multiple functions in Lessing's aesthetic interrogation of the porous boundaries between fact and fiction and, psychologically, the porous emotional boundaries between intimate partners. Moreover, Lessing's unauthorized literary appropriations ultimately benefited both her and Clancy Sigal artistically: Lessing gave aesthetic form to her most intense and psychologically probing explorations of a complex intimate relationship between a man and a woman, while Sigal's discovery of Lessing's writing about him ultimately released him to write fiction of his own. By the time *The Golden Notebook* was published in 1962, he had resolved his writer's block, publishing both the documentary novel, *Weekend in Dinlock* (1961), and the autobiographical novel, *Going Away: A Report, a Memoir* (1962). Yet the points of resemblance that I demonstrate here between autobiographical "raw material" and fiction bear close attention from both directions and for both writers: Doris Lessing and Clancy Sigal each drew significantly on the facts of their actual relationship. Along the way, they both drew on the notes that Sigal recorded in his private journals, which became—first inadvertently and later deliberately—a pivotal resource for each of them for their separate literary purposes. As I explore in chapter 2, the literary technique of disguising autobiography has not only aesthetic but ethical implications.

Chapter 2

Truth Values and Mining Claims

"Not necessarily facts, but emotional truth is all there." Doris Lessing
(Walking in the Shade)

"Raw Materials": Aesthetic Considerations

Virtually since *The Golden Notebook* was published in 1962, Doris Lessing objected, usually with pique, to any claim that the novel is autobiographical, directing critics and readers to appreciate its formal structure rather than simply its content. As she complained in an interview not long after the novel's publication, "the point of that book was the relation of its part to each other. But the book they [reviewers] tried to turn it into was: The Confessions of Doris Lessing.... The writer who tosses a scrap of autobiography into an otherwise fictional piece (which writers always have done and always will do), he's not credited with any imagination. Everyone says, 'Oh, that character's so and so'..." (interview by Roy Newquist October 1963, 51–2).[1] Lessing's objections notwithstanding, the permeable borderline between fact and fiction is the central aesthetic matter of *The Golden Notebook*, beginning with its author's creation of a fictional persona who, like herself, grew up in southern Africa; was briefly married to a German Marxist with whom she had a son; emigrated to England at the beginning of her writing career; was a single parent; and was a member of the British Communist Party until she left it in disillusionment in 1956; to say nothing of her fraught love affair with an American Leftist and aspiring writer with a writer's block who rented a room in her flat and became her lover.

To complicate the matter, if *The Golden Notebook* is at several points disguised autobiography, it is further transformed through the interposition of its fictitious author, Anna Wulf, whose experiences are not identical with those of Doris Lessing. Early in the novel, Anna Wulf describes, as if for her creator, "that game writers play with themselves when writing, the psychological game—that written incident came from that real incident, that character was transposed from that one in life, this relationship was the psychological twin of that. I am simply asking myself: Why a story at all.... Why not, simply, the truth?" (*GN* 60). The answer to that question is far from simple. Indeed, it takes Anna Wulf—to say nothing of Lessing's readers—most of *The Golden Notebook* to sort out the fluid and unstable relationships among "fact" (autobiography as aesthetically shaped life-writing), "fiction" (invented and aesthetically shaped narrative), and "truth" (the unmediated raw material of experience). To further complicate the slippages among these categories, Anna Wulf is ultimately revealed as the author of *Free Women*, a (fictitious) "autobiographical" novel-within-the-novel that overlaps with but does not duplicate material in the notebooks. Moreover, even details that might be regarded as "autobiographical" within the frame of *The Golden Notebook* are doubly fictitious, given both Anna's position as author of the novel-within-the-novel, *Free Women*, and her status as Doris Lessing's invented character. On the other hand, because *The Golden Notebook* includes transformed details from Doris Lessing's life, including (but not limited to) her relationship with Clancy Sigal, at least some of the "invented" material of the novel is closer to fact—that is, closer to disguised autobiography—than to strictly imaginative invention.

Of any of the possible correspondences between Lessing and her fictional protagonist, the one most pertinent for my consideration of *roman à clef* and disguised autobiography is Anna Wulf's strategy of transforming the raw material of her life into fiction, sometimes intentionally and sometimes because she cannot prevent herself from doing so. In virtually every segment of *The Golden Notebook*, she examines and struggles with the difficulty of writing about her experiences and feelings without distortion. Her multiple attempts to put her experiences into words range from almost transparent autobiography—fictitious autobiography, of course, since Anna Wulf is an invented character—to segments of the narrative that are specifically identified as fiction.

A considerable body of scholarship focuses on the aesthetics of autobiography. Regardless of critical persuasion, most theorists of the genre acknowledge that life-writing contains elements of fiction and that, conversely, fiction contains elements of autobiography. Both the title and subtitle of one study of life-writing—Paul John

Eakin's *Fictions in Autobiography: Studies in the Art of Self-Invention*—capture this interpenetrating relationship. Eakin contends that "autobiographical truth is not a fixed but an evolving content in an intricate process of self-discovery and self-creation and, further, that the self that is the center of all autobiographical narrative is necessarily a fictive structure" (3).Taking a different approach, Louis A. Renza argues that "autobiography is neither fictive nor nonfictive, not even a mixture of the two. We might view it instead as a unique, self-defining mode of self-referential expression, one that allows, then inhibits, its ostensible project of self-representation, of converting oneself into the present promised by language" ("Veto of the Imagination" 295).

Marie-Laure Ryan further theorizes three different approaches to the relationship between autobiography and fiction. In the first, "There is no need for a borderline, because all history, indeed all narratives are a form of fiction." In the second, "Fiction and history are distinct forms of discourse...linked by a continuum of hybrid forms" without a "definite boundary between the fictional and the historical. The position of a text along the continuum is determined by the distance between the textual world and the real world.... [H]istory is the true-to-life, fiction is the imaginary." In the third, "Fiction and history are the two poles of a binary opposition." The border between them, although "clearly marked," is also "somewhat porous." Moreover, "hybridization is possible, if by hybridization one understands not the disappearance of the boundary but the borrowing of elements from the other side of the divide. Rather than gray texts, hybrids are thus patchworks of black and white" ("Fiction and Its Other" 354, 355, 356). Without privileging one approach over the other two, Ryan suggests that fiction may be "like light: sometimes it is best described as a wave (the continuous axis), sometimes more efficiently modeled as particles (the binary approach)" (357).

Of course, *The Golden Notebook* is not an actual autobiographical account but a novel that depends centrally on fictionalized—and, at times, doubly fictionalized—autobiography. In narratological terms, the difference between fictional and historical autobiography (life-writing) is signaled by the name of the narrator. As Dorrit Cohn contends,

> A fictional work that presents itself in the form of a self-narrated story normally imitates its nonfictional counterpart, historical autobiography, in every respect.

...Such fictional autobiographies...look exactly like accounts that real persons bearing their narrators' names might give of their own lives. If we nonetheless know that these narrators are *not* real persons, it is because their imaginary status is signaled by...the fact that they don't bear the same names as their authors. (*The Distinction of Fiction* 42, Cohn's italics)

However, fictional autobiography has an unacknowledged half sister. What I term *disguised autobiography*—the underlying method of *roman à clef* that blends indeterminate elements of fact and invention in the service of *fiction* rather in the service of historical autobiography on the one hand or fictional autobiography on the other—falls in the theoretical cracks. Doris Lessing's *The Golden Notebook* is a particularly good example because, as a fiction in itself, it includes both disguised autobiography and fictional autobiography. The narrator of all portions of the narrative is the invented character, Anna Wulf, narrator of four color-labeled notebooks, behind whom stands the implicit narrating author, Doris Lessing. Adding several further degrees of slippage among the narrative layers, the fictitious Anna Wulf not only writes from both first and third person perspectives but also creates her own named (but not narrating) fictitious alter ego, Ella. Several sections of the yellow notebook include what might be termed Anna's meta-commentary, through Ella, on her fictionalizations of her own experiences. Late in the novel, she ponders the peculiar relationship between herself and what Suzette Henke terms her "autobiographical self-projection" ("Doris Lessing's *Golden Notebook*" 164) who is both like and unlike her: "the moment I, Anna, write: Ella rings up Julia to announce, etc., then Ella floats away from me and becomes someone else" (*GN* 430), much as Anna Wulf, whatever her resemblances to and differences from Doris Lessing, "floated away" from Lessing and became someone else: a fictional character.

Like the author of *The Golden Notebook*, both the fictitious Anna and the doubly fictitious Ella are writers: Anna is the author of a successful first novel set in southern Africa, *Frontiers of War*, who is currently both unwilling and unable to write a second one; unlike her, Ella—author of "half a dozen stories" (*GN* 159)—completes and publishes her "quite good...small, honest novel" (199) on the theme of suicide—a theme that hints at Anna Wulf's own deep despair. Because *The Shadow of the Third*, in which Ella is her alter ego, is too painfully close to her recent emotional loss, the "story" necessarily remains unfinished; Anna struggles with the impossibility of writing a narrative whose key moments are distorted by her painful retrospective knowledge of how it ends. As she laments, "The trouble with this story is that it is written in terms of analysis of the laws of dissolution of the relationship between Paul and Ella.... As soon as one has lived through something, it falls into a pattern" (*GN* 213). Marie-Laure Ryan observes more generally that "memories are always forged to some extent, since the I-of-the-past is (re)constructed by an I-of-the-present who has access to other sources of knowledge than authentic recollections" (352).

According to late-twentieth-century scholars of the genre of autobiography who for the first time foregrounded considerations of gender, life-writing by women has diverged both formally and substantively from that of men because of significant differences in socially conditioned gender roles and the resulting life-experiences. In a key observation that has influenced the study of the genre by taking gender into account, Estelle C. Jelinek argues that, by contrast with autobiographies written by men, "irregularity rather than orderliness informs the self-portraits by women. The narratives of their lives are often not chronological and progressive but disconnected, fragmentary, or organized into self-sustained units rather than connecting chapters" (Introduction, *Women's Autobiography* 17). Allowing for the fact that even the most "autobiographical" aspects of *The Golden Notebook* are aesthetically shaped fictions, Jelinek's observation might almost be read as a description of Lessing's novel. Furthermore, Jelinek claims, "one is struck by the number of women writing diaries, journals, and notebooks, in contrast to the many more men writing autobiographies proper. From earliest times, these discontinuous forms have been important to women because they are analogous to the fragmented, interrupted, and formless nature of their lives" (19).

Elaborating on the influence of the author's gender on the form of autobiography, Sidonie Smith proposes that the female autobiographer, engaged in a "doubled subjectivity" as both the protagonist and the narrator of her story, "pursues her fictions of selfhood by fits and starts" (*A Poetics of Women's Autobiography* 17–18). Moreover,

> Trying to tell the story she wants to tell about herself, she is seduced into a tantalizing and yet elusive adventure that makes of her both creator and creation, writer and that which is written about....
> [W]ords cannot capture the full sense of being and narratives explode

in multiple directions on their own.... Because the autobiographer can never capture the fullness of her subjectivity or understand the entire range of her experience, the narrative 'I' becomes a fictive persona.... [*The autobiographer*] *may even create several, sometimes competing stories about or versions of herself as her subjectivity is displaced by one or multiple textual representations.* (Smith 46–47, my italics)

Jelinek's and Smith's observations are remarkably applicable to the fictitious Anna Wulf's creation of several narrators and multiple narrative representations of her complex artistic/political/emotional life.

Indeed, in *The Golden Notebook*, the distinctions between "fact" and "fiction" are blurred throughout. In the initial installment of the black notebook, Anna Wulf describes in exhaustive detail the social, political, and emotional experiences of her young adulthood and that of her close friends in Southern Rhodesia during the war years of the early 1940s. Recalling the precise moment when her attempt to express these experiences "was born," in her words, as *Frontiers of War*, Anna ponders but cannot explain why she did not "write an account of what had happened, instead of shaping a 'story' which had nothing to do with the material that fuelled it" (*GN* 59–60). In the first of several disclaimers that appear throughout *The Golden Notebook* when Anna attempts to distinguish aesthetically and substantively between the "raw material" of her experiences and her imaginative transformations of that material, she insists that "the two 'stories' have nothing at all in common" (*GN* 143). More critically, she repudiates her novel because she regards it as emotionally dishonest—flawed by what she terms its "lying nostalgia" (*GN* 60).

Just as Lessing fictionally transformed her autographical experiences, so—as readers of *The Golden Notebook* discover—does Anna Wulf. Even her apparently true account of her young adulthood in southern Africa is revealed to be to some degree fictionalized. Tellingly, she later reveals that the name of the German refugee through whom she became involved in Leftist politics and to whom she was briefly married is not named Willi Rodde, as he is identified in the black notebook (*GN* 66), but Max Wulf, as he is named in the blue notebook (*GN* 437). This discrepancy and others destabilize a reader's trust in what Beth Boehm terms the "ontological boundaries" between fact and invention. "The black notebook, in calling into question the 'truthfulness' of a particular fiction which was based on 'real' events, begins to blur the ontological boundaries between fact and fiction, but we naturalize this notebook by reading it as Anna's attempt to tell the truth about the past, a truth which her novel, *Frontiers of War*, distorted" (Boehm 92). In either case, the model for Willi Rodde/Max Wulf is Lessing's second husband, Gottfried Lessing, a refugee from Germany whom she met in Southern Rhodesia and whose socialist philosophy decisively influenced her and her friends. Taking his surname, she became, and remained, Doris Lessing, even though the marriage lasted only four years.

At other points in *The Golden Note*, Anna Wulf underscores more overtly her fiction-making propensity. In the red notebook, for example, she parodies or fictionally exaggerates the naïve fantasies and intellectual oversimplifications of socialism that—as she explores through her younger self in the first segment of the black notebook—she had earlier failed to question. The yellow notebook foregrounds her most explicit ruminations on the porous boundary between autobiography and fiction. In *The Shadow of the Third*, the draft of a novel-in-progress that remains incomplete, she reconstructs and examines from the perspective of the invented persona that she names Ella the critical phases of her recently and painfully concluded five-year love affair with Michael, a married psychiatrist. Michael's fictional counterpart, Paul Tanner, is also married and is also a "witch-doctor" (*GN* 171) at an unnamed London psychiatric clinic. The Ella/Paul relationship thus fictionalizes key aspects of Anna's relationship with Michael, which—in the manner of nested Russian Matroushka dolls—fictionally transforms key aspects of Lessing's relationship with a married émigré Czech psychiatrist who served on the clinical staff of London's Maudsley Hospital and whom she regarded as the most significant love of her life (*Walking* 41). Several other characters in *The Shadow of the Third* are drawn from Anna's (and Lessing's) "real" life, including Anna's friend Molly, named Julia in the inner novel. Anna's son, Michael, whose "real" name duplicates that of Anna's lover, is fictionalized as a daughter of the same age named Janet.

At several points, Anna steps back from the detailed literary reconstruction of her concluded love affair to examine from both aesthetic and psychological perspectives the stages of its unfolding and the sources of its failure. She compels herself to recognize troubling incidents—signals that she willingly ignored at the time—that foreshadowed the end of the relationship. Her retrospective analysis leads her to conclude that there is no privileged position from which to articulate the authentic version of her, or anyone's, experience. Regardless of the writer's chronological, aesthetic, or emotional proximity to or distance from the original events, not only recollection but also literary expression and analysis introduce distortion—indeed, *are* forms of distortion—that inevitably affect the "truth" of what can be articulated. Any prose written after the fact or "after the event" (*GN* 213) necessarily alters the fact or event; there is no neutral position. As Jay Parini and others have observed, "Anything processed by memory is fiction. That is to say, anything that has been shaped and reconstructed is fiction" (*Essays on Writing and Politics* 249).[2]

Anna Wulf ultimately concedes this point. Regardless of the degree of authorial distance from her subject, it is impossible for her to capture in language the "truth" of her past experiences. Even writing about current experiences just after they occur introduces distortions and inconsistencies. All 22 segments of *The Golden Notebook*—16 notebook sections (four each of black, red, yellow, and blue notebook installments) plus the singular inner golden notebook plus five installments of *Free Women*—regardless of whether told from the first-person or third-person perspective—are narrated in the past tense, introducing the element of retrospection in relation to immediate experience. Regarding more generally the illusion of immediacy—as if events could simultaneously occur and be narratively reported—Dorrit Cohn artfully observes, "Life tells us that we cannot tell it while we live it or live it while we tell it. Live now, tell later" (*The Distinction of Fiction* 96). Phenomenologically, as Daniel N. Stern observes, "the present moment, while lived, can not [*sic*] be seized by language which (re?)constitutes it after the fact" (*The Present Moment in Psychotherapy and Everyday Life* 8, Stern's parentheses and question mark).

Yet in *The Golden Notebook* Anna Wulf repeatedly tests that truth, aspiring both to "live now" and "tell now." In the blue notebook/diary sections, she sheds the aesthetic distance that her fictional persona, Ella, and the third-person narrative perspective provided her, attempting to narrate the raw material of her experiences in the first-person without aesthetic shaping or embellishment. Her account of the events of September 15, 1954, describes in detail a single day—not a random day but the one on which she realizes that her relationship with Michael has ended when he fails to appear that evening for the meal she has lovingly prepared for him. She concludes that her minutely detailed account of the day's events and her feelings about them—so exhaustively reported that she frets that mention of her menstrual period and other bodily details distorts her account—is "[a] failure as usual" (*GN* 344). Summarizing the same fateful day in a drastically condensed paragraph, she concludes that, despite her effort to capture the "truth" in minimalist form, the brief version of that day is no less a failure than the exhaustive account.

In a later section of the blue notebook, Anna writes an even further reduced summary of strictly neutral biographical details, as if to convey that the only form of personal information that resists distortion is the purest of uncontestable facts: her date of birth; her parents' names; bare facts concerning her educational history; the dates (by year) of her marriage, her (unnamed) daughter's birth, and her divorce; and the dates (by year) when she joined and left the Communist Party (*GN* 437). It is here that Anna's husband—named Willi Rodde in the black notebook—is identified as Max Wulf, one discrepancy among many that highlight the fluidity between fact and fiction or narrative "truth" and invention. Which details represent the "authentic" version of Anna's life? Or, indeed—a fundamental question not only for Anna but for readers of *The Golden Notebook*—can any version of her narrative be construed as "true"? By both design and necessity, Anna Wulf is an unreliable narrator.

Concerning more generally the matter of autobiographical "unreliability," Sidonie Smith parenthetically observes that

> In autobiography the reader recognizes the inevitability of unreliability but suppresses the recognition in a tenacious effort to expect "truth" of some kind. The nature of that truth is best understood as the struggle of a historical rather than a fictional person to come to terms with her own past, with the result that she renders in words the confrontation between the dramatic present and the narrative past, between the psychological pressures of discourse and the narrative pressures of story. (*A Poetics of Women's Autobiography* 46)

No version of the experiences that Anna Wulf expresses in language—including the supposedly unmediated diary that she expected to be the "most truthful" (*GN* 438)—escapes distortion. Every attempt to give verbal form to feelings and experiences, regardless of differences in aesthetic distance, narrative persona, and point of view, is a "failure." Lessing herself judged *The Golden Notebook* itself a "failure." As she phrased it in a 1966 interview with Florence Howe, "I like *The Golden Notebook* even though I believe it to be a failure, because it at least hints at complexity" ("A Talk with Doris Lessing," *Small Personal Voice*, ed. Schlueter 82). Regarding Anna's—and Lessing's—perceived "failures" as the author's postmodern literary accomplishment, Molly

Hite contends that "'the truth' is not a fixed reality that lurks behind the distortions of narrative form but a product of tellings and retellings. Or rather, that there is no truth apart from the telling, no real story, no authorized version, no vantage point that allows experience to be viewed as a whole" (*The Other Side of the Story* 90).

* * *

Nearly four decades after the fact—I use the phrase advisedly—Lessing attempted once again to lasso her past into words, this time choosing the form of historical autobiography without fictionalized intermediaries. However, as the aesthetics of the genre suggest and as Lessing herself acknowledged, even the most ostensibly "true" version of life-writing is not entirely transparent. Since it depends on aesthetic shaping, it inevitably introduces discrepancies and distortions. In her essay titled, "Writing Autobiography," she elaborates,

> when you are shaping an autobiography, just as when you shape a novel, you have to decide what to leave out.... Yet it should be like life, sprawling, big, baggy, full of false starts, loose ends, people you met once and never think of again.... And as you write your autobiography it has to have a good deal in common with a novel.... In short, we have a story. What doesn't fit into the story, the theme, gets cut out. (*Time Bites* 98–9)[3]

The process is further complicated by the capriciousness of recollection itself. Lessing explains quite matter-of-factly the insight that comes only with difficulty and acute frustration to the fictitious Anna Wulf:

> Memory isn't fixed: it slips and slides about. It's hard to match one's memories of one's life with the solid fixed account of it that is written down.... Our own views of our lives change all the time, different at different ages.... Once I read autobiography as what the writer thought about his or her life. Now I think, 'That is what they thought *at that time*.' An interim report—that is what an autobiography is. ("Writing Autobiography," 92, Lessing's italics)

Nonetheless, Lessing's effort to describe more transparently her emotionally wrenching relationship with Clancy Sigal is instructive for readers interested in the fluid boundaries between historical and disguised autobiography and between both forms and declared fiction. According to the autobiographical and retrospective Lessing, Clancy Sigal "caused as severe a dislocation of my picture of myself as ever in my life" (*Walking* 173). She acknowledges her "shame at [her] stupidity" in succumbing to loneliness following the end of her love affair with the émigré Czech psychiatrist to whom she refers as Jack. She slept with Sigal "I think on the first night" (*Walking* 172)—a detail that is corroborated by Sigal's multiple fictional renderings of their first evening together after he moved into her flat. Regretting her emotional neediness at the time, Lessing admits, "There is no fool like a woman in need of a man ... to have and to hold" (172). Without departing from her insistence that *The Golden Notebook* is not autobiographical, she acknowledges, both implicitly and explicitly, several parallels between Clancy Sigal and the fictitious Saul Green.

Alternatively, in the life/art/life hall of mirrors that exemplifies the relationship between Lessing and Sigal and its half-lives in their overlapping fictionalizations of it and each other, one might venture to say that details in Lessing's much-later-written autobiography were colored by her creation of the character Saul Green. For example, she describes Sigal's entrance into her life with an image that duplicates Anna Wulf's first meeting with Saul in *The Golden Notebook* "[a]s if off a film set. He was in the style of young Americans then, jeans, sweatshirt, a low-slung belt where you could not help but see a ghostly gun. The lonely outlaw" (*Walking* 167; see *GN* 517). Moreover, like Saul Green, Clancy Sigal had "an immediate, intelligent understanding of women, not as females, but of our situation, our difficulties.... In *The Golden Notebook* I call it 'naming'. He 'named' us. Every woman he ever met he got into bed, or tried, and as a matter of principle" (*Walking* 171; see *GN* 515). Of note, the autobiographical Lessing uses the phrase "heroic figure" to describe Sigal, though it was apparently his conception of himself, not hers of him. The younger Sigal's self-image, according to her, was inspired by "a thousand film epics and the heroes and heroines of the Left, who inhabited his imagination like close friends" as well as by "the great figures of American history" (*Walking* 167). Before coming to Europe, he had completed a cross-country car trip in the United States—the raw material for his novel, *Going Away*—during which he was, according to Lessing, "crazy as a loon, conversing with Abraham Lincoln, Clarence Darrow, Sacco and Vanzetti, Jefferson, ... Rosa Luxemburg, ... Trotsky, and anyone else who turned up" (*Walking* 167–8).

Whatever the differences that ultimately compelled their separation, Lessing and Sigal were initially strongly united by their political views. Sigal's sophisticated political understanding came from his experience as the son of radical labor union organizers. His and Lessing's mutual interest in schisms developing in the Left and the disillusionment that followed the discovery of Stalin's atrocities during the 1950s and the Soviet invasion of Hungary in 1956 were of particular importance for Lessing, prompting her disaffection from the Communist Party and, ultimately, from politics altogether. She identifies important changes occurring in her at the time that she could only much later identify as fracture lines in her relationship with Sigal: he was "a mirror of everything I was beginning to be uneasy about in myself," particularly the "left-wing romanticism" of the era (*Walking* 168). From the perspective of several intervening decades, she concluded that she and Sigal were "ill suited emotionally—that above all—and sexually... but intellectually it was a match, all right, for a time" (*Walking* 169).

Lessing credited Sigal for educating her about the "squalid parts" of London (*Walking* 175) and was grateful that he introduced her to contemporary music. "He instructed me in the history of jazz, of the blues, how to listen to different instruments, how to tell false from true, how to appreciate the way a group plays together, the instruments as a family" (174). At the same time, her listening to jazz with Sigal was associated with "suffering, the enjoyment of the pain of loss." As she phrases it, "listening to the blues... went together with a time of pain, and the one reinforced the other" (174). Four decades later, she could clearly recognize that such feelings had helped to "fuel" *The Golden Notebook*. The novel

> was written at high pressure—pressure from within.... Sometimes the emotional pressures that fuel a novel are very far from its subject matter.... *The Golden Notebook*'s fuel was feelings of loss, change: that I had been dragged to my emotional limits by Jack and then Clancy—rather, I had been dragged by *my* emotional needs, which really had nothing to do with them as individuals.... Loss, departures, the ending of dramas begun long ago, the need for drawing lines—*finis*. All this dynamic energy went into *The Golden Notebook*: *emotional energy*.... (*Walking* 337–8, Lessing's italics)

With her intelligence and her emotions at odds, Lessing found herself "dragged along like a fish on a line. With Clancy I hit the extremes in myself and had from the start, and this had nothing very much to do with Clancy the person. Partly it was because he was in 'breakdown'...[as] described (not defined) in *The Golden Notebook*" (*Walking* 285).

* * *

Porous Boundaries: Psychological Considerations

Doris Lessing emphasizes that to "describe" breakdown is not to "define" it. *The Golden Notebook* minutely describes (among other things) the process of mental and emotional breakdown in Anna Wulf and Saul Green, who break down into each other. Narratively, readers have only Anna's subjective experience of a process in which Saul is both a catalyst and a collaborator. The matter of porous boundaries in the novel thus has psychological as well as formal implications. According to Lessing's autobiographical recollection, Clancy Sigal was in a psychologically fragile state when they met; he was "pretty ill when he arrived, just about holding himself together. He had come from Paris, where a close friend, an American woman living in Paris, told him he was crazy....He made no secret about finding in me a good substitute for a psychotherapist" (*Walking* 169). Sigal's fictional counterpart in *The Golden Notebook*, Saul Green, is similarly ill with both physical and psychosomatic symptoms. Moreover, Anna Wulf comes to identify so closely with her lover intersubjectively that she often finds it difficult to distinguish between his moods and feelings and her own.

As Daniel N. Stern theorizes the "intersubjective matrix"—the porous psychological boundaries between people who know each other that exist even under normal circumstances—"our mental life is cocreated [*sic*]" through our interactions with others. Therefore, "what is ours and what belongs to others starts to break down. Our intentions are modified or born in a shifting dialogue with the felt intentions of others. Our feelings are shaped by the intentions, thoughts, and feelings of others. And our thoughts are cocreated in dialogue, even when it is only with ourselves" (*The Present Moment* 77). More metaphorically, Jessica Benjamin describes intersubjectivity as "the shadow cast by the other in the space in-between [individual consciousnesses]..." (*Shadow of the Other* xii). Coincidentally but instructively, in *The Golden Notebook*, the unfinished novel-within-the-novel that Anna Wulf writes about herself through her invented persona, Ella, is titled *The Shadow of the Third*. The identity of the shadowy "third" that occupies the psychological zone between individual consciousnesses changes as Anna examines the emotional fault lines in her intimate relationships. In the final segment of the yellow notebook—by then, no longer a novel in progress but a series of sketches for stories Anna might compose—porous psychological or intersubjective boundaries are expressed almost exclusively in negative terms, such as the transfer or exchange of symptoms of emotional illness between a man and a woman. For example, Sketch 4 describes "[a] healthy woman, in love with a man. She becomes ill with symptoms she has never had in her life. She slowly understands that this illness is not hers.... She understands the nature of the illness, not from him, how he acts or what he says, but from how his illness is reflected in herself" (*GN* 499). The sketch that follows (#5) expresses another variation of the porous boundaries between psychologically enmeshed lovers: a woman who has "fallen in love, against her will" awakens in fear one night and asks her lover, "Is that your heart beating?" to which he replies, "No, it's yours" (*GN* 499). In sketch 11, Anna imagines a relationship in which "the neurotic hands on his or her state to the other, who takes it over, leaving the sick one well, the well one sick" (*GN* 502).

In the blue notebook, fluid psychological boundaries and negative intersubjectivity are expressed not from the detached perspective of invented story sketches but through immediate and disturbing visceral experiences that actualize—one might say "real"-ize—scenes and events sketched in the yellow notebook. Soon after Saul Green arrives in her flat, Anna finds herself suffering from acute anxiety and "undirected apprehension" (*GN* 519). Yet it is not she but Saul who is ill, as she confirms when she goes to his room to inform him of a phone call and finds him asleep, unnaturally pale and "deadly" cold (*GN* 520). Feeling her stomach "clench," she realizes that somehow she has absorbed the symptoms of his emotional illness into herself, "as if a stranger, afflicted with symptoms I had never experienced, had taken possession of my body" (*GN* 521).

In sketch 18 in the yellow notebook, Anna describes a "psychological chameleon" who, reminiscent of Chekhov's "the darling" but with the gender roles reversed, becomes "half a dozen different personalities, either in opposition to or in harmony with" the same man (*GN* 505). Similarly, in the blue notebook, Anna is disconcerted by the "five or six different people" (536) Saul Green appears to be during a single conversation. Though she cannot be certain which of his several distinct personalities is the "real" Saul, she prefers to believe that the gentle, brotherly, responsible man is more real than the crazy, gibberish-speaking man who occasionally appears for breakfast (552–3). As Anna breaks down and careens uncontrollably between states of sanity and madness, she too becomes an emotional chameleon. At one point, she embodies the personalities of several people who were important to her during her young adulthood in southern Africa years before.

According to Lessing, one of the most significant ideas she attempted to express in *The Golden Notebook* was that "to divide off and compartmentalise living was dangerous and led to nothing but trouble" (*Walking* 338). As the narrative demonstrates, the compartments cannot hold. However, the opposite circumstance, "formlessness" (*GN* xiii)—the dissolution of "compartments" and boundaries, including those between self and other—also leads to "trouble." As Anna and Saul undergo a mutual mental breakdown, ego boundaries and the intersubjective space between them dissolve. In the 1971 preface to the novel, Lessing describes the psychological fluidity between the two characters that she endeavored to convey: Anna and Saul

> [reflect] each other, [are] aspects of each other, [give] birth to each other's thoughts and behavior—*are* each other, form wholes.... [They] "break down" into each other, into other people.... They hear each other's thoughts, recognise each other in themselves.... In the inner Golden Notebook, which is written by both of them, you can no longer distinguish between what is Saul and what is Anna, and between them and the other people in the book. (*GN* xiii–xiv, Lessing's italics)

* * *

What's Yours, What's Mine?

The fluid boundaries between self and other and between fact and fiction—two aspects of the correspondences between Anna Wulf/Saul Green and Doris Lessing/Clancy Sigal that emerge when one reads *The Golden Notebook* alongside autobiographical materials, including Sigal's journals and other unpublished writings, and Lessing's letters, later-authored autobiography, and other writings—also have ethical implications. One may well ask: What is the responsibility, if any, of authors who "use" for their own literary purposes material based on their own lives that typically also depends on details drawn from the lives of their friends, acquaintances, and intimate companions?

Wayne C. Booth briefly touches on this subject in his exploration of the ethics of literature, querying whether there are "limits to the author's freedom to expose, in the service of art or self, the most delicate secrets of those whose lives provide material?" (*The Company We Keep* 130). However, having raised the provocative question, Booth leaves it unanswered. More concerned with the ethical dimension of critical reading from a reader's perspective than with authorial sources, he regards such appropriations as a matter of interest only for readers who possess "more or less accidental knowledge about the author's life" (131).

Admittedly, no ground rules govern what is permitted or proscribed in *roman à clef*. Disguised autobiography, whatever its literary purposes from an author's perspective, may impinge on the privacy of actual people, details about whom are typically used without their knowledge or consent. Considering the ethical responsibility of writers who appropriate such details for the purpose of historical autobiographies, Paul John Eakin argues that "life writing that constitutes a violation of privacy has the potential to harm the very self of the other" (*How our Lives Become Stories* 168). According to the contemporary ethicist Claudia Mills, if experiences can be said to "belong" to the individuals to whom they occur, then writers' literary use of such material for their fiction constitutes a violation not only of privacy but ownership ("Appropriating Others' Stories" 202). William Amos, compiler of a veritable who's who of the "originals" who were or are the unwitting models for characters in fiction, suggests that the real-life prototypes may suffer "the pain of being fictionalised" (*The Originals* xvii). Similarly, Mills ponders the "psychological pain" as well as feelings of betrayal or exploitation that may result when individuals find that they have been used as models for literary characters (197). Since people rarely object to flattering fictional versions of themselves, the harm usually results only from "untruthfully or unfairly negative portraits" (199).

Another form of harm that may be caused by authorial appropriation of actual lives and experiences is the perceived damage to an individual's reputation, which intersects more publicly with libel matters. However, parallels between actual people and their fictional counterparts are subjectively measured and difficult to substantiate unambiguously, as legal actions concerning defamation of character reveal. Peter Duffy cites a recent libel suit "brought against Joe Klein and Random House by a woman who believed she was the model for a character who has an affair with a Clintonesque presidential candidate in Klein's *Primary Colors...*" ("Character Assassination" 23). The court ruled that "superficial similarities were not enough: the depiction 'must be so closely akin' to the real person claiming to be defamed that 'a reader of the book, knowing the real person, would have no difficulty linking the two'" (Duffy 23). Duffy also describes an unusual case that occurred early in the twentieth century in which a person took an action far more extreme than a libel suit to settle his claim that a writer had wrongfully appropriated details from another person's life for his fiction. Fitzhugh Coyle Goldsborough, a concert violinist, was convinced that the satirical novel *The Fashionable Adventures of Joshua Craig* (1909) by David Graham Phillips featured a character closely based on his sister and that the writer had thus defamed her. Two years later, the distraught and by-then mentally unstable Goldsborough fatally shot the author. Duffy imagines the shooting as an act of all-too-literal "character assassination" in response to perceived literary character assassination. Yet, fact may be stranger than fiction and life imitates art as well as the reverse: Duffy concludes, "But what of Goldsborough's charges? Had a distinguished Washington family really been libeled? Phillips' friends and family insisted he had never heard of the Goldsboroughs" (Duffy 23).

Another celebrated example of literary "character assassination," along with reciprocal and overlapping literary appropriations, is a group of three novels and a memoir based on a scandalous affair between Ford Madox Ford and Jean Rhys early in the twentieth century. Rhys's first novel, *Quartet* (1927), is a thinly fictionalized representation of her liaison with Ford. Her French–Dutch husband during the time of the affair, Jean Lenglet, wrote, under the pseudonym Edward de Nève, *his roman à clef*, published in French as *Sous les verrous* and, astonishingly, dedicated to the adulterous Rhys. The novel was translated into English as *Barred* (1931) by none other than Jean Rhys—the pseudonym of Ella Gwendolyn Rees Williams—who took it upon herself to omit portions that she regarded as "unfair to herself" (Weisenfarth 78). During the same year, Ford returned the literary favor, publishing *When the Wicked Man* (1931), a *roman à clef* based on *his* perspective on his affair with Rhys. To neatly round out the quartet, Stella Bowen—Ford's partner while he and Rhys were adulterously involved—later published *her* version of events, a memoir whose title, *Drawn from Life* (1940), aptly captures the boundary-straddling spirit of *roman à clef*. Betsy Draine observes that virtually everyone but Jean Rhys herself understood *Quartet* to be "an autobiographical act of vengeance against her erstwhile lover and literary patron," whereas Rhys, "astonished" that people regarded it as autobiographical, nonetheless conceded that "some of it was lived of course" ("Chronotope and Intertext" 318).[4]

What complicates judgment—whether aesthetic, ethical, or legal—in such cases is that novelists are traditionally accorded "'poetic license' to break moral rules in the service of artistic creation" (Mills 195). Moreover, since "[n]o one can write of her own life without writing, in detail and in depth, about the lives of those intimately connected with her...[,] our only normative concerns are with the infliction of pain on those depicted..." (203). However, it is highly unlikely that writers, even if confronted with such ethical considerations, will henceforth ask consent to use for their literary purposes material based on the lives of relatives, intimate friends, and acquaintances. Nor are their models entitled to royalties or—unless they successfully press a libel suit—other forms of compensation.

Among Doris Lessing's intimate friends and acquaintances who apparently experienced psychological pain upon finding thinly fictionalized (or dramatic) depictions of themselves in her fiction and drama were her lover, Clancy Sigal, the model for Saul Green of *The Golden Notebook* and Dave Miller of *Play with a Tiger*. As Lessing later defended her method in her autobiography, "Both Jack and Clancy are in *The Golden Notebook*. Not necessarily facts, but emotional truth is all there. *Play with a Tiger* too" (*Walking* 172). The ethical matter hinges on the distinction between "facts" and "emotional truth" as differently assessed by writers and their "originals." In his own writing over time, both disguised autobiography and fiction, Clancy Sigal has expressed a complex range of responses to Doris Lessing's invented characters based on him, ranging from initial shock and outrage to fascination and admiration and, eventually, to detached amusement. Moreover, as will be discussed in subsequent chapters of this study, Sigal amply returned the favor. His novels, *Zone of the Interior* and *The Secret Defector*—both of which may be regarded as *romans à clef* that depend on the technique of disguised autobiography—include caricatures of, among others, Doris Lessing.

Another one of Lessing's own models was her friend Joan Rodker. For several years beginning in 1950, when she first arrived in England and before she met Clancy Sigal, Lessing lived with Rodker in the latter's flat near Portobello Road, Kensington. Over the kitchen table, the two women discussed politics and the state of the world and confided to each other the intimate details of their personal lives. Fictional transformations of their friendship and conversations were later woven into the fabric of *The Golden Notebook*. Lessing later acknowledged that she "mined" her conversations with Rodker, who became "Molly, much altered, of course, and I, Ella [and Anna]. It ought not to be necessary to say that this was not a strict use of what happened, or of what was said; but such is the hunger of readers for the autobiographical that one has to repeat: no, it did not happen just like that.... Molly was a composite of several women I've known" (*Walking* 336). She laments that "the author who has tried so hard to take the story out of the strictly personal, to generalise personal and private experience, sometimes feels he or she need not have bothered, might as well have set down a strict and accurate record of what happened—autobiography, in fact" (*Walking* 336). Despite her impassioned defense of her method, it is not always possible to regard as "generalizations" a number of Lessing's apparently invented characters and other details described with such specificity in *The Golden Notebook*.

Whatever the close bond between Doris Lessing and Joan Rodker during the 1950s, Rodker later came to regard Lessing's literary appropriations with a certain degree of ambivalence. In an introductory cover page that she prepared in 2000 for her archive for the Harry Ransom Center at the University of Texas, she mentions her surprise when *The Golden Notebook* was published (1962) when she realized that Lessing had not offered to show her proofs of the novel prior to its publication, as she had done with her previous novels. Rodker recalls having lunch with her friend Joseph Barnes, who, coincidentally, was the editor of *The Golden Notebook* for Simon and Schuster. Barnes "made a little grimace or did something that made me ask whether he was trying to tell me something," after which he remarked to Rodker, "'I don't think you're going to like [the book]'... and would, in his professional capacity I suppose, be drawn no further" (Introductory comments 1, Rodker Archive[5]). Later, Rodker recognized in *The Golden Notebook*—despite Lessing's later disclaimer—a fictionalized version of herself as Anna Wulf's close friend, Molly Jacobs—"much altered, of course," in Lessing's opinion (*Walking* 336). Identifying friends and associates whose correspondence and other materials she includes in her archive, Rodker describes Clancy Sigal as Lessing's "American lover—each having written extensively about the other. DL, in particular 'uses' (her own expression) him in various recognisable guises" (Introductory comments 2). In her introductory overview of her archive, she explains, although I was angry at the way some of my friends were depicted and so ill-disguised [in *The Golden Notebook*], I'd never felt particularly indignant on my own behalf. Now, after all this time, and with the production of WALKING IN THE SHADE I've come to agree with most of my friends who strongly disapprove at [*sic*] what DL considers her "author's right" to freely exploit and "use" (her word) dear friends and casual acquaintances alike—regardless. (Introductory comments 1, Rodker's caps)

She explains that she decided to make public her conversation with Barnes because, 35 years later when she read the prepublication copy of the second volume of Lessing's autobiography, *Walking in the Shade*—its author, this time, having shared the proofs with her—her attitude changed. Preparing for Lessing a two-page single-spaced typed response to the proof copy of the book, she began by remarking, "lots of interesting stuff here...enjoyed the read" (comments on proof copy of Lessing's *Walking in the Shade*, Rodker's ellipsis). She then proceeded to demur, listing a number of errors of fact and inference, particularly but not exclusively those concerning herself. At one point, she remarked, "Of course I don't agree with everything...but then it's your story and viewpoint. Perhaps I'll have to write a biog[raphy] myself..." (*Walking* proof comments 2, Rodker's ellipses). The list of corrections concludes with a blunt objection to Lessing's appropriative method: "And, Doris, if in other references to me you have conversations in quotes (i.e., supposedly as really happened verbatim), do check or take out quote marks....[P]lease" (2, Rodker's ellipsis). Lessing, responding point for point to Rodker's list of corrections, also expressed her dismay that, four decades after their time together under the same roof, Rodker had come to resent her and had "turned on" her (letter to Rodker dated March 9, 1997, Rodker Archive).

Rodker may also have been perturbed, in retrospect, by the fact that Lessing had incorporated details of her life and their conversational dialogues not only for her autobiography but also, years earlier, for her fiction and dramatic works. In Lessing's first play, *Each His Own Wilderness* (1959), the two central characters are, by Lessing's own admission, based on Joan and her son, Ernest. The latter was a model for the character Tony, the apolitical and jaded young man in the play; in addition, although Lessing does not mention it, Ernest was likely a source for the character, Tommy, Molly Jacobs's politically disaffected and suicidal adolescent son in *The Golden Notebook*. In the play, Lessing gave dramatic form to what she regarded as the disheartening discrepancies between the heady if naïve Communist idealism to which she and her friends had subscribed during the 1950s and the later-documented brutalities of Joseph Stalin. To compound their elders' disillusionment, the younger generation seemed disinterested in politics altogether, as Lessing clearly observed in the circumstances of a friend and her son. Without naming names, she describes the context for her play as "a communist, being harassed by her non-political son, week in and week out, for months, about her politics. Then she gave up politics, and he, overnight, became extremely, not to say violently political—everything he had criticised her for being" (*Walking* 226).

Each His Own Wilderness was produced by the English Stage Society and performed on March 23, 1958, for one of the well-regarded Royal Court Theater Sunday Nights (*Walking* 226). Disappointingly for Lessing, the play, despite garnering "good reviews," was not granted a run. Three decades later, responding defensively to Rodker's dismay at finding herself exposed in her friend's autobiography, Lessing explained that the play was "not a direct transcript of things said" between Rodker and her son (letter to Rodker dated March 9, 1997). Apparently Ernest Rodker never saw *Each His Own Wilderness* during its brief stage performance; when recently asked by me, he acknowledged that, at the time the play was written and produced, he was unaware that the central characters bore resemblances to his mother and himself. However, he knew that characters with recognizable resemblances to them appear in *The Golden Notebook* as Molly Jacobs and her disaffected adolescent son, Tommy. While Ernest Rodker and his mother were not deeply troubled at the time by what Lessing wrote, he later regretted Lessing's failure "to acknowledge, even to my mother, that she was using her closest friends as raw material for characters in her books" and now feels that "sometimes this went too far" (e-mail message to the author dated July 4, 2012).

For her part, Doris Lessing, recalling her friendship with Joan Rodker with mixed feelings of her own, expressed her dismay that Rodker "criticised me—or so it felt—for everything.... To withstand the pressure of [her] continual disapproval, I got more defensive and more cool.... Joan was unable to see that I found her overpowering because I admired her" (*Walking* 46–7). In fairness and in tribute to her good friend during her critical early years in London, Lessing also praised Rodker's "kindness and charity" and regarded their time together in Rodker's flat on Kensington Church Street as among her "best times in London." As she phrases it, "I see Joan and me sitting at her little table in the kitchen, talking, gossiping, setting life, love, men, and politics to rights, the best part of my time there..." (*Walking* 249).

Despite Joan Rodker's disappointments and disagreements with Doris Lessing, she kept her own counsel until she prepared her archive for the Harry Ransom Center. She consistently declined to speak either on or off the record with Carole Klein, who repeatedly pressed her for cooperation in connection with an unauthorized biography of Lessing then in progress. Klein's biography appeared in 2000, the same year that Rodker's archive was acquired by the Harry Ransom Center. In the introduction to her archive, Rodker provides a capsule description of the section that contains correspondence "relating entirely to [Klein's] efforts to persuade me 'to talk.' DL [Doris Lessing] had specifically phoned me and most other friends (not all of whom obliged) NOT to cooperate. I agreed and stuck to it (more fool me?)" (Introductory comments 2, Rodker's caps). In one of her letters to Klein, Rodker wrote, "Of course I considered the fact that Doris writes and has written about friends and acquaintances[,] myself very much included, at least in THE GOLDEN NOTEBOOK. However, I'm not under my own name, *I am somewhat disguised and only people who know us both recognise the clues*. The end result comes under fiction I believe" (letter to Carol Klein dated April 22, 1996, Rodker's caps; my italics).

Rodker's observation to Klein, as well as her retrospective objections concerning Doris Lessing's literary method, perfectly captures—from the perspective of the "original"—the literary and ethical considerations that shadow historical autobiography, disguised autobiography, and *roman à clef*. In the latter two forms, the "key" to the real identities behind the fictional ones initially may be known only to the author. However, friends and acquaintances who recognize themselves as models may experience—as did Clancy Sigal at the time of composition, publication, or performance of several of Doris Lessing's literary works and as did Joan and Ernest Rodker years later—the psychological pain resulting from recognizing oneself as the "raw material" for others' fictions (or dramas, as the case may be).[6] No critic of *roman à clef* and disguised autobiography can fully resolve the question of a writer's ethical responsibility to his or her models and the real-life consequences of "mining" the details of people's characters and lives for artistic purposes. The degree to which psychological harm or pain may obtain depends on several factors, including the nature of the relationship and the degree of closeness and trust assumed between one who recognizes himself or herself as the model for an invented character and the writer who has chosen to mine such personal details for literary purposes. One can speculate that Clancy Sigal's initial shock and outrage and Joan Rodker's later dismay concerning Doris Lessing's literary method were based on their sense of a breach of personal trust. From the writer's perspective, Lessing insisted that she merely practiced what all writers practice: the creative transformation of experience, which may draw on personal relationships with friends and intimate acquaintances, among others. Indeed, Clancy Sigal—perhaps initially in self-defense but ultimately because it served his own creative purposes—perfected the same "mining" technique himself, as will be illustrated in subsequent chapters in this study. Regarding the imaginative enterprise, the interests of authors and their "originals" simply do not converge.

Chapter 3

Plays and Power Plays

"The characters of The Golden Notebook *came from* Play with a Tiger.*" Doris Lessing ("The Older I Get, the Less I Believe")*

Dream Tigers

At the beginning of the inner golden notebook, Anna Wulf enters a dream state, during which the light she observes on the ceiling of her room in the darkness transmogrifies into a tiger. Threatened, she feels as if she is "inside a cage into which the animal could leap when it wished. I was ill with the smell of dead flesh, the reek of the tiger[,] and with fear" (*The Golden Notebook* 574). On the one hand, she fears the animal and is alarmed when it attacks her directly, lacerating her forearm with its claws. However, as the flesh wound instantly heals, her feelings turn to concern; she worries that the tiger will be captured by men who are coming for it. Anna quickly decodes the transparent symbolism, understanding that the dream embodies her complicated feelings about Saul Green: "The tiger is Saul, I don't want him to be caught, I want him to be running wild through the world" (575). The dream also inspires her creative imagination, an aspect of her personality that remains intact even during her most emotionally disintegrated moments of breakdown. She is inspired to "write a play about Anna and Saul and the tiger" in which "the 'story'...would be shaped by pain..." (575).

Of significant consequence for the actual relationship between Doris Lessing and Clancy Sigal, Lessing indeed wrote that play, titled *Play with a Tiger*, in 1958, concurrent with the period of her composition of *The Golden Notebook*. Regarding which literary transformation of her idea came first, she explained that "the characters of *The Golden Notebook* came from *Play with a Tiger*" ("The Older I Get, the Less I Believe," September 11, 1991, 201). In the novel, the correspondences between Saul Green and the dream tiger that Anna regards as both threatening and in need of her protection suggest that Lessing concurrently envisioned two different literary forms whose focus and subject matter converged: the emotional collision between a woman who aspires to liberate herself from traditional gender roles and a feisty, independent man who refuses to be "caged" in an exclusive relationship with her or any one woman. Between novel and play, several crucial details overlap, including the name of the protagonist: Anna Freeman in *Play with a Tiger* is "all in pieces" (*Play with a Tiger* 37); Anna Freeman Wulf in *The Golden Notebook* is similarly emotionally split. In the latter text, in the final installment of the yellow notebook, the man who prefigures Saul Green is mentioned by name only once—as Dave (sketch 10, *GN* 501), the name of the antagonist in *Play with a Tiger*. In both texts, several key elements of Anna's fraught intimate relationship with her American lover mirror Doris Lessing's fraught relationship with Clancy Sigal. At one point in the inner golden notebook, Anna Wulf describes Saul Green as "a talking animal" with green eyes who aims words at her like bullets and who expostulates, "I'm not going to be shut up, caged, tamed, told be quiet..." (*GN* 587).

As a result of casting complications for *Play with a Tiger*—the producer, Oscar Lowenstein, insisted that Siobhan McKenna play the female lead, but she was not available for four years (*Walking in the Shade* 254)—the play did not reach the stage until 1962, four years after its composition. Produced by Lowenstein and directed by Ted Kotcheff, the play finally opened at the Comedy Theatre on March 22, 1962, with McKenna as Anna Freeman. Lessing was disappointed not only by the protracted delay between composition and stage performance of the play but by several other aspects of the production, including the size of the theater—"I believe if they had done it in a smaller theater it would have succeeded" ("The Older I Get" 201)—and the miscasting of the male lead. The young American actor who played Dave Miller, Alex Viespi, was, in her view, "a sexist stud" (201).

Though Harold Hobson—according to Lessing, "the most influential [drama] critic" at the time—praised the play as "the most troublingly poetic play in London," most reviewers were, in Lessing's word, "indifferent" to it (*Walking in the Shade* 255). *Play with a Tiger* closed, "just under its break-even point" (255), after a two-month run. The accumulated disappointments of *Play with a Tiger* and several other works for the theater that went nowhere led Lessing to cease writing plays altogether. She concluded that to continue to do so would be an exercise in frustration. As she explained, "Why should one go through this humiliation and torture when you can write a novel and get it printed the way you wrote it?" ("The Older I Get" 201).

Of the six characters in *Play with a Tiger*, four are secondary characters whose function is to reinforce the central drama concerning stereotyped gender roles and vexed heterosexual intimate relationships. Anna Freeman, an Australian woman in her mid-thirties, and her somewhat older widowed flatmate, Mary Jackson, decry the sexual double standard, including the norm of chronic male philandering. One of their friends, Harry Paine, an aspiring middle-aged writer, is a perfect illustration of the problem. Early in the first act, he expresses dismay that his young "poppet" (*Tiger* 21) is about to marry a man her own age who, unlike him, is actually available. Bereft, the older man admits to having earlier suggested to his wife that she, he, and his girlfriend "live together in the same house" (34).

The antagonist of Lessing's unacknowledged *drame à clef*, Dave Miller, is, like Clancy Sigal, a Jewish American Communist filmscript writer in his early thirties who grew up on the streets of Chicago. The son of two professional union organizers, he is "rootless on principle" (*Tiger*, character list and descriptions, unnumbered front page). Although Lessing never acknowledged the similarities in character, behavior, and idiom between Dave Miller and Clancy Sigal that stunned Sigal, in her autobiography she remarks that elements of the play's setting—specifically, the rough street scene suggested outside the room in which the action takes place—were inspired by "Clancy's tales of his street-corner adolescence in Chicago, on the 'wrong side of the tracks,' the prostitutes' house a diagonal glance away, where the girls sometimes emerged on to the pavement to attract customers or to quarrel" (*Walking* 254). In the play, Dave describes himself as "still a twelve-year-old slum kid standing on a street corner in Chicago, watching the expensive broads go by and wishing I had the dough to buy them all" (*Tiger* 32). At another point, he mentions his "old buddy Jedd"—Lessing's barely disguised allusion to Jed, Sigal's alter ego and protagonist of his semiautobiographical first novel, *Going Away: A Report, a Memoir* (*Tiger* 48). When the play begins, Anna and Dave have split up, Dave has a girlfriend, and Anna is engaged to marry another man, an underdeveloped character named Tom Lattimer. The engagement is quickly dissolved for several reasons, including Anna's need for greater personal freedom than marriage offers her and Tom's awareness that his fiancée is still in love with her former lover. Dave's current girlfriend, a young American woman named

Janet Stevens, means little to him, although the reverse is not true: she arrives on the scene in distress, hoping for Anna's assistance in pinning Dave to marriage because she is five months pregnant with his child.

However, these are side issues. The central drama of *Play with a Tiger* is the extended confrontation between Anna and Dave, whose feelings for each other ricochet rapidly between affection and hostility, appreciation and mockery. Dave embodies the reigning patriarchal attitude of the 1950s that so rankled Doris Lessing in her relationship with Sigal: that women should accept male promiscuity as the norm. Dave even exclaims to Anna, "how any man can be faithful to one woman beats me" (*Tiger* 32). Anna and Dave had split up over precisely this issue, exacerbated by Anna's conviction that he repeatedly lied to her about his liaisons with other women. She castigates Dave's capacity to deny his two-timing behavior in the face of the evidence, remarking, "[I]f I walked into your room and found you in bed with a girl and said Dave, who is that girl, you'd say what girl? I don't see any girl, it's just your sordid imagination" (39).

Anna's accusations highlight Clancy Sigal's view, as expressed in several of his journal entries and related writing during the period, that Doris Lessing routinely assumed infidelity when it may not have been the case. Five months into their relationship and just a few weeks before Sigal recorded his discovery that Lessing was reading his journal, he wrote, "Doris zeroed in with a highly-charged accusation that I am lying to her, forcing her into the jealous woman role. It was a stunner; I was confused as to how to handle it. . . . Doris claims she is not jealous but detests my feeding her half truths about how I live & what I am; insulting her intelligence" ("Going Away" Journal, October 10, 1957).

By the fall of 1957, Sigal knew that Lessing was secretly reading his journals and had begun to fashion his entries with his prying reader in mind. In that context, a long entry penned on October 28, in which he mulled over the visit to London of his former French girlfriend, is especially pertinent. Sigal belatedly understood that he had put Lessing in a difficult position and admitted that, if the situation were reversed, "no matter how logically or eloquently the woman argues the case I would feel betrayed." He added that "the old Clancy" would have

> little trouble figuring out what to do. He would, if it were necessary to teach Doris that Clancy, *if he is an animal, is an uncaged animal,* go

out to the French girl & let Doris suffer sharply[?] a little at 1st....
[I]f, however, he felt that it were doing great damage he would write
the French girl & tell her all was off. Instead, he drifts. Perhaps it is
a new, passive way for him to get his message across to Doris that
Clancy is a friend & not a husband; that out of deference to her needs
his own are being starved & thus his nerves frayed. (October 28, 1957;
Sigal's underscoring in pencil; my italics)

At an undetermined point, Sigal indicated in the margin of the journal entry he wrote two days later (October 30) his discovery that Lessing had been reading what he wrote there. Of particular significance in this passage, his reference to himself as an "uncaged animal" may have inspired Lessing to imagine Anna Wulf's dream of a wild tiger whose demand for freedom evokes not only her fear but her concern for its safety. In *Play with a Tiger*, the promiscuous prowess of the tiger, Dave Miller, clashes with Anna Freeman's need for emotional and sexual fidelity.

In the play, Anna and Dave retain intense, albeit ambivalent, feelings for each other even though their relationship has ended. Indeed, Dave admits to Anna that he is lost without her. When she touches his chest, he "begin[s] to breathe" (*Tiger* 33). Later, Anna similarly acknowledges that Dave is her "soul" (50). The first act of the play ends with Dave's question to Anna, echoed as the opening line of Act Two: "Who are you?" (*Tiger* 36, 37). His former lover responds by describing her younger self—Anna MacClure from Brisbane, Australia (37)—as a woman who wanted choices for herself and who emphatically rejected the stultifying gender roles represented by her conventional parents, particularly her discontented mother. In Anna's view, her parents consented to mutual entrapment in a relationship in which their primary feeling for each other was "a kind of ironical compassion—the compassion of one prisoner for another..." (54, Lessing's ellipsis). She vows that she would prefer "anything rather than the man and woman, the jailed and the jailer, living together, talking to themselves, and wondering what happened that made them strangers. I won't, I'll die alone first" (54–5).

Dave describes his own unconventional path to his current life, beginning with his youth in Chicago. More recently, he has had a brief and unsatisfactory experience with psychoanalysis, the recapitulation of which provides not only the details of his disturbed emotional history but a vehicle for Lessing's extended critique of the psychoanalytic process. When, as Dave explains, he had tried to describe to the shrink what was troubling him, the doctor had seemed much more interested in his sex life, asking him how many women he had "had" (45). Amusingly, the psychiatrist was offended when his patient turned the same question to him. Dave regards his problem not as his relationships with women but his resistance to being "integrated into society" along the lines of conventional expectations, particularly the psychiatrist's recommendation—echoing social norms of the time—that he "get married, have two well-spaced children and a settled job" (47). Dave challenges the cliché, explaining, "I don't want to fit into [society], I want society to fit itself to me..." (49). Anna and Dave concur in their refusal to be guided by the norms of the time regarding heterosexual intimate relationships. Yet the only alternative seems to be a "sex-war" (58) in which men and women—particularly women like Anna Freeman who aspire to the kind of independence that men take for granted—square off as antagonists.

Ironically, Anna regards the sex war as "the only clean war left. It's the only war that won't destroy us all. That's why we are fighting it" (58). Dave argues that the resistance of people like Anna and himself to conventional social formulas is what enables them to remain open to change: "if there's anything new in the world anywhere, any new thought, or new way of living, we'll be ready to hear the first whisper of it" (60–1); he is waiting for "something new to be born" (61). In *The Golden Notebook*, Lessing gives this central insight not to Saul Green but to Anna Wulf, who remarks to *her* psychiatrist, Mother Sugar, "I want to be able to separate in myself what is old and cyclic, the recurring history, the myth, from what is new.... [S]ometimes I meet people, and it seems to me the fact they are cracked across, they're split, means they are keeping themselves open for something" (*GN* 442–3).

In *Play with a Tiger*, the "something" is embodied in and by the tiger itself, "an enormous glossy padding tiger" (61)—like the "beautiful glossy animal" of Anna's dream in *The Golden Notebook* (*GN* 575)—whose appearance in the second act comes as no surprise to Anna Freeman. As she explains to Dave, she had been thinking that "if we can't breed something better than we are, we've had it, the human race has had it," when suddenly a male tiger had appeared in her room, "twitching his tail" (61). She had fondled the tiger, which—again, analogous to the tiger of Anna Wulf's dream in *The Golden Notebook*—had responded first by purring and then by lashing her with his claws. Dave, excited, immediately grasps that the tiger represents Anna's view of him—an animal by turns "purring" and aggressive. Perhaps preferring to regard himself as more of a pussy-cat than a wild cat, he asks her why she did not offer the dream tiger a "saucer of milk" (62). Instead, the tiger had left Anna's bed only to be captured on the street, as Anna had feared, by men wheeling a large cage. Anna explains to Dave, "I tried hard, but that was the best [I could do]—a tiger. And I'm covered with scars" (62). Ignoring her emphasis on the "scars," Dave cautions Anna that "anything you shut out because you're scared of it becomes more dangerous" (63), to which Anna replies, "Yes, but I've lived longer than you, and I'm tired" (63).

As the third act of *Play with a Tiger* opens, the tone of intimate exchange abruptly ends. Anna concludes that she must be crazy because she keeps forgetting that her relationship with Dave is over. By this point in the play, she has "frozen up on him" (stage directions, 65) to insulate herself from further emotional injury. She feels that if she expresses her unhappiness, he will interpret her petulance as a curtailment of his freedom (65). Because she cannot be emotionally honest with him, she must withdraw from him. Though Dave apologizes for having made her unhappy, he reminds her that he cannot help being who he is. In effect, the tiger cannot change its stripes. Anna nakedly exposes the depth of her hurt and pain, remarking, "I sometimes think if my skin were taken off I'd be just one enormous bruise" (69).

Turning more combative, she speaks "with malice" about the degrading vocabulary that Dave and other American men use when they speak of sex: "getting laid" (72) incorrectly implies that the man is a helpless creature at the mercy of a sexually aggressive woman. In *The Golden Notebook*, Anna Wulf expresses the same grievance, complaining to Saul Green that, "whenever you talk about sex or love you say: he got laid, I got laid[,] or they got laid (male).... [S]urely *I* get laid, *she* gets laid, they (female) get laid, but surely you, as a man, don't get laid, you lay" (*GN* 523, Lessing's italics). Loathing the way "language degrade[s] sex," she decries the crude and dehumanizing or infantilizing diction that Saul routinely uses when he speaks about women: "you never say a woman, you say a broad, a lay, a baby, a doll, a bird, you talk about butts and boobs, every time you mention a woman I see her either as a sort of window-dresser's dummy or as a heap of dismembered parts, breasts, or legs or buttocks" (*GN* 523). In both *The Golden Notebook* and *Play with a Tiger*, Saul/Dave frequently addresses Anna as "Baby," a patronizing generic term that irritates her intensely. In the play, Anna reproaches Dave, pointing out that "Every woman is baby, for fear you'd whisper the wrong name into the wrong ear in the dark" (*Tiger* 32)

The implication of such degraded communications—and relations—between the sexes is a central preoccupation of both *The Golden Notebook* and *Play with a Tiger*. In the play, Anna Freeman is determined to have an honest relationship with a man "or nothing" (*Tiger* 74). As she explains to Dave, "I watch women buttering up their men...and despising them while they do it. It makes me sick" (74). In her view, Dave's real sin is less his womanizing than his hypocrisy. Though he encourages Anna's independence, he will likely marry Janet, even though he does not love her, because she is pregnant with their child. Anna briefly regrets that she didn't employ the same devious strategy for entrapping Dave herself. When the phone rings and the caller is Janet, Dave responds by leaving Anna to return to his girlfriend. Anna, bitterly concluding that her former lover will marry Janet because, as Dave puts it, she has "manacles" on him (78), begins to cry but interrupts her tears to pour herself a glass of Scotch. The stage directions fill in what Lessing's distressed character does not say: "Anna sits holding herself together, because if she cracked up now, it would be too terrible" (79). Soon, her flatmate, Mary, enters, so concerned about her own inebriated condition earlier that evening that she is virtually oblivious to Anna's grief. *Play with a Tiger* concludes with Anna moving alone toward her bed as "the city comes up around her and the curtain comes down" (stage directions 80).

Though *Play with a Tiger* dramatically expresses Anna Freeman's—and her creator's—emotional grievances, from Clancy Sigal's perspective, *he*, not Doris Lessing, was the injured party. He was deeply distressed by the play, feeling betrayed by Lessing's appropriation for her artistic purposes of many details of their most intimate exchanges during a period that included his emotional breakdown and his unsatisfactory experience with psychoanalysis. He first learned of these borrowings for the dramatic character, Dave Miller, when one of their reconciliations in 1959—achieved despite their growing recognition of their incompatibility—reinforced their mutual dependence. In a journal entry that expresses his ambivalence, he faults both Lessing and himself for the impasses in their relationship:

> Our reconciliations were always beautiful. I knew I needed her badly. For the first time, I saw that she needed me with equal poignance. She said she loved me but I believe it was that other men bored her.

Preeminently she was a woman who required an equal partner, and inasmuch as she was my superior in moral strength and creative talent I had no choice but to treat her as an equal. For the next few days we lazed about August London, slowly, almost dreamily, while our bruises, we hoped, healed. (Journal, July 1959: 6 [unnumbered TS])

In the same entry, Sigal records his shocked discovery that Lessing "had begun to write a play about the two of us. I was, at first, unconcerned, and then, as I understood, furious. I issued a veiled threat that to continue to write such a play might cleave us inseparably, but I knew she would write it. She would never, for some very good reasons, sacrifice her personal life to art.... I do not believe she could have existed without her art. In the meantime, we continued our reconciliation. As usual, the flies in the ointment were of my own making" (6).

Two months later, in September 1959, Sigal learned from Lessing that she was involved in discussions with Oscar Lowenstein concerning casting one of her plays, though not which one. By phone, he expressed his sympathy over the protracted delay resulting from the producer's insistence on a particular actress. When he learned that the play in question was "To play w/ Tiger" [*sic*] it was, he writes, "like the wind is sucked out of me. A proof of superiority, of the fact that I am not paramount. I feel awful, sulk..." (Journal 1959–60, September 19, 1959). The following day, he reports feeling "sick and dizzy all day, as tho D's play had sucked soul-wind out of me" (September 20, 1959).

Several days later, Sigal traveled to Yorkshire to visit miner friends whom he had interviewed for his documentary fiction, *Weekend in Dinlock*, which was soon to appear in print. He returned to London early and unannounced, having just received news of his mother's death in California. Since Lessing was not in the flat at the time, Sigal apparently felt free to wander into her room and read what he found there, ironically mirroring her behavior during his absences from the flat. What is noteworthy in his typed—and therefore presumably somewhat more polished—journal entry in response to what he discovered is his undisguised emotional shock, accentuated by his references to Lessing not by name but by a generic term. Almost replicating the scene in which he discovered the character sketch of himself on a page in Lessing's typewriter while she was drafting *The Golden Notebook*, he wrote,

> I found my woman's play open at a certain page and I let my eye idle over a few lines. It hit me between the eyes. The play she was writing,

in fact had completed, was about our relationship. But those lines of dialog! They were exactly what I had said to her, in my worst, most intimate moments of a severe nervous breakdown in the year previous. My emotions are indescribable. Never, I felt, had I been so profoundly betrayed. It instantly occurred to me that my rage might be a convenient way to excuse an estrangement, but when all was said and done I was deeply and painfully hurt. I spent the night with her. I tried to be normal. All to no avail. (Late September 1959 Journal: 2 [unnumbered page])

Sigal's sense of shock, which persisted for several days, affected him quite viscerally. As he elaborated in his journal,

By the following Monday I had become ill with symptoms which I suspected were highly psychological. I became feverish and unbalanced, and took to my bed with a sense of collapse and weariness. I wrote a letter to the woman, an angry letter, [to] which she replied in like mind, reminding me how much she had done for me. She was perfectly correct in this.... I could not remove from my mind my woman's betrayal.... I needed her, depended upon her, defined much of my life and work by her—and now she had done this. I suspected and believed that consciously or otherwise this was her way of writing finis to a relationship which had begun to seriously exhaust her. (Late September 1959 Journal: 2 [unnumbered page])

As if nursing a wound that must be repeatedly probed for its exquisite pain, Sigal, at several other points in his unpublished and published writings, expressed this development as a breach of trust on Lessing's part. For example, in an unfinished novel draft titled "Ceiling Spike," possibly begun in 1959, he fictionalized Lessing not as a playwright but as an actress and producer named Sophie Ravenscroft. The author's alter ego, Matthew, attends one of Sophie's star turns in the theatre as Hedda Gabler. Watching her performance, he remarks, "The soul-wind, the breath, had rushed out of me in the theatre" ("Ceiling Spike" seg. 2: 140). However, he later admits that his extreme response was in part due to his shock at the news of his mother's death.

Although Lessing characterized Sigal as a wild tiger who was ambiguously both dangerous and in need of her protection, Sigal regarded Doris Lessing as the tiger. He saw himself not as a destructive partner in their relationship but a vulnerable one in need of her nurturance. Expressing that conviction in "Ceiling Spike," he rings changes on Lessing's tiger images: Sigal's narrative stand-in, knowing that Sophie Ravenscroft (Doris Lessing) is fond of describing herself as a tigress, asks her, "'If you are a tiger'... 'what am I?' 'Oh you,' she shrugged, 'you're a bird of passage of course.' 'In other words,' I said, trying to be careful to keep my anger under control..., 'you're the cat and I'm the canary.' 'Don't be so literal,' she snapped..." ("Spike" seg. 1: 60).

Later in the same draft, Sigal approaches the subject from another direction. Sophie is working with a playwright and "companion," Max Wexler, on elements of dialogue in a play in which she will appear as the female lead. When Matthew, Sigal's alter ego, overhears their discussion in the kitchen, his heart "freezes."

> The "line of dialogue" given by Sophie to Max was all too familiar. It was something I had been in the habit of saying to her in our most intimate moments. I suddenly knew, without a shadow of doubt, the basis of this strange collaboration.... A couple of days later... I whirled on Sophie, "Are you writing a play?"... "Yes," she said.... "But it's about me?" I said, "isn't it?"....She looked at me with amusement. "If you mean is there a character based on what I know of you: yes."... "You know," I said as levelly as I could, "if you go through with this play about me—we're through. Finished. Kaput." "Threats? At this late stage. Well well." That was the closest I had come to knocking Sophie down. We might be married today if I had. ("Spike" 2: 156–7)

Later, Matthew accepts an assignment to review the suspect play produced by Sophie, who is also its lead actress. As the play, pointedly titled *The Liar*, unfolds on stage, he runs angrily out of the theater ("Spike" 3: 203).

In both *The Golden Notebook* and *Play with a Tiger*, Doris Lessing alludes to a neurotic and destructive aspect of Anna Wulf (Freeman)'s relationship with Saul Green/Dave Miller that was also true of her fraught relationship with Clancy Sigal: a regressive mother/son dynamic. In the novel, soon after Saul Green arrives to rent the room in her flat, Anna Wulf enters his room to notify him of a phone call and finds him asleep. When she awakens him, he "put[s] his arms up round [her] neck, in a frightened child's gesture..." (*GN* 519). Later, Anna accuses Saul of "mother-trouble. You've fixed on me for your mother. You have to outwit me all the time. [...]Then, when I get hurt, your murderous feelings for me, for the mother, frighten you, so that you have to comfort and soothe me..." (*GN* 543, Lessing's ellipses unless bracketed). When their affair reaches its nadir and they recognize that they must separate, the negative mother–son pattern reappears one last time, as parody. Anna, trying to resist the urge to embrace Saul because she knows they must part, nonetheless cradles him in her arms; at the same time she recognizes the inauthenticity of her gesture. However, the maternal quality in her embrace triggers a filial response from Saul, who murmurs to her in the voice of a child, "'Ise a good boy,' not as he had ever whispered to his own mother, for those words could never have been his, they were out of literature. And he murmured them mawkishly, in parody. But not quite" (*GN* 598). They both agree that, as Saul phrases it, "We can't either of us ever go lower than that" (599), at which point he packs his bags to leave Anna's flat. *Play with a Tiger* hints directly at the same disturbing Oedipal undercurrent. Early in the encounter between Anna Freeman and Dave Miller, Dave insists that he won't be "any woman's pet" (*Tiger* 32), adding combatively, "And I'm not going to stand for you either—mother of the world, the great womb, the eternal conscience. I like women, but I'm going to like them my way and not according to the rules laid down by the incorporated mothers of the universe" (33).

At various points in his journals and autobiographical/fictional writing, Clancy Sigal examined Doris Lessing's persistent contention that he was projecting onto her his unresolved feelings about his dominating mother, a dynamic that seriously undermined their intimacy. In one of his earliest attempts to write about this subject—the Coral typescript chapters in which he lightly fictionalized the early phase of his relationship with Lessing—he describes Coral's psychoanalytic diagnosis of his fictional double's problem:

> Coral says I am probably looking for the Eternal Mother.... She talks a lot about the "good" mother and "bad" mother, good and bad nipple.... But how does it apply to me? She says, a little smugly, that one day I will understand. She went, she says, to a Jungian lady psychoanalyst for three years to learn about herself. I am amazed. I would have bet a thousand dollars Doris [*sic*] had never been to a shrink. ("CS writing about DL" 112)

In the draft of an unfinished story that Sigal eventually incorporated into his loosely autobiographical third novel, *The Secret Defector* (1992), the fictional substitutes for himself and Lessing are characters named, respectively, Sid Bell and Lily Sloan, who meet and even occasionally sleep together during the two years following the end of their relationship. By that point, Sigal had apparently achieved sufficient emotional distance from Lessing to write about their complicated relationship with a touch of humor as well as with a nod at their shared technique of transforming autobiography into fiction. During one such encounter between their narrative alter egos, Lily says, "My dear Sid, why didn't we ever get married?" which Sid regards with tolerant amusement as a clear signal that his former lover is "about to publish something about me. First it was a short story, then a play, then a section of a novel. I read them without much interest but carefully, *noting now the parts I thought I might want to use myself later.* I was infuriated only by the casting of 'my' part in her play" ("CS on DL" 1, my italics).

From Lessing's perspective, the stand-off between Anna Freeman and Dave Miller—like the one between Anna Freeman Wulf and Saul Green—reproduces the clashing emotional scripts and the traditional but nonviable gender roles, still in place at mid-twentieth century, available to women and men in heterosexual intimate relationships. By the end of *Play with a Tiger*, the tiger has escaped, leaving the despairing Anna alone to nurse her wounds. In *The Golden Notebook*, when Ella and Julia discuss the difficulty of being "free women"—a phrase expressed mostly with irony—Julia exclaims, "Free! What's the use of us being free if [men] aren't?" (*GN* 429).

* * *

Dramatic Skirmishes

Beginning after he and Doris Lessing separated, Clancy Sigal wrote a dozen plays that were not published, produced, or performed, most of them concerning subjects that are unrelated to his relationship with Doris Lessing.[1] However, two plays—including "A Visit with Rose," the only play that was produced—feature a central character named Rose O'Malley who bears a number of resemblances to Lessing, albeit in skewed, exaggerated, or satirical form. Both plays are five-scene dramas. The unproduced "Little Big Horn, N.W. 6" is a sharp-toned play with three characters whose positions within a rather-too-obvious Oedipal triangle constantly shift: Jerry (Clancy Sigal), Rose (Doris Lessing), and Oliver—awkwardly nicknamed Ockie—the stand-in for Lessing's son on the cusp of adolescence. The apprentice piece suggests Sigal's attempt to work through and resolve in dramatic form his complicated feelings about his relationship not only with Lessing but with her adolescent son, Peter. His dramatic alter ego, Jerry, naively argues that his relationship with Rose's son is independent of his relationship with her. The action of the play ultimately undermines that assumption, with Rose's son Ockie as the catalyst.

Other details in the script draw on the significant matter of Lessing's intrusion into Sigal's private journals—an incident to which Sigal returned almost obsessively in his narrative and dramatic writings. In this version, Jerry, reiterating a version of the strategy that Sigal describes with various twists in his fiction, plays, and sketches, ties a thread across the knobs of the dresser drawer where he hides the journal each day and repeatedly finds it broken ("Little Big Horn, N.W. 6" 17). He remarks to Rose that the "new section" of her novel in progress is "all about an American named Paul Blue"—Sigal's play on Saul Green's name—"and what you say about him sounds remarkably like what I say about myself in my journal" (17). However, this time Sigal also gives the incident a comic turn by reversing the roles of sinner and sinned-against: Rose's response to Jerry's accusation is to accuse him of "prying" into her "new novel" (17). Jerry defends his literary eavesdropping as an opportunity to "look over your shoulder to see how you do it. Call it on the job training" (17). When Rose insists that "Paul Blue is not you," he puns in response, "Stay out of my drawers—figuratively, I mean" (18).

The plot thickens when Ockie asks whether Jerry intends to marry his mother, a question Jerry cannot answer, given the tensions between himself and Rose. Jerry attempts to enlist the boy's confidence by explaining that because he, too, grew up fatherless, he can readily sympathize with Ockie's anxieties about the men in his mother's life. Following a series of dramatic skirmishes that highlight the tensions between each pair in the triangulated relationship, the characters gather for the climactic final scene, during which each attempts to ally himself/herself with one member of the triangle and against the other. Jerry and Rose each self-servingly attempt to enlist Ockie on their side, while the boy, who in earlier scenes has self-protectively allied himself with each of them, resists both of their overtures and calls their bluffs.

Although "Little Big Horn, N.W. 6" suffers from a strident tone that is insufficiently rescued by the humor it occasionally attempts, the play is revealing for its treatment of the triangulations with Lessing's son that Sigal recognized as a complicating feature of his relationship with her. In the play, the Oedipal triangle is a convincing, albeit rather obvious, trope for dramatizing the tensions produced by their living arrangement. Sigal's genuine regard and affection for Lessing's son was complicated by his own unresolved feelings as a son who was abandoned by his father during his youth. As Sigal later wrote in his nonfictional account of growing up fatherless, "When a father abandons a son, the son takes on the role of guilty party. If you have admired your father, then you must see his wisdom in ditching you. You deserve punishing because he knows you for the piece of shit you know yourself to be.... *He left because you exist*" (*A Woman of Uncertain Character* 182, Sigal's italics). However, during the time of his relationship with Doris Lessing, Sigal did not want his ambiguous position as her lover—but not inevitably her future spouse and therefore not inevitably Peter Lessing's future stepfather—to dictate the terms of their relationship. In the play, the wise but troubled child absorbs and amplifies the strains between the lovers, only some of which are due to him. He lacks power to change the adult script except in fantasy, a strategy that Sigal effectively and even poignantly dramatizes through Ockie's imaginative but ultimately limited strategy for empowerment: his role-playing as the Indian chief Crazy Horse, the defiant hero of the battle of Little Big Horn.

Sigal's only produced play, "A Visit with Rose," like "Little Big Horn, N. W. 6," dramatizes clashes among three characters, in this case all adults, who are fictionalized versions of Sigal (Jack Barker), Sigal's then-wife, Margaret Walters (Shirley Barker), and Doris Lessing (Rose O'Malley). The play, which aired on BBC Radio sometime in 1983,[2] is the most accomplished of Sigal's dramatic works, recasting several themes and preoccupations that appear in his short stories and introducing new ones. The dialogues range— more successfully in tone and expression than those in "Little Big Horn, N.W. 6"—from sarcasm and critical attack to sympathy and grudging admiration of Rose O'Malley. Through Sigal's treatment, a skewed but recognizable version of Doris Lessing, along with several prescient views of the direction of her writing and the development of her ideas, emerges.

The drama opens in the London home of Jack and Shirley Barker as Jack, reading the *Guardian* arts page, mentions to his wife a rave review of Rose O'Malley's newest play. Learning from the review that Rose is laid up in the hospital with a broken leg, he asks Shirley whether he should phone her. The remark precipitates tensions between husband and wife that apparently have been simmering for some time. Shirley, irritated at Jack's undiminished preoccupation with his former "mistress" (her term), reminds him of his earlier scandalous public behavior with regard to her. On one occasion, he had "knock[ed] down that actor she was sleeping with at the Royal Court—I mean the Royal Court actor she was sleeping with—when he called her a trollop for making time with you as well" ("A Visit with Rose" 1). On another occasion, he had "broke[n] up [Rose's] play at the Aldwych" by shouting at Rose—with reference to the actor who was impersonating him—"I never uttered putrid lines like that—the least you could have done was get a better actor in the role!" ("Visit" 2). Shirley's reminders are thinly disguised references to Sigal's outrage at finding himself so transparently characterized in Lessing's *Play with a Tiger*, staged at the Comedy Theater in 1962.

The conflict escalates as Jack complains that his wife wants him to "work" all the time while Rose had seemed satisfied with him as he was—certainly not an accurate reflection of Clancy Sigal's relationship with Doris Lessing, though the matter of contention in their relationship was philandering rather than employment. Through Shirley's retort, Sigal also airs some of his own grievances: Shirley snaps, "Of course she liked you as you were—a perfect patsy for her next play and book. A sex object she could show off at parties" (2). She concludes with the stinger, "You were her male geisha" (2). The source of Shirley's antagonism is her husband's persistent comparisons of her with Rose. In her view, Jack's "basic" relationship is still with his former lover rather than with her (3, Sigal's underscoring). Jack attempts to placate his wife by reminding her that it is she, not Rose O'Malley, whom he married.

The next four scenes of "A Visit with Rose" are set in a hospital room where Rose—described in the stage directions as "a middle[-]aged woman of great attractiveness" (4)—lies in bed with a cast on her broken leg, a detail based on an actual event in Doris Lessing's life (Klein, *Doris Lessing* 245). She is pleased to see Jack enter her room, somewhat less so when she notices his wife with him. She quickly perceives the strain between them. Before long, tensions also develop between Rose and Shirley: stage directions for the first sarcastic exchange between them indicates "snarls" for Rose and "declaring war" for Shirley (5). As the opening scene implies, Jack's wife feels herself in competition with her husband's former lover. However, Rose is similarly on the defensive. Early on, she directs a caustic comment toward the younger woman, cattily remarking that Jack "was always betraying me with teenage dollie birds. I didn't actually expect him to marry one" (5). Jack attempts to break up what increasingly resembles a "cat fight" (5) between the two women. When Rose "narrows her eyes into a cool stare at Shirley" (stage directions 7)—one questions whether this and other silent expressions could have been conveyed in audio-only delivery—the older woman's expression prompts an even stronger verbal cut from Shirley: "I take it that is your notorious x-ray look—the one that lets you eviscerate your friends and lay them out on your literary dissecting table like butterflies in formaldehyde" (7). The scene ends with Shirley stalking angrily out of the hospital room, leaving Jack and Rose to themselves.

With the former lovers alone together in Rose's room, the third scene begins with Jack assuring Rose that Shirley "understands about you and me" and that he and Rose are "important to each other in a way other people can't interfere with" (8). Rose indicates that she has gotten over her anger that Jack left her and sincerely wants his marriage to Shirley to succeed. However, the dialogue becomes more combative as it unfolds. Jack, needling Rose for her excessive commitment to her writing, snidely remarks, "as long as you have a pair of eyes and can work a typewriter you'll write. And that's all that's really important to you" (9). Rose, stung by his inclination to "push [her] off into some sexually neutral corner—Rose The Writer" (9), shifts the conversation to intimate matters, asking him bluntly, "How is your sex life?...How do Shirley and you get along—in bed?" (10). Jack, clearly irritated by her tactlessness, replies that her question "[s]eems an awfully lazy way for you to dig out your raw material" (10). Rose's probing questions and blunt remarks prompt Jack to defend his wife, as they gave Clancy Sigal an opportunity to vent his spleen on several matters of contention between himself and Doris Lessing when they were lovers.

Less defensively, Jack recognizes the generational divide between the two important women in his life; as he reminds Rose, his wife worships Rose O'Malley and "reads every book of [hers]" (11). The fourth scene of the play foregrounds that conflict when, while Jack is absent from the room, Shirley enjoys a turn at verbal combat with Rose. The stage directions—again, directed more toward readers than listeners—indicate, "You can practically see [Rose] taking out a mental pad and paper" (13). Shirley, refusing Rose's invitation to talk about trouble between her and Jack, responds with one of the most acerbic lines in the play: "Jack warned me you carry an invisible tape recorder in your head and you play back all your friends' intimate conversations in your books" (13), a line that exposes Sigal's lingering pique at Lessing's appropriative literary method. However, Rose's persistence overrides Shirley's resistance. The younger woman tearfully confesses her fear that Jack still loves Rose. Though the stage directions for Rose's response are especially revealing—"loves it, but comes to" (14)—one must again wonder how her important but unspoken expressions could have been communicated in audio form. Such details strongly suggest that the play was originally intended for stage rather than radio performance.

Shirley's opening gives Rose an opportunity to criticize Jack directly for his insufficiencies. Sigal, attempting to see himself through Lessing's eyes, lets Rose diagnose her former lover's problem as a fear of emotional commitment that prompts him to create obstacles where there are none. Expressing a view that appears repeatedly throughout Sigal's writing about his relationship with Lessing—her insistence that the source of both his philandering and his writer's block was his unresolved feelings about his mother—Rose explains knowingly to Shirley, "He can never get too close to a woman—he used up so much energy fighting off his beautiful, shrewd, sexually aggressive mama. I told you it was straight out of a Freudian primer" ("Visit" 14). Shirley is offended by Rose's armchair—or, rather, bedside—psychology. To the older woman's insistence that she does not want to get "involved" in the "messes" between Jack and his wife, Shirley rebuts, "of course you do.... You're precisely the emotional vulture Jack always said you were" (15). The venomous remark hits its target, after which Shirley backpedals, reluctantly admitting that Rose was "the best thing that ever happened" to Jack (15).

With Shirley's concession softening the tone of their exchange, Rose adds, "Why can't it be: I was then but now you are. Sort of passing the torch on in a sexual relay race" (16). The two women "laugh, then giggle like schoolgirls" (stage directions 16), after which Rose asks Shirley why the women of her generation are so "anti-male" (16). Shirley defends her "generation of women [who] had many of its ideas about men formed by your work, your stories, even your example. Like it or not we're—at least partly—your daughters and disciples" (16). Following several exchanges on the subject, Rose responds indignantly, "my 'books' are not a manifesto to be waved like flirtatious banners.... I didn't write as a call to arms.... I wrote those stories for myself, to help clear my own path. I never intended them as a pocket torch to light up anyone else's confusion" (17).

Sigal's representations of Rose O'Malley's artistic motivation and her irritation concerning feminist idolatry accurately render positions that Doris Lessing herself expressed over time. In her autobiography, she describes herself as the kind of writer who "uses the process of writing to find out what you think, and even what you are..." (*Walking* 250). Moreover, beginning with her 1971 preface to *The Golden Notebook*, she repeatedly emphasized her distance from feminists and feminism. A decade later, in a 1982 interview with Lesley Hazleton for the *New York Times Magazine*, she complained,

> What the feminists want of me is something they haven't examined because it comes from religion. They want me to bear witness. What they would really like me to say is, "Ha, sisters, I stand with you side by side in your struggle toward the golden dawn where all those beastly men are no more." Do they really want people to make oversimplified statements about men and women? In fact, they do. I've come with great regret to this conclusion. (Hazleton 21)

Two decades later, her position on the subject had not changed. Barbara Ellen, interviewing her when *The Sweetest Dream* was published in 2001, observed,

> The interesting thing about Doris Lessing is not that she's not a feminist, but how insistent she is that she's not a feminist. Moreover...Lessing claims never to have embraced feminism in the first place...still stoutly refusing to be claimed as a feminist icon whole decades after her most famous work, *The Golden Notebook*, was widely hailed as one of the great inflammatory emancipating texts of the 70s. ("I Have Nothing in Common with Feminists")

Ellen also cites a similar comment Lessing made in 1994; she distanced herself from feminists, because they "never seem to think that one might like men, or enjoy them."

In "A Visit with Rose," as Rose and Shirley continue to spar over the writer Rose O'Malley's retreat from her previous ideological positions, Clancy Sigal presciently dramatized the tensions between women a generation apart in age who represent different generations of feminists—if one may use that term for Lessing despite her vehement objection to the label—as the emphasis and goals shifted from the "second wave" women's movement of the 1970s to its ideological offspring in later decades. However, the terms "second wave" and "third wave" feminism are a matter of debate and must be used advisedly. As Rhonda Hammer and Douglas Kellner representatively observe, "Some have associated [the term 'third wave'] with young feminists who were influenced by the legacies of feminism's second wave, which began in the mid-1960s. Yet the term is highly contested and has been employed to describe a number of diverse feminist and antifeminist theories and practices. Like 'feminism' in general, there is no definitive description or agreed upon consensus of what constitutes a feminist third wave" ("Third Wave Feminism, Sexualities, and the Adventures of the Posts" 220).

In Sigal's play, the exasperated Rose O'Malley drops the sensitive subject of feminism. However, she remains curious about personal matters, wondering whether Jack still talks about her. Shirley admits that he does, "[e]ven in his sleep. Once, in the middle of my orgasm, he called me Rosie" (18), to which Rose replies in sympathy—as Sigal injects into their altercation a dash of humor at his own expense— "In the middle of my orgasms he called me Louise. God knows who she is" (16, Sigal's underscoring). On the vexed subject of sexual fidelity, at least (and at last) Sigal was able to poke a critical finger at himself. The similarities between the two women's intimate experiences with Jack temporarily bring them closer together. When Shirley bluntly presses Rose, "Were you in love with Jack?" (18), Rose replies, "No. But don't you dare tell him. He was terrific in bed. And I was lonely. And he needed someone. And I loved the envious looks some of my women friends gave me when I took him to parties" (18). Her comment accords closely with Sigal's concern that Lessing (and others) came to regard him as her "male geisha." In the final yellow notebook section of *The Golden Notebook*, Anna Wulf enters a sketch for a story in which "[a] wandering man happens to land in the house of a woman whom he likes and whom he needs. He is a man with a long experience of women needing love" (*GN* 500).

The last scene of "A Visit with Rose" brings the three characters together for the play's dramatic resolution. Rose remains irritated by Shirley's sycophantic and tin-eared insistence that her feminist elder should not "back out of the sex battle" because she still has "so much to teach us," while Jack laments Rose's retreat from what was once her political "element" (22). Finally, the Barkers make their exit, offering conciliatory comments to Rose that shade toward condescension. The play concludes with a brief exchange between Rose and a minor character who appears for the only time, the nurse matron who stops in to check on her patient after the guests have left. To her query whether the woman with Rose's male visitor is his wife, Rose replies, "No. She's me. Once upon a time" and adds, "Oh God, Sarah—why do we have to grow old and up and so incredibly wise and stupid?" (23).

Placing in direct verbal combat women of different generations who were closely modeled on the two important women in his life,

Sigal lamented Lessing's ideological disaffections, including her refusal to be associated with feminism, as he astutely dramatized the generation gap between feminists of different "waves." He also anticipated another subject and a different kind of generation gap that was to become increasingly significant in Doris Lessing's fiction: the subject of aging. Over time, Lessing, born in 1919, drew on the different life stages through which she passed to illuminate the experiences of her female characters, beginning with Martha Quest, as they face the physical and emotional challenges of middle age and later years. Kate Brown, the protagonist of *The Summer Before the Dark* (1973), experiences a midlife crisis that obliges her to reorient herself toward new roles. Under the pressure of circumstances and her growing awareness that her four children are young adults or nearly so, she begins to let go of outdated elements of her maternal role; her process of self-discovery is aided by her friendship with a young woman who is not much older than her own daughter. In *The Diary of a Good Neighbor* (1983, published pseudonymously by Lessing under the name, Jane Somers), the gap between generations offers lessons in the opposite direction: Janna Somers, a woman in her fifties and the successful editor of a women's magazine, is deeply influenced by her association with Maudie Fowler, a cantankerous and fiercely independent woman in her nineties through whom she develops compassion and insight into the ravages of the body and compromises of the soul that accompany old age. *Love, again* (1996) focuses on Sarah Durham, a scriptwriter and youthful-looking widow in her mid-sixties who is dismayed by her helpless erotic attraction to men who are significantly younger than she.[3]

Although in Sigal's "A Visit with Rose" the character Shirley Barker is an important vehicle for the action, the real dramatic conflict is between the thinly fictionalized versions of Doris Lessing and Clancy Sigal. The play highlights from Sigal's then-defensive perspective several matters between himself and his former lover that had become recurring set pieces in his fiction and plays. Both "Little Big Horn, N. W. 6" and "A Visit with Rose" demonstrate Sigal's developing skill in using dramatic dialogue as a method for distributing ideas and creating tension and resolution among several characters. In addition, in the latter, more accomplished play—allowing for his occasionally acerbic and satirical tone—he charted or presciently anticipated several developments and shifts in Lessing's literary preoccupations during the years following their liaison.

Chapter 4

Will the Real Saul Green Please Stand Up?

"It was like taking a postgraduate course in Creative Writing." Clancy Sigal ("How to Live with a Lady Writer")

"'So you believe everything you read in the papers? Why take as God's truth what's in a novel?'" Clancy Sigal ("In Pursuit of Saul Green")

Living with a "Lady Writer"

Two important distinctions between the literary methods of Doris Lessing and Clancy Sigal are their approaches to the subject of their relationship and the time periods during which they drew on and adapted details about each other. Lessing fictionalized Sigal primarily in the play and novel she wrote and published during the active years of their liaison (1957–60)—although Sigal has hinted that he recognizes versions of himself in one or two of her short stories. Unless evidence exists in Lessing's unpublished writing that is not currently available for scholarly scrutiny, after *The Golden Notebook* and *Play with a Tiger* were published in 1962 Lessing did not write again about Sigal or their relationship until the second volume of her autobiography, published 35 years later in 1997, by which time she had acquired considerable distance, both emotionally and temporally, from their emotionally and artistically complicated liaison. By contrast, for Sigal the relationship continued to have a literary half-life for a number of years, beginning with his opening parry in a long-running imaginary literary dialogue between himself and Lessing: "Now it's my turn" ("The Sexual History of Jake Blue" 1). Conversations, ideas, and scenes drawn from autobiographical experience made their way into his unpublished sketches, stories, and plays and eventually into his published works, including two novels, a play produced by BBC Radio, and several stories that feature thinly fictionalized and occasionally parodied characterizations of Doris Lessing and himself. To borrow a phrase from the title of the first volume of Lessing's autobiography, Doris apparently remained "under his skin" for many years. Indeed, if living well is the best revenge, perhaps the second-best revenge is writing about it, which Clancy Sigal has done repeatedly, in both overtly fictional and disguised autobiographical forms. By the time Lessing's *Play with a Tiger* was performed in March 1962, he and Lessing had separated. During the same year, Sigal, then still angry with and obsessed by her as he worked on his unpublished novel, "Ceiling Spike," wrote in his journal, "I think the worst thing I learned from Doris was this 'tough' line about writing: oh well, we're scavengers, & that's all there to say, we have to go on scavenging" (Journal, August 28, 1962). Several weeks later, he wrote, "Sometimes my rage at D. is almost overpowering, a desire to curse & physically smash her. The play was my tombstone. I see clearly! There can be no quarter in this relationship" (September 14, 1962). Driven initially by a sense of injury and only later by humor and affection, Sigal took "his turn" to correct the record, so to speak, transforming details of their shared if not identical experiences for a variety of his literary pieces. Mining the raw material of his liaison with Lessing, he reworked for fictional purposes a number of incidents that he had first recorded in his journals. At several points in his then-nascent writing career, he even marked and highlighted in his journal details that he apparently identified as potential seeds for fiction. For example, in March 1958, he noted several ideas for possible literary development, including a crisis between him and Lessing in which he saw comic potential.[1]

An early unpublished example of these autobiographical transformations offers a humorous "take" on Sigal himself. Several draft versions of what he described as a "5000-word piece on Doris Lessing and me" probably written sometime during the early 1960s, judging from internal evidence, offer his partly serious, partly comic treatment of his relationship with Lessing. One version has the long title, expanded for humorous effect, "HOW TO LIVE WITH A LADY WRITER. FIRST LESSON, DON'T CALL HER A LADY WRITER; or, Writers are Writers' Best Friends, Even When They're Rivals, Lovers, Enemies" (caps in original). Another draft of the sketch retains the capitalized portion of the title but substitutes the more acerbic subtitle, "A Kiss and Tell Story." An extended fictionalization of Sigal's relationship with Lessing appears in the incomplete, unpublished novel draft noted above. Both the comic sketch and the more serious novelistic treatment of the same material, "Ceiling Spike," written sometime between 1959 and 1962, offer instructive insights into Sigal's attempts to give his own spin to his relationship with Lessing. Each provides a hall-of-mirrors version of Lessing from his perspective.

The most polished version of "Lady Writer" opens with Sigal's exaggerated fantasy of having an affair with Simone de Beauvoir during his pre-London sojourn in Paris. As it turned out, he became the lover of de Beauvoir's "foster daughter," Riva Lanzmann, instead; coincidentally, de Beauvoir herself was romantically involved with Riva's brother-in-law, the filmmaker Claude Lanzmann.[2] Having failed to actualize his romantic fantasy with the unavailable de Beauvoir, Sigal arrived in England after seven months in France with—as he humorously phrases it—"an unassuaged appetite to link up with any small sexy European lady writer" ("How to Live with a Lady Writer 2). When he actually met his "lady writer," Sigal was "still in [his] James Dean phase": "crew cut, GI combat boots, black high[-]neck sweater, tight blue jeans, fingers stuck in belt with silver cowboy buckle point suggestively at my groin" ("Lady Writer" 7). In effect, Sigal reappropriated Lessing's exaggerated image of him as a Hollywood stud. The pose and attire he describes closely resemble Anna Wulf's description of the fictitious Saul Green of *The Golden Notebook*, who, on first arriving at Anna's flat, is described as a caricature of a caricature: the "young American we see in the films—sexy he-man, all balls and strenuous erection...his thumbs hitched through his belt, fingers loose, but pointed as it were to his genitals . . . " (*GN* 517). Saul soon changes into new clothes that better fit his gaunt frame—"neat blue jeans, tight-fitting, and a close dark blue sweater" (517).

In various drafts of the "Lady Writer" sketch, Sigal describes how he and his first "landlady" became lovers, connecting through their Leftist political persuasions and their vocation as writers—though his own literary career at the time was only embryonic. Several other thinly disguised details include his recognition that Lessing had modeled two of her characters on him; he expresses his ambivalence about being her "kept man": "Among literary gossips it's fairly common knowledge that I once lived with the writer Doris Lessing, Myself, I'm a gentleman and wouldn't breathe a word. But ever since she nailed me in her novel, The Golden Notebook, a play (To Play With A Tiger [sic]) and one or two of her short stories, I've been community property" ("Lady Writer" 2). Giving his own humorous spin to Lessing's diagnosis of the Oedipal dimension of their relationship, he remarks, "Doris was the first woman I'd ever lived with—aside from my mother, that, is. And Doris rarely let me forget it. 'Of course I'm your mother substitute,' she'd say with calm, no-nonsense assurance as if only an idiot would deny it. And then would follow a fiery hail of psychoanalytical bullets that had me jumping like a tenderfoot in a tough cowboy bar" (3).

If Sigal had qualms about Lessing's penchant for armchair psychoanalysis, he had none concerning her culinary talents, about which he apparently enjoyed lavishing details throughout his literary characterizations of her. "She was the second best cook I ever met.... Maybe even the finest" (2), he writes. In fact, it was her "wonderful, inventive, imaginative cooking" that enabled them to get through "the bad times" (3). Indulging in a further bit of hyperbole, Sigal adds that he was so enamored of Lessing's culinary skills that he would

> wade through a sea of fire to get to her mushroom meat loaf, lamb stew Provencale [sic], lasagna al forno, pork and red cabbage. And her home-made jams! She was never happier, not even at the typewriter, than when messing about in her large unkempt kitchen.... Like my mother, she never asked me to help. Nor wash the dishes afterwards. The food appeared as if by magic, the dishes wiped themselves clean, and our best sex was just before or after meals.... Compared to her writing, cooking was her real genius, I felt. (4)

Sigal also credits Lessing with supporting his literary ambitions before he had succeeded in publishing a single word and at a time when he seriously doubted that he had any talent. During his acute anxiety attacks, she assured him that the terrors he experienced were simply "writing pains" (5) and continued to nourish him with her superb cooking.

But, as Sigal later reconstructed the trajectory of their failed relationship, their pleasure in each other's company was undercut by antagonisms whose sources were multiple: not only their different personalities and experiences but their different social conditioning by gender, particularly regarding intimate relationships. "From some point on, Doris stopped believing in the possibility of simple love between a man and woman. Inevitably, my crafty callowness and her profoundly knowledgeable view of the sex war stripped our gears. She was talking to the past men in her life, I was psychologically still with my last few girlfriends in America" (5). Their episodes of psychological combat sometimes took the form of name-calling, during which Sigal hurled insulting epithets such as "memsahib" at her ("Spike" seg. 1: 32), baiting her—without success—to lose her temper. A version of that epithet dates back to the early months of their relationship. In a journal entry written in September 1957, Sigal complains about Lessing's patronizing criticism of his novel in progress—eventually published as *Going Away*—remarking, "I was a fool to show her the novel synopsis; if only because it helps destroy illusions she may have had about my 'creative persona'. In some ways she is still the white settler lady sahib" ("Going Away" Journal, September 6, 1957). The epithet that most irritated Lessing, according to Sigal, was his intentionally taunting labeling of her as a "lady writer." In retaliation, she called him a "Jewish guttersnipe," which he found laughable rather than cutting because "it was so accurate" ("Lady Writer" 6). Given their knife-edged rounds of verbal combat as well as their manifestly different personalities and cultural backgrounds, "it was amazing how well we got along so much of the time" (7).

In "Lady Writer," Sigal reprises the cardinal developments in his relationship with Lessing—still with considerable heat but from greater aesthetic distance and humor than are apparent in his two early and thinly disguised autobiographical pieces, "The Sexual History of Jake Blue" and the untitled lightly disguised autobiographical Coral typescript chapters: her prying into and appropriation of details from his private journals; her transparent character sketch of him for *The Golden Notebook*; and her appropriation of elements of his character, background, and intimate conversations as models for Saul Green in *The Golden Notebook* and Dave Miller in her play, *Play with a Tiger*. In the "Lady Writer" sketch, these developments are drained of some of the shock of their initial discovery, first expressed in Sigal's private journal. Describing what he continued to regard as Lessing's appropriation of features of his character and personal history for the creation of Saul Green, Sigal describes his discovery of the "paper stuck in her [typewriter] roller. I knew, all too well, what was written on it. 'The Case of C.S...Ex Hollywood Red. Comes to London. No money, no friends. A wandering man, happens to land in the house of a woman whom he likes and whom he needs'" ("Lady Writer" 8, Sigal's ellipsis). As noted in chapter 1 above, several phrases in this passage duplicate those written by Anna Wulf in the yellow notebook, in the opening sentences of two of her sketches for a short novel (sketches 7 and 9, *GN* 500, 501). In deliberately echoing Lessing's idiom and phrasing, Sigal hints that she drew too freely on the details of his identity and biography, to say nothing of his private writing. Apparently, he was initially puzzled by her literary method. "What was she up to? Clearly, she wanted me to read her manuscript. In case I didn't get the point, Doris left copies of her notes all over the house..." ("Lady Writer" 8). In "Ceiling Spike," Sigal's fictional alter ego, Matthew Maynard, reprises that scene, writing,

> With a pounding heart I read the topmost page of the "profile" she had written. I was impressed, even amused, at the manner in which she had constructed out of the person in her house a scheming, intensely complicated Lothario of nearly mythical proportions, imputing to this person designs and aggressions on women I was positive had not occurred to me. The person she had written about had made a career of deliberately and persistently wrecking women. At first much relieved I retired to my room. And then I doubled over with an attack of anxiety. ("Spike" seg. 1: 57–8)

As is expressed from several perspectives—in Lessing's *The Golden Notebook* and *Play with a Tiger* as well as in Sigal's "How to Live with a Lady Writer"—a fundamental fault line in the relationship between him and Lessing was their clashing assumptions about sexual fidelity. From Lessing's point of view, Sigal's philandering undermined the integrity of their relationship, a problem compounded by what she saw as his repeated dissimulations about it. In return, he was irritated by what he regarded as her sexual possessiveness and unwarranted jealousy. He viewed his occasional dalliances with other women as inconsequential and therefore not a threat to her or their relationship. He apparently attempted more than once to analyze for himself this problematic dimension of their association, hoping to gain more insight into what seemed to him Lessing's irrational jealousy. "How to Live with a Lady Writer" reflects, among other things, Sigal's effort to mount his defense. As he writes,

> After searching my journals and wracking my memory, I'm at a loss to accurately recall whether Doris had a case or not. I had ex-girlfriends all over the joint.... But, hand on heart, I cannot remember if I made love to all those Bradford factory girls, London absolute beginners and Midlands bus clippies she incessantly accused me of screwing. Anyway, we never had a clear understanding about extra-marital flings.... (For the record, I add that Doris quickly rebounded from her jealousy by going to bed with one or two of the poets who swanned through the house.) ("Lady Writer" 8–9)

Similarly and equally defensively, Matthew Maynard observes early in "Ceiling Spike" that Sophie Ravenscroft's jealousy was "the 'third man' in our relationship (the other two were the boy [Sophie's son] and the Ceylonese [lodger]).... My way of being in the world was to flirt. Her disapproval was not calculated but came from the depths of her being and took a form which frightened and disorganized me" ("Spike" 1: 12). Later in the novel draft, the narrator concludes that he and his lover are trapped in a neurotic cycle in which the behavior of each invariably brings out the worst in the other. In the process of analyzing this pattern, however, Matthew disingenuously assigns the blame to his partner; as he observes,

> Sophie had begun our relationship by protesting that the last thing on earth she wanted was to be placed in the role of jealous female.... She had, in fact, been waiting, and dreading, the "trigger" for this something, this spring-coiled fury she had in her. I was that trigger. But I don't really think you can trigger a person off into something that he, too hasn't in some sense been waiting for. Though Sophie's power of suggestion was strong it wasn't strong enough to induce in me desires I did not have. Very likely, sooner or later, I would have "met my situation" by becoming unfaithful. What Sophie did was to ensure that my latent talent for infidelity would conform inch-by-inch to her latent talent to have someone near her who was infiditous.... Looking back on it, I think I can say that the soil out of which I began to grow my present character was the neurotic compulsion of my lady love to believe in my unfaithfulness. ("Spike" 2: 98)

In "How to Live with a Lady Writer," Sigal addresses not only sexual but professional jealousy, given the potential of the latter to affect the relationship between two strong-willed and ambitious writers, one of whom was already successful while the other was a mere fledgling with aspirations. "I don't recall feeling any rivalry. I might have done if I had been further in my own work. But for most of the time I knew Doris I was wrestling to have word one printed.... And anyway [she] strongly, practically backed my ambition.... [A]ll the time we lived together I felt the tangible force of her breath at my back pushing, willing, me to literary success" ("Lady Writer" 10). In fact, Sigal credits Lessing with introducing him to Len Doherty, the South Yorkshire coal miner who became his "tightest buddy" ("Lady Writer" 10) and who figures centrally as the lightly fictionalized Davie in his first book, *Weekend in Dinlock*.[3] In "Ceiling Spike," Sigal expresses through his fictional persona his sincere gratitude for this aspect of his relationship with Lessing, who perhaps even erred in the direction of convincing him that he had more talent than he believed he had.

> I rushed down from my room several times a day to shout, pour out, show her plans for a new novel, a new story. She listened patiently, even when I was blindly interrupting her own work. She was tactful, she was encouraging, she pointed me in useful directions and with immense delicacy tried to touch me off literary blind alleys.... She patronized me mercilessly[,] never flatly judged my work to be unspeakably inferior to hers: it would have saved me time. She was honest on every score but this. ("Spike" seg. 1: 16)

Nonetheless, Lessing's appropriation of aspects of Sigal's character and their intimate dialogues for *Play with a Tiger* was the proverbial straw that broke the camel's back. It pushed to the limit his tolerance of her literary method when it applied to him, producing choking "bile" ("Lady Writer" 10). Lessing apparently saw her literary method quite differently. Years later, she directly defended her use of autobiographical materials in *Play with a Tiger*, claiming as "hers" aspects of their relationship that Sigal could legitimately claim as "his." She also lamented the double standard that had resulted in her being criticized more than were her "Angry Young Man" counterparts in British drama for exercising the same kind of artistic license. Less in response to Sigal's personal grievance than to her literary critics in general, she argued, "[Y]ou put your own life into the play. Just as if John Osborne's *Look Back in Anger* were not direct from life, and as if Arnold Wesker's plays were not from life. No one had said to John or Arnold anything like the unpleasant things that were said to me" (*Walking* 256).

Of note, in the same sketch in which he denies any professional jealousy, Sigal also admits it: he suggests that he could have forgiven Lessing's direct references to his supposed infidelity—"the usual stuff about neurotic philandering" ("Lady Writer" 10). What he found more difficult to accept was the bruise to his ego: her success in "working behind scenes at Britain's best theatre, the Royal Court, then still basking in the fame of its glory with Osborne's *Look Back in Anger*" ("Lady Writer" 11). Although *Play with a Tiger* was not produced at the Royal Court, Lessing's first play, *Each His Own Wilderness*, was briefly staged there. Sigal, then still a struggling unpublished writer, "yearned to be a playwright" ("Lady Writer" 11).

When he gave Lessing a draft of his own first play to read, she was tactfully but pointedly critical of it. Subsequently, he wrote a dozen plays, only one of which—a BBC radio play, "A Visit with Rose," which draws directly on his relationship with Doris Lessing (Rose O'Malley)—was produced.[4]

It continued to rankle Sigal that, after they separated, Lessing regarded his eventual success as a writer as a result of her mentoring and influence. Although he readily credited her for supporting his writing ambitions, he did not appreciate the way she aggrandized and exaggerated that credit. In "Ceiling Spike," his narrative persona describes a party he attends just after his own publishing career has finally begun to flourish. Matthew joins a conversation in progress between the successful playwright and actress Sophie Ravenscroft and another female playwright "whose newest play, loosely based on the series of articles I had written for the Sunday newspaper, was then running in Sloane Square. Both women were drunk and tuggeing [sic] at each of my arms. 'Matthew,' cried the young female playwright, 'I created him.' Sophie drew away slightly to appraise us. 'He's my creation,' she said plainly and with no particular emphasis" ("Spike" seg. 2: 132–3).

In both "Ceiling Spike," and "How to Live with a Lady Writer," Sigal achieves a degree of aesthetic distance from—and even manages to inject occasional humor into—the circumstances of the literary identity theft that had shocked him at the time it happened. Though he marvels at his lover's prurient interest in his "sexual nuttiness," he also credits her literary method as a valuable model for his own education as a writer. In a condensed variation of the "primal scene" to which he returned obsessively in his early writing, Sigal describes Lessing-as-mentor intentionally leaving chapters of her "raw new novel" around for him to "stumble on, knowing that I'd then go upstairs and scribble furious responses in my journal, which she'd then creep up to look at [...] which was then translated, sometimes verbatim, to her novel.... It was like taking a postgraduate course in Creative Writing" ("Lady Writer" 11, Sigal's ellipses unless bracketed).

Sigal prided himself on never asking Lessing to cease prying into his private journal. Rather—at least, in his disguised-autobiographical representation of this sensitive subject—he employed that curious form of communication between them "almost exclusively to supply data for her novel," even as he adds the dig that he did not particularly admire her "turgid style" ("Lady Writer" 12). Moreover, taking control of the process and privately styling himself her unsung collaborator, he apparently enjoyed playing what he regarded as a kind of game. He maintains that, through his journal entries, he offered Lessing suggestions to make more believable the character for whom he was the model. Close perusal of Sigal's journals does not corroborate this assertion. In any case, although Lessing may have ignored Sigal's editorial advice, she apparently secretly continued to read his journal.

Ultimately, according to both Sigal's and Lessing's accounts, the lovers drifted apart for multiple reasons, including not only what both came to see as sexual and emotional incompatibilities but also differences in the political commitment that had once been such a strong bond between them. While Lessing's politics took a "rightward swerve," Sigal maintained his radical socialist position. Nonetheless, even after the couple separated in 1960, they continued to see each other occasionally. In the final line of "Lady Writer," Sigal observes, "There's a lot we don't talk about" (12). Another fragmentary variant of the sketch concludes, more humorously, "All I really regret is calling her a lady writer. If only I'd kept my mouth shut" ("Lady Writer" fragment headed "Doris" 15–16).

Years later, Doris Lessing disparaged the epithet that Sigal used for her, regarding "English lady"—not Sigal's actual label, "Lady Writer"—as an illustrative example of his misunderstanding of her. As she protests in her autobiography,

> I had always been seen as a maverick—tactless, intransigent, "difficult"—and now, all at once, I was accused [by Clancy] of being an English lady. It was no good saying that any real English lady would at once repudiate me as a bogus sister. This English lady was ignorant of the harsh realities of life, which meant, for him, the struggles of the poor. Clancy was never one to spare unfavourable comment, and I was tongue-lashed, but I gave back as good as I got. (*Walking* 173)

* * *

In the curious saga of reciprocal literary appropriations between Doris Lessing and Clancy Sigal, one of Sigal's early unpublished stories pivots on an experience that he and Lessing shared but in which the focus is only marginally on their intimate relationship. The seven-page narrative is suggestively titled "Dolores." Despite the echo of Doris' name, it is not Dolores but the unnamed narrator's landlady and lover, Sophie Ravenscroft, who occupies the position of Lessing's fictional double. The fictional name suggests that Sigal wrote "Dolores" and "Ceiling Spike" during the same time period. In this version of the couple's early days together, Sophie is not a playwright but an actress with whom the narrator is "desperately in love" ("Dolores" 2). Sophie's first words in the story echo almost verbatim the remark that appears in several other versions of Sigal's sketches and fictions based on his early days with Lessing: Sophie cautions him, "I have been badly treated by men. I won't have it any more. I'd rather live alone" ("Dolores" 2). Though the narrator enjoys being Sophie's "kept man," he must stay out of her way when she is rehearsing a dramatic role, which is often. With no work of his own, he occupies himself by shepherding her daughters around London.

Sigal's fictional alter ego almost seems to set himself up for a destructive emotional struggle with his lover. "I insulted Sophie, tried to teach her how to make love, went out and dated bus clippies and generally conducted myself in a way that offended and pleased both of us" ("Dolores" 3). In this fictionalization of the early phase of the Lessing/Sigal relationship, Sophie is, in marked contrast to Doris Lessing, completely apolitical; she "didn't have a political brain in her head" (3). More surprisingly, Lessing's *Play with a Tiger*, which struck such a nerve in Clancy Sigal when it was performed on stage, is casually dismissed. As the unnamed narrator of the story observes, "Eventually [Sophie] and one of her sometime lovers got together to write a play 'about me'. I never went to see it" (3).

Reluctantly giving up his role as Sophie's "kept man" without income, the narrator begins to write and eventually finds a New Left audience for his journalistic pieces. In his guise as a "writer-reporter," he describes the disaffected young people he meets while socializing with youths in social clubs in the scruffier London suburbs. His subjects include a girl named Dolores, who lives with an older Turkish restaurant owner in a situation of virtual sexual slavery. Dropping his journalistic distance, he decides to rescue the young woman by taking her home with him. The story shifts to a confrontation between Sophie and Dolores, with the attractive girl innocently asking the older woman to tell her "all about acting" (6). Even though the narrator virtuously dismisses the girl's advances when she comes to his bedroom one night, Sophie jealously concludes that the nocturnal encounter was less than innocent and sends Dolores packing. The story ends, weakly, with the narrator's observation that he and Sophie have resumed their previous combative routines. Although

"Dolores" is a slight piece, it demonstrates one of Sigal's several early attempts to fictionalize details and themes to which he returned more successfully in his later fictional transformations of his relationship with Lessing, including their complicated emotional parrying, his ambivalence about being a "kept man," and his professed innocence regarding liaisons with other women. As the choice of name almost transparently suggests, the young, beautiful, and defenseless Dolores may represent qualities that Sigal wished for and found lacking in the older and by then somewhat man-weary if not also world-weary Doris.

Perhaps more noteworthy than the story itself is the fact that it is apparently based fairly closely on an actual encounter that affected not only Sigal but Lessing. In fact, the episode was memorable enough for Lessing to devote several pages of her autobiography to it. In her version, an 18-year-old girl whose name Lessing does not provide, a "plump fair frail beauty, with hazy blue eyes" (*Walking* 177), was apparently being kept in virtual sexual bondage by a married Greek restaurant proprietor. Sigal and a friend, inspired by their "protectiveness for the deprived" (176), brought the girl to Lessing's flat, seeking her assistance in their effort to rescue her from her enslavement. As Lessing describes what followed, "Exciting times with this famous writer—so they had told her I was. She hinted she would like to be a model, a film star.... She made free with my clothes..." (178), lounging in Lessing's "cherry-coloured dressing gown" (179) for ten days. When the girl realized that her fantasies of a better future were unlikely to be realized, she left, presumably to return to the abusive Dmitri—who, she insisted, "never bruises me, Mrs. Lessing..." (179). Lessing closes her sketch of the incident by remarking, "[b]y now she must be a fat, dyed old woman, probably a lush, and the thought hurts" (179).

In several of Clancy Sigal's literary transformations of his intermittently combative relationship with Doris Lessing, a strain of suppressed—and occasionally even overt—aggression appears, with different fictionalized outcomes. In "Ceiling Spike," Sigal's alter ego, Matthew, observes that he and Sophie Ravenscroft "lived together in mounting fury, though we never struck each other. (How different my history had I found the courage to do so!).... Sophie held the whip hand" ("Spike" seg. 1: 52–3). At some point—Sigal gives the date as 1965—he intended to transform and develop the unfinished novel draft into a play with a similar title, "The Ceiling and the Spike."[5] Although he apparently never wrote the dramatic version, he drafted a detailed 22-page synopsis of it, retaining several characters and a number of details that appear in the unfinished narrative version. In the anticipated dramatic version, the actress/playwright Sophie (now Manion rather than Ravenscroft) rather amusingly "lives and works in a ramshackle riverboat, of maisonette proportions, anchored permanently on the Thames in Putney, London" ("The Ceiling and the Spike," synopsis for unpublished play).

Eventually, "Ceiling Spike" and "The Ceiling and the Spike" evolved into the published novel, *The Secret Defector*, in which Sigal finally permits his fictional alter ego, by then named Gus Black, to act out his aggressive feelings. Agitated by his former lover's nonchalance about her current lover—in his judgment, a "hack poet who hasn't written an original line in his life"—Gus gives in to the anger that still simmers beneath the surface by slugging Doris Lessing's narrative double, Rose O'Malley, in the chin. (*The Secret Defector* 69)[6]

* * *

Pursuing the "Real" Saul Green

Among Clancy Sigal's multiple literary transformations of his complicated relationship with Doris Lessing is an early story, "In Pursuit of Saul Green," that must have been written with tongue firmly in cheek. Its mellow comic tone and allusions to events in Sigal's life after he and Lessing separated suggest substantial, and perhaps later, transformations of the raw material of their relationship. The story is an entertaining *histoire à clef* in which the "key" figures—Clancy Sigal, Doris Lessing, and Sigal's own comic version of the fictitious Saul Green—are comically caricatured.

The protagonist of the story, Abner Briskin, is a divorced American man in his thirties—Sigal's age while he and Lessing were lovers—whose surname echoes the name of one of Sigal's associates at R. D. Laing's Kingsley Hall during the 1960s, Sid Briskin, whose first name he later gave to the protagonist of *Zone of the Interior*. Abner Briskin, who regards himself as a "combat veteran of the Sixties" even though he did not fight in Vietnam, has returned to school to pursue a PhD in American Studies, hoping that the degree will lead him to "a small, stable corner from which to continue resisting Amerika [*sic*]" ("In Pursuit of Saul Green" 1). After several false starts on his dissertation, he has established as its focus American characters in the works of European writers. Not surprisingly, given

Sigal's biography and his literary method, among the books that Abner Briskin has already subjected to literary analysis is Simone de Beauvoir's celebrated *roman à clef, The Mandarins* (1960), in which the character Lewis Brogan is a thinly disguised version of de Beauvoir's lover, Nelson Algren.[7] Recently Briskin has determined that the "jewel in [his] thesis" will be a "detailed, brilliant exploration of the personna [sic] of 'Saul Green' in Doris Lessing's monumental novel, *The Golden Notebook*" ("Pursuit" 2). While illuminating his protagonist's scholarly progress, Sigal pokes fun not only at academe but at other sacred cows as well, including feminism. Although Briskin "[does] not particularly admire Lessing's work" ("Pursuit" 2), he does understand politics, including academic politics: the subject of his thesis is calculated to win the favor of a feminist scholar on his dissertation committee. "And, by some lucky stroke, 'Saul Green'—the great neurotic whale to his Ahab—seemed to be just wallowing around Lessing's prose, waiting for Abner's harpoon" (3).

To support his critical exegesis of the character in *The Golden Notebook*, Abner determines, he must locate and speak with the real Saul Green. After reaching several dead ends in his effort to track down the elusive man, Briskin wonders—as Sigal caricatures details of his own biography—whether Saul Green had "gone irretrievably mad in a Laingian half-way asylum in London's East End" or "defected to the East bloc" or "joined a Buddhist monastery in Sri Lanka after a bad acid trip" (3). But Abner is not discouraged. Rather, digging more energetically into his research task by "cross-referencing Lessing's short stories, her novels and a stage play 'To Play With A Tiger' [sic], he began to build up a vivid portrait of his quarry who appeared, in one guise or another, in [Lessing's] work. Clearly even by the author's own account, Green had been important to her creative development at a certain major crisis she had faced just before her 'middle period'" (4). Finally, as Briskin's investigative efforts begin to bear fruit, Sigal skewers Lessing's fictionalized version of him in *The Golden Notebook*. The "real" Saul Green, Briskin discovers, is a man named Stanley Feldman, the unprepossessing owner of a small electronics shop in Encino, California, "Progressive Electrical Emporia." Feldman is "on his third marriage" and drives an Oldsmobile Cutlass (4).

Unlike Sigal, who was educated at UCLA and worked in Hollywood, Abner Briskin is a wide-eyed first-time visitor to Los Angeles. After making his way to Feldman's electronics shop, he meets the older man and is taken aback by his physical appearance.

Based on Doris Lessing's characterization of Saul Green in *The Golden Notebook*, he had expected a "communist Marlon Brando" (13) rather than "a small guy; wiry; with slightly nervous, staccato[,] even birdlike movements. And, of all things, a crew cut. He resembled photographs Abner had seen of Nelson Algren..." (6)—Sigal's nod to a fellow Chicago writer whom he knew and admired. Briskin, concealing his surprise and "instinctive disdain" (6) for the elusive man whom he has finally tracked down, promptly gets down to business, starting his tape recorder to capture his research subject's words for later analysis. He begins by asking Feldman what brought him to England and how he met Doris Lessing. The amiable Feldman speaks, somewhat improbably, in a working-class Jewish vernacular that may channel the speech patterns of Sigal's father, Leo Sigal, a radical Jewish union organizer who disowned him as a child. In fact, the portrait of Feldman, including his working class idiom, suggests other details based on Sigal's father and on Nelson Algren.

Feldman explains that he had originally gone to Paris "to be another Hemingway or at least Dos Passos" but that his poor French accent had soon stalled his ambitions. En route back to the United States, he had decided to stop in London to see the sights. "I took a room...you know the rest" ("Pursuit" 6, Sigal's ellipsis). Feldman had regarded Doris Lessing as his "dream woman" (6) and had particularly relished her cooking. The ingenuous Abner, who doesn't quite know what to make of what he is hearing, briefly considers that Feldman may be putting him on. "He had come three thousand miles, on a quest to locate the source of the fire of one of the world's leading writers and feminists, and parenthetically to track down an obscure socialist who might shed light on the hidden history of the lost years of American radicalism, and it was boiling down to a question of...roast mutton and parsnips" (7, Sigal's ellipsis).

As Feldman waxes poetic about Lessing's culinary talents, Briskin is tempted to put his tape recorder on "pause" until the conversation returns to topics more relevant to his research project. Lessing's fictitious ex-lover reminisces that he had urged her to write a cookbook, musing—as Sigal wrings full comedy out of the subject and situation—"I even offered to collaborate on it with her. But all she ever wanted my collaboration on was having a baby" ("Pursuit" 8). However, fatherhood did not figure in Stanley Feldman's plans for himself. Briskin, listening to the "real" Saul Green's rambling reminiscences concerning his long-ago love affair with the author of *The Golden Notebook*, struggles to find either the point or the truth. The older man tries to explain that their union was complicated: "something to do with Creation. And Sex. Politics. The interface of exile cultures. The subtle confluence of hate, rage, lust and envy—even penis and the-other envy?—in making the powerful undeniable force that broke blockages, flung souls in torment high into the dark cosmos. The explosive overlap of radical commitment and personal relationships. All that" (8).

Abner bluntly asks Feldman whether he had had "girl friends" during his "tenure with Lessing" (9). On this subject, Feldman's position—like Sigal's own on the matter—is decidedly equivocal: "Guilty as charged.... I think" (9). The earnest graduate student, irritated that Feldman is unable to clarify a matter of such significance in his relationship with Doris Lessing, presses further. In an explanation that—with allowances for its comic tone and exaggerated diction—closely echoes Sigal's own views on the subject dating back to journal entries written while he lived with Lessing, Feldman muses—with "affectionate distaste"—

> "She had this...this ability to make me think I'd done things I hadn't and hadn't done things I had.[...] [S]he'd put this kind of ray, like a vibration, all over me like a sort of net and I was this character she had invented, or was inventing and he was guilty of all these things and I, you know me, was left on some lonely pocket of the moon wondering what the hell was going on." (9; Sigal's ellipses unless bracketed)

Later, Feldman recalls—as Sigal has elsewhere suggested—that Lessing "minded the lies more than the dolly birds" (10), her disparaging term for his other women. But he defends his behavior by emphasizing that he "liked" the working-girls and "bus clippies" with whom he spent time because they revealed a side of London that Doris did not know (11, Sigal's underscoring). Abner is puzzled by the discrepancies he discerns between the man before him who was ostensibly the model for Saul Green and the considerably more psychologically complex character who appears in *The Golden Notebook*. As he phrases it, "'Saul Green' had had genuine stature as a romantic neurotic—if not a titan[,] certainly a minor giant of self-torture and mental instability" (9). Stanley Feldman's very ordinariness, Abner Briskin suggests, is evidence of Lessing's imaginative and artistic skill.

Briskin asks Feldman whether it was the "sexual quarrels and...jealousy" (10) that had prompted Lessing to make him into a character in her novel. Feldman admits his difficulty in understanding her motivation; "the comradeship thing and the sex thing got all mixed up in the work thing" (11). Yet he confirms that Lessing "was climbing into my diaries and journal.... She told herself it was jealousy, an insatiable need to know what I was up to" (10, Sigal's ellipsis). Once he discovered what she was doing, Feldman explains to Briskin—as Clancy Sigal has highlighted in other literary variants of this decisive development in his relationship with Doris Lessing—"I started writing my diaries for her. It gave me this big kick, knowing that even if I couldn't get going as a writer I was contributing to literature some-other-how" (11). The dialogue that follows is both amusing and trenchant:

> But according to *The Golden Notebook*, Lessing was trapped in a major creative block when you two met, Abner objected.
> "So you believe everything you read in the papers? Why take as God's truth what's in a novel? It just makes a better story."
> But Lessing has given interviews declaring her gratitude to you for breaking that block, Abner reminded Feldman.
> Benignly Feldman said, "Doris is a liar. Okay a writer. Same thing. Maybe it was a block. Sure didn't look like it to me." (11)

Briskin speculates that it must have been difficult for Feldman to live intimately with a woman while she was making him into a character in her fiction. Feldman assumes that Briskin must mean professional rather than sexual jealousy since, when Lessing and Sigal first became lovers, she was already a successful writer, while Saul Green/Clancy Sigal, regardless of his literary aspirations, was as yet unpublished. On that subject, Feldman indicates that, although he was not professionally jealous of Lessing, his nonliterary activities had very different consequences for him than for her. His interest in London bus clippies, which so inflamed Lessing's jealousy, led to his breakthrough as a writer. In particular, through his friendly and, he insists, only occasionally, sexual involvement with an East End Cockney bus clippie named Loreen, he met members of her working-class family, including her brothers and their "j.d." (juvenile delinquent) friends. What he learned by observing the disaffected London youths inspired his first successful publication—a journalistic piece about "'working class youth alienation' for the New Statesman," after which he "never looked back" (11–12). With this detail, Sigal identifies what one might term his own origin-story as a writer; one of his first published pieces, "Short talk with a Fascist beast," appeared in the *New Statesman* in October 1958. Through his alter ego's interview with Stanley Feldman, Sigal also generously acknowledges that, while Lessing indeed surreptitiously read his journals, he received something valuable in return. As the "original" for Saul Green phrases it through his twice-removed comic persona, Stanley Feldman, "If [Doris] was copying my diaries, unconsciously I was probably finding out from her how a real writer went about it. Fair exchange, I'd say, wouldn't you?" (12) However, in response to Briskin's query whether he loved Lessing, the older man reproaches the naïve graduate student for his tactlessness. Even though the relationship ended "badly," Feldman nonetheless believes that "if you both took that much crap from each other, something had to be working for you. Call it love" (12). Briskin hazards that it might have been need rather than love, an interpretation that Feldman finds too "psycho-ass-alytical" (12).

Privately deciding to leave the older man to his "illusions" (12) on that point, Briskin turns his attention to the subject of politics. Ironically, while Feldman has been (or so it appears) quite candid about his relationship with Lessing, he is uncharacteristically guarded about his radical politics, as if he might inadvertently divulge something that could still get him into trouble all these years later. He explains that in his youth he had done some "army and union organizing" in the United States but that his urge to be a writer and the right-wing zealousness of the McCarthy era had compelled him to leave the country. When both "the affair [with Lessing] and his involvement with the British new left [*sic*] simultaneously fizzled" (13), he—unlike Clancy Sigal, who remained in England for another 30 years—had soon returned to America, drifted for a while, married several times, and tried various working-class jobs. Finally, he had assumed ownership of the electronics business that he still manages. Somewhere along the way, he had lost the desire to write.

If the story up to this point seems like a mellow correction of the record, the final pages of Sigal's story betray a sharper edge. Abner Briskin can't help but wonder whether Feldman's life would have been any different if he had never met Doris Lessing. "Had she stolen some vital flame of his sacred fire...?" Approaching the end of his interview, Briskin unleashes what he regards as the proverbial coup de grace: the sword "aimed straight at the hump just above the bull's heart muscle" (14). He asks the older man, "How did you feel at [*sic*] what she wrote about you?" (14), to which Stanley Feldman/Saul

Green almost sputters, resorting to a more colorful diction and more agitated affect than has been true of his previous responses to the graduate student's often blunt questions. "How would you feel? Like a piece of garbage. Human junk, a bunch of mangled guts thrown away in a black plastic sack. That's how" (14). When Briskin asks him how long such strong feelings lasted, Feldman retorts in a clipped statement, "Till now" (15). Although he eventually got over his anger, at the time it had felt like "getting stomped on by an elephant—even after the blood dries the imprint stays" (15).

Without flinching at Feldman's vivid metaphors, Briskin follows up by asking him whether he had ever attempted to stop Doris Lessing from writing about him. Feldman, striking a surprisingly conciliatory note after his vituperative exclamations, defends his former lover's artistic method. "It was her work. You don't stop nobody from their work" (15). As Sigal deadpans, Feldman adds that, though he had seriously considered leaving Lessing once he discovered that she was writing him into her novel, he stayed because she was "one great cook—and London is a lousy place for food..." (15). Briskin privately wonders, as he has wondered at several other points during the interview, whether Stanley Feldman is "putting him on" (15). However, still curious about Saul Green's embryonic writing career at the time, he returns to the subject, wondering whether Feldman thinks that his former lover damaged his literary promise by "scooping out all the best that was in you and using it for herself?" (15) Feldman—and, implicitly, Sigal—responds with generosity and humor, although the working-class vernacular is grammatically awkward and hardly resembles the "real" Saul Green's idiom: "She never stole nothing from me that she didn't have in the first place. I never stole anything from her.... I loved that woman. Still do, as a matter of fact. It's just that I wouldn't wanna ever meet her in a dark alley—again" (15–16).

Once the interview officially ends and Abner Briskin has promised to send Stanley Feldman a copy of his doctoral dissertation when it is published, the older man delivers his own coup de grace to the very green graduate student who thinks he has found the "real" Saul Green. Using a pet name for Doris that startles Abner, he remarks, "DeeDee didn't put me, not the real me, into her stuff. But you're going to, right?" (16). Whatever Clancy Sigal may have intended with this twist on the methods of disguised autobiography and *roman à clef* concerning who is "the real me," it is difficult to imagine him— or anyone—calling Doris Lessing "DeeDee." Briskin awkwardly replies, "Sure thing" (16), as he proceeds to pack up his tape recorder and interview materials. After he leaves, Stanley Feldman briefly wonders whether he had spoken too freely to a stranger. "Sure why not. The best way to keep a secret, he had always figured, was to tell it" (17).

In his send-up of the "true" story of Saul Green and *The Golden Notebook*, Clancy Sigal caricatures both his and Doris Lessing's invented characters and their implied models as he also satirizes academic research and the genre of *roman à clef* itself. Moreover, he apparently enjoyed the comic opportunity to return a favor to the creator of the fictitious Saul Green: his own invented "original" for the character in *The Golden Notebook* is intentionally less colorful and considerably less complex than is Doris Lessing's invented character based on Clancy Sigal. The "real" Saul Green in this case is a feckless old man who, far from having any literary pretensions of his own, still doesn't know quite what hit him all those years ago in Doris Lessing's London flat. Moreover, while Stanley Feldman resembles—if he resembles anyone—Nelson Algren or the vanished father of Sigal's youth, Leo Sigal, more than he does either Clancy Sigal or the fictitious Saul Green, the credulous would-be literary scholar who interviews him is green to a fault. Sigal's comic story may be read as a dialogue between actual and invented, younger and more mature, versions of the author himself. "In Pursuit of Saul Green"—one of Sigal's most engaging unpublished pieces—exaggerates the interplay between fact and fiction, adding new images to the hall of mirrors in which the half-lives of Clancy Sigal and Doris Lessing continue to refract.

Chapter 5

A Rose by Any Other Name

"She was an indelible part of my bloodstream. We didn't 'owe' each other a thing. Except faithfulness to that funny old whatever-it-was we once shared." Clancy Sigal ("Lunch with Rose")

For several decades after Doris Lessing and Clancy Sigal parted as lovers, Sigal continued to draw extensively on aspects of their relationship for his fictional and dramatic writing. One might say that, whatever Lessing's overly zealous literary appropriations of aspects of Sigal's character and their relationship during their time together, Sigal more than got his own back, creating multiple fictionalized versions of Lessing beginning before or soon after their separation in 1960 and continuing over the next 30-plus years. It took him considerably longer than it did Lessing to get the relationship out of his system—and to exhaust its literary possibilities. While Clancy Sigal was the model for the fictitious Saul Green of *The Golden Notebook* and Dave Miller of *Play with a Tiger*, Doris Lessing in turn inspired several of Sigal's characters who resemble—with varying degrees of exaggeration, oversimplification, and parody—Doris Lessing. It is instructive for readers to see the fun house mirror distortions of Sigal's former lover as his literary skill and comic gifts developed.

Although Sigal also drafted a number of unpublished stories and plays on other subjects, literary versions of his former lover appear throughout his unpublished writing in both narrative and dramatic forms: as the barely disguised Coral Brand; briefly as Lily Sloan; as the actress/director/playwright, Sophie Ravenscroft/Manion; and finally, as Rose O'Malley, the rather vain novelist and author of *Loose Leaves from a Random Life*, Sigal's send-up title for *The Golden Notebook*. The changing names of Lessing's fictional personas reflect stages in Sigal's emotional and aesthetic distancing from her as time passed. His own narrative personas appear variously in his fiction and plays with the names Jake Blue, Paul Blue, Abner Briskin, Matthew Maynard/Sirota/Kane, Robert Wasserman, Jerry (no surname), Sid Bell, Gus Black, and the occasional nameless "I" who functions as the author's narrative double. As Lessing's and Sigal's romantic and postromantic relationship evolved over time, Sigal in particular continued to re-work the original raw material. Several pivotal episodes, including Lessing's surreptitious reading of his journals, as well as certain themes and preoccupations—particularly her jealousy regarding his liaisons with other women, her armchair psychoanalysis of his oedipal problem, and her culinary talents—appear frequently in Sigal's fiction, both published and unpublished. His literary treatment of them ranges from thinly disguised autobiography to satirical and comic representations.

The character Rose O'Malley features in several of Sigal's most pointed and—from the perspective of publication—successful treatments of the Lessing "raw material" to that date: three stories with the overarching title, "Rose & Her Friends," published in the *North American Review* (1983); the play, "A Visit with Rose," aired on BBC radio in 1983 (discussed in chapter 3); and *The Secret Defector*, Sigal's third novel, published in 1992. By the time the Rose stories were published, Sigal not only had achieved emotional and aesthetic distance from Lessing but also had become an accomplished practitioner of the techniques of literary "mining" and disguised biography and the form of *roman à clef*. As he examined his own role in their relationship, he satirized Doris Lessing but also endeavored to represent her view of him.

Sigal's literary and personal preoccupation with Lessing, whom he continued to see occasionally during the 1970s and early 1980s, apparently continued even while he was living with and eventually married to (and later divorced from) Margaret Walters, an Australian feminist activist and writer. An undated, unpublished story, "The Corpuscle Quartet Rides Again," which focuses on Sigal's adolescence in Chicago and otherwise has nothing to do with Doris Lessing or their relationship, opens with a paragraph-long defensive nod in her direction. He laments that Rose O'Malley, his fictionalized version of Lessing, is incapable of seeing him as he is because her own imaginative—and imaginary—version obstructs her view of him. The story begins,

> Rose O'Malley and I work differently. Once she has written about somebody, that's it. Fini. "Life itself"...may go on but the portrait

is finished for all time. And because it embodies artistic truth it is somehow more life-like than the living person himself. That is why I at times get this peculiar feeling that Rose is talking to "Paul Blue" not me when we have our little get-togethers. She seems happy to do this—except when I do something that massively contradicts her picture of me-as-Paul. Such as make a durable marriage and keep writing, or do my share of the washing-up, or not fall apart. ("The Corpuscle Quartet Rides Again" 1, Sigal's underscoring)[1]

The name Paul Blue is a variant of Jake Blue, Sigal's alter ego in his earliest disguised-autobiographical writing about himself and Lessing. Both names obviously ring changes on Lessing's invented Saul Green.

The overlaps between art and life functioned in the other direction as well. By the early 1980s, Sigal's fictionalized version of Doris Lessing as Rose O'Malley had become equally "alive" for her creator. His early Rose period, so to speak, reflects the apprentice stage of his efforts to turn the experiences—his, hers, and theirs—of the Sigal/Lessing years into publishable fiction. Of the three "Rose & Her Friends" stories published by Sigal, Rose O'Malley is central in one and stands just offstage in the other two. The tone of the first and most significant of the stories, "Lunch with Rose," ranges from reflective to caustic, revealing several aspects of an intimate liaison whose scars and sensitive points lingered on for years after the relationship ended. For old time's sake, Robert Wasserman, the narrator and Sigal's fictional alter ego, and Rose O'Malley, his former lover, meet annually for lunch. This time, Robert arrives at the designated restaurant to find Rose already seated. Her posture as she greets him reminds him of the way she had, from the very beginning, regarded her lover as raw material for her writing: "she used to [straighten up] from her typewriter when I came into her room. Without irritation, swiftly slipping a thought, an image, into her memory bank for later use. Once I'd found that maddeningly sexy" ("Lunch with Rose"[2]). From the outset, the language suggests veiled combat. Robert anticipates their time together "*mano [à] mano*" ("Lunch" 41, Sigal's italics); soon after he joins Rose at the table, they raise their menus "like shields" (41).

Since their last meeting, each has experienced a temporarily disabling medical condition. Their responses to these conditions are distinctly different, as the narrator emphasizes in the sardonic tone that saturates the story. Robert had regarded his esophageal surgery as a signal to moderate his pace; by contrast, Rose, when incapacitated by a broken leg, had "practically seized the chance... to study Sanskrit and also become an expert in homeopathy" (41). While Robert privately regards himself as Rose's inferior, "Professor Emeritus only of alleys and street corners," his former lover has achieved her place as "Britain's most active literary Grand Lady" (42). The phrase captures Sigal's uncanny anticipation of Lessing's recognition as a grande dame of letters, even though she refused the honorific title of Dame Commander of the British Empire in 1992.[3]

Overall, however, the tone of the story is critical. Like Doris Lessing as seen through the eyes of Clancy Sigal, the fictitious Rose O'Malley has changed in ways that Robert does not admire. He recalls how central "politics had once been... to our lives" and regrets that his former lover has abandoned that "irksome relic of her now-despised radical past" (42). During one of their previous lunch reunions, he had attempted to discuss political subjects, provoking Rose to "almost [hiss], 'Politics is a bad joke. It's primitive thinking. My God, won't you ever grow up?'" (42) He had been shocked at her vehemence, "as if she had stepped over a thin but dreadful line between being a humorously self-critical Communist and a spiteful renegade" (42). Doris Lessing turned her back on New Left politics when she left the British Communist Party in 1956, admitting that she was thoroughly disillusioned with the "straightjacket" of Marxist communism (*Walking in the Shade* 214). In an interview in 1980, three years before Sigal's "Lunch with Rose" was published, she underscored her political disengagement in the same emphatic tone that Sigal captures in his story, remarking, "Certainly I would never have anything to do with politics again unless I was forced at the point of a gun, having seen what happens" (interview with Christopher Bigsby, "The Need to Tell Stories" April 23, 1980, 74).

Through the sardonic and at times even disparaging tone that Sigal sustains throughout "Lunch with Rose," his narrative double privately admits that he had been slow to take seriously Rose's move into "Sufism and science fiction" (42). At an earlier lunch reunion, he had chided her for "'futzing around with that drugstore sheikh.'... I meant Ibraham Hassan, a Surrey guru who looked like Valentino and talked like W. C. Fields as The Great Swami" (42)—Sigal's jab at Idries Shah, the popularizer of Islamic mysticism with whom Lessing studied Sufism for many years. Robert knows Rose well enough to assume that her relationship with the Indian/Afghan spiritual teacher whom he mistakenly describes as an "Arab prankster" (42) is likely something other than platonic. However, he also mocks his own equally dubious psychological and spiritual adventures—the period of his "Laingean, Sartrean, Zen-Buddhist Siberian shamanistic 'spiritual wanderings'" (42).

Quite apart from Clancy Sigal's negative spin on the subject and the man, Idries Shah was a significant guide and catalyst for a fundamental shift in Doris Lessing's spiritual orientation during the 1960s and afterward. She was deeply attracted to Sufi philosophy because it offered her the possibility of being "in the world, but not of it" ("In the World, Not of It" [1972], *A Small Personal Voice* 133). Through Shah's book, *The Sufis* (1964) and later through her discipleship under him and a friendship that ended only with his death 30 years later, in 1996,[4] she adopted the belief that each person is a "mere concoction of transient influences" ("On Sufism and Idries Shah's *The Commanding Self*"). When she first encountered this and other Sufi ideas, she felt "liberated," "as if at last hearing news I had been waiting for" ("On Sufism"). She regarded Idries Shah's book as "the most surprising book I had read, and yet it was as if I had been waiting to read just that book all my life. It is a cliché to say that such and such a book changed one's life, but that book changed mine" ("On the Death of Idries Shah" and "Summing Up" 357). A number of Lessing's novels reveal the influence of Sufi thought on her fiction. Both *Landlocked* (1965)—the fourth volume of *Children of Violence* and the first of her novels published after her turn to Sufism—and *The Four-Gated City* (1969), the final volume of the series, not only include quotations from Sufi teachings as epigraphs to several sections of the novels but also incorporate Sufi ideas about spiritual growth. *Briefing for a Descent into Hell* (1971) and *The Memoirs of a Survivor* (1975) also express Lessing's ongoing interest in giving literary expression to the path to spiritual enlightenment.[5]

In "Lunch with Rose," Sigal's narrator also chastens Rose O'Malley/Doris Lessing as a writer whose literary success has led her—in Sigal's less-than-neutral judgment—to become rather vain and self-preoccupied. She "reel[s] off the books she ha[s] written, prizes awarded, kudos bestowed since we last met" ("Lunch" 42). By contrast, all Robert Wasserman has to offer by way of personal news is prosaic details about his new house in a London suburb. Privately, he admits that this is his way of reminding Rose of his success in an area of his life that she had seriously doubted he was capable of achieving: sustaining a stable long-term relationship with a woman. His strategy does not entirely succeed because, to his irritation, Rose prefers her own imaginary typecast Hollywood caricature of him as "a reincarnation of James Dean out of Brendan Behan: the ragged-trousered urban cowboy, handsome creature of moods, dark prince of neurosis, stunted Oedipal child" (42). As in the opening paragraph of Sigal's unpublished "The Corpuscle Quartet Rides Again," the phrasing suggests that, long after he and Lessing separated, Sigal was disturbed that she persisted in retaining an image of him that was more fiction than fact—as if her literary creation, Saul Green, remained more real than the "original" on whom he was modeled. Sigal's fictional alter ego in "Lunch with Rose," having achieved literary success, marriage, and personal tranquility, regrets that his former lover has not relinquished her outdated and patronizing image of him as the "Unsung Genius of Too Many Words" (42). Wondering whether Rose is lonely in her worldly and literary success, he concludes, on the contrary, that she enjoys "being Next in Line for the Nobel Prize" (43). Although the comment is sardonic, one must give Sigal credit for his prescience; two decades later, in 2007, Doris Lessing, then just shy of her 88th birthday, was awarded the Nobel Prize in Literature.

The lunch-time chat turns to Robert's imminent departure for America, where he will assume a position as a visiting professor at an unspecified university. (For several years during the 1970s, Clancy Sigal was a visiting professor at the Annenberg School for Communication and Journalism at the University of Southern California.) The subject of academe leads Rose O'Malley to a particular, and repeated, sore point, her appropriation by "The Movement"—feminists who, in their "illiterate literalness," reduced her imaginative literary creations, notably *The Golden Notebook*, to "tracts" (43). In Sigal's retelling, Lessing/Rose O'Malley blames American feminists in particular for their position as oversimplifiers who were blind to the "ironic complexities" of her work (43). With a touch of sarcasm, Robert privately muses that Rose regrets having to "bear the heavy burden of once having lighted a path forward for women which she herself now felt to be a false trail" (43). Yet he also identifies an element of hypocrisy in her position, for her worshipful feminist admirers were instrumental to her literary and financial success.

On the subject of feminist appropriations, Clancy Sigal had his own ax to grind. As his fictional alter ego in "Lunch with Rose" phrases it, "I understood about acolytes. I could have screwed myself to death with all the American feminists who looked me up as a way of knowing Rose. (They all agreed I was the 'Paul Blue' of her trail-breaking novel *Loose Leaves from a Random Life*)" (43). Robert's strategy for deflecting such embarrassing and even humiliating attention has been to remark to Rose O'Malley's worshippers that she is "a fuckin-A great cook." Such comments outraged American feminists who, missing his irreverent attempt at humor, regarded it as "100% evidence that Paul Blue hadn't changed his spots" (43). Or, one might say, his stripes.

What dismays Robert most about this particular lunch with Rose O'Malley is his recognition of the growing distance between them, illustrated by the ever-shrinking list of permissible topics of conversation. "Politics, sex, feminism, Alex [Rose's son], the news— out" (43); the only safe topics are travel, books, and his wife, about whom Robert would rather not share personal details. He regrets the uneasy armistice that prevails between him and Rose as both have become increasingly protective of "the trade secrets of our inmost lives. It was a big, felt loss for me. She was, when all was said and done, my best non-fucking woman friend in England. I didn't mind the divorce, I had even got used to the distance, emotionally. But she was an indelible part of my bloodstream. We didn't 'owe' each other a thing. Except faithfulness to that funny old whatever-it-was we once shared" (44). Though he still follows Rose O'Malley's literary career, he regrets that her "[g]reat sense of fun, in life" (44), which he valued while they were lovers, seems utterly absent from her fiction, particularly her recent speculative fiction. As he notes condescendingly, he abandoned that particular "space ship" when he was 14. He is aware of Rose's "linked series of novels about catastrophe and after" (44), a direct allusion to Lessing's five-volume series then in progress, *Canopus in Argos: Archives*, beginning with *Re: Colonised Planet 5, Shikasta* (1979) and continuing with *The Marriages Between Zones Three, Four, and Five* (1980) and *The Sirian Experiments* (1981).

Clancy Sigal was not the only reader of Doris Lessing's work to lament her turn to speculative fiction. In a major piece for the *New York Times Book Review* in 1982, the editor John Leonard penned what was virtually a critical screed concerning the four novels in the *Canopus in Argos* series that Lessing had published to date. As he phrased it,

> The question: Why does Doris Lessing—one of the half dozen most interesting minds to have chosen to write fiction in English in this century—insist on propagating books that confound and dismay her loyal readers? The answer: She intends to confound and

dismay.... Mrs. Lessing is no longer very interested in people. She has come to feel that individuality is a "degenerative disease." The "archeologist" of human relations, so celebrated by Irving Howe in his review of *The Golden Notebook*, has gone intergalactic.... Nor are we likely to hear any more from her on racism, capitalism, colonialism, Marxism, sexism, psychoanalysis, science and technology. Having eaten too many -isms, she is still hungry. She has gone beyond—and transcended. ("The Spacing Out of Doris Lessing")

In "Lunch with Rose," Clancy Sigal has his stand-in reminisce about the old days when he and Rose O'Malley/Doris Lessing were still on the same wave length politically, emotionally, sexually—and culinarily. Sigal clearly enjoys lavishing details on the elaborate breakfasts that Lessing had once lavished on him:

> Warm home-baked bread, Rose-preserved strawberry jam, hot strong coffee (from the Venezuelan mountain beans I liked and she trekked all the way to Golders Green to get), bacon streaky crisp, three sunny-side-up eggs with the yolk slightly runny, butcher-fresh...sausages, grilled tomatoes, *News-Chronicle* and *Daily Worker* at the side of plate. A banquet. Often followed by a digestive screw, sometimes on the kitchen floor.... Who knows, maybe she was trying to kill me with a premature coronary? ("Lunch" 44)

But Robert's paean to Rose's culinary skills and their erotic postscripts reminds him of the incompatibilities that ultimately resulted in their breakup. Still defensive about what he regarded as Lessing's irrational jealousy, Sigal proposes through his fictional persona that it was not simply their differences concerning his occasional girlfriends—a matter that he and Rose "could have settled in five minutes" (44)—but their colliding core assumptions about intimate relationships. Perhaps Clancy Sigal's awkward position as both lodger and lover compounded the problem. What he regarded as his privilege as a single male to engage in casual liaisons with other women, Doris Lessing regarded as sexual and emotional infidelity. Sigal/Robert and Lessing/Rose quarreled mightily and with "elegant venom" (44) over this subject of great consequence for their relationship.

Another matter that apparently continued to irk Clancy Sigal was Lessing's habit of invoking the subject of his mother, particularly during their quarrels concerning his other women. Thinking back to those altercations, his narrator in "Lunch with Rose" recalls Rose challenging him, "'how *can* you be faithful to me when I'm your damn mother every time.' And then, instead of cursing me, she'd pour down upon my aching head a witch's cauldron of Jungian epithets and Freudian pronouncements that petrified the awed-of-doctors Jewish kid in me" (44, Sigal's italics). Robert prides himself on having resisted most of Rose's attempts to fit him into such psychoanalytic oversimplifications.

The lunch concludes on a humorous note as the former lovers have one last "little spat" (45), as if for old time's sake. The subject is Rose's recommended treatment for Robert's gastrointestinal troubles. With a straight face, she prescribes a "paste of garlic, pressed daffodils and Spanish onions, taken with camomile [*sic*] tea and a few tiny pills she offered to let me try" (45). Robert, without directly challenging the unorthodox concoction itself, protests that her nostrum was intended to treat a broken leg rather than an ailing stomach; Rose turns his objection to criticism of him. In the retort that concludes the story—and with a sly allusion to a central theme of *The Golden Notebook*—Sigal gives Lessing's literary substitute the last word: "'You still compartmentalize, don't you,' she smiled tolerantly. 'Ah well, take care of yourself, darling. There aren't too many of us left any more, are there?'" (45)

In "Lunch with Rose," Clancy Sigal, by turns acerbic and reflective, gives literary expression to his lingering ambivalent feelings about Lessing, still present more than two decades after they separated, and defends his own behavior. Although the fictitious lunch date ends in détente—one that apparently remained in force for many years after Sigal and Lessing parted company romantically—the defensive, sardonic, and critical tone of this story is characteristic of several of Sigal's apprentice literary treatments of their relationship. Yet, despite his rather jaundiced view of his former lover, one can see that he knew Doris Lessing well. His story highlights significant literary developments as well as personal changes in her—albeit tinged with criticism—that he observed after they separated.

The other two stories in Sigal's Rose trilogy—"An Abuse of Hospitality" and "Two Cats on a Mantelpiece"—are both set earlier in time than "Lunch with Rose" and, despite their shared 1983 publication date, suggest an earlier date of composition. In both stories, Sigal continued to work through the legacy of his liaison with Lessing and was apparently still licking some of his wounds, so to speak. The fictitious Rose O'Malley is strongly present in the stories, not only as their pretext but as the reference point for the narrator's continuing feeling of emotional entanglement and his sense of grievance. In

"An Abuse of Hospitality," Robert—Sigal's fictional alter ego who also appears in "Lunch with Rose"—is shakily recovering from his journey through mental breakdown and madness. As with the opening paragraph of Sigal's unpublished story, "The Corpuscle Quartet Rides Again," noted above, the double-edged references to his former lover literally begin with the finger-pointing opening lines of "An Abuse of Hospitality": "Rose O'Malley isn't responsible for her fans. Yet I blame her for Sally Wilner and her doting husband Randal" ("Abuse" 45). Courtesy of Rose's recommendation, Robert finds himself the fawned-over house guest of a social-climbing Beverly Hills couple who regard the writer/shaman they have snared as a kind of social trophy. Sally Wilner, "a leading young feminist" (45) and author of a "mad-housewife novel, *Domestic Affairs*," and her husband are curious about Robert's recent heroic "spiritual pilgrimage" (46). Robert finds it impossible to live up to the reputation that the Wilners expect as a result of Rose O'Malley's recommendation.

The couple offers Robert a place in California to stay and write while he recovers from his emotionally draining mind trip. Before long, he finds himself fending off sexual overtures from Sally, who seeks to seduce him as a way of learning more intimate details about her feminist idol, Rose O'Malley. He is torn between vanity—he can't entirely resist his status as privileged guest whom the Wilners worshipfully parade before their friends as "a worthy successor to R. D. Laing" (48)—and his self-protective instinct. Alone one night, feeling trapped in his circumstances, he "talks" to Rose, who has by now become an inner voice in his head. "We had a bitter argument over what I should do next" (49). The following morning, he springs himself free of the Wilners' clutches; by implication, he also sheds some of his own pretensions.

The final story in the Rose trilogy, "Two Cats on a Mantelpiece," reprises the theme of the manipulative woman who uses the narrator's relationship with Rose O'Malley to get something for herself, suggesting Sigal's lingering grievance that he was valued less for himself than for his association with Doris Lessing. The story opens with the narrator's hyperbolic statement, "Have you ever fallen for three women at the same time—but they were the same woman? No, I'm not into schizophrenia again. Just London literary life" ("Two Cats" 50). The woman in question is Freda Balcon, a beautiful writer with features like "a great Aztec queen," who "used Rose O'Malley to get to me" (50). Initially, the narrator sees Freda as the "Literary Lady" of his dreams who will "wipe out the bloody painful memory of Rose O'Malley" (50). Falling hard for her despite the inconvenient fact that she is married, he figuratively embraces "all three of her": not only the "stunning, elusively maternal Freda" but the invented heroine of Freda's "divorce novel, *The Hungry Vessel*, and Julie Christie, the actress who plays the character in the film version of it. A further cinematic connection, though coincidental, is suggested by the character's name, Freda, along with her "marvelous Mexican-eyed face" (52): nearly 20 years after "Two Cats on a Mantelpiece" appeared in print in 1983, Sigal—by then a Hollywood film-script writer—was the principal script writer for *Frida* (2002), a biopic based on the life of the Mexican artist, Frida Kahlo.[6]

Sigal's feckless alter ego eventually learns that he has been set up: Freda and her husband had "cooked...up" the seduction plan as a strategy to satisfy Freda's curiosity about "her great literary rival, Rose" (51). Taken in by the scheme, the naïve narrator, channeling one of Woody Allen's comic schlemiels, marvels, "I'd never done it with three women at once" (51). After their unsatisfying sexual encounter, Freda quickly proceeds to her studio, where Robert can hear "a pen scratching on a pad" (52), presumably as she writes about their intimate encounter. With that detail, Sigal lampoons Lessing's writing method in the portion of *The Golden Notebook* that concerns Saul Green, exaggerated as an accelerated version of kiss-and-tell, with the female writer recording intimate details virtually moments after they occur. Not long afterward, the narrator, sadder if not wiser, flees the Balcons' Hampstead mansion.

The Rose trilogy of stories, while apprentice literary pieces, demonstrate several features of Sigal's developing writing practice, including his method of mining autobiographical experience, including variations on points of tension in his long-since-ended relationship with Doris Lessing. In "Lunch with Rose"—as in the BBC radio play, "A Visit with Rose," produced the same year—Lessing is the object of criticism and complaint as well as sarcasm and grudging admiration; Sigal gives his fictional stand-in the upper hand in both insight and equilibrium. In the two slighter stories, Rose O'Malley functions behind the scenes, as it were. As an accessory to the plot, she is the figure only barely in the background, the source of the narrator's wounded pride and humiliation when he recognizes that he is sought after not for himself but for his connection to his more famous former lover. Through these stories, readers may capture glimpses of a fictionally transformed and at times satirically skewered Doris Lessing, as filtered through the imagination of her once—if not, at the time of writing, still—disgruntled former lover. The Rose O'Malley of the Rose trilogy and play was not only the prototype for a character that Sigal continued to develop and embellish in his later fiction; in addition, she represents and illustrates Lessing's indelible presence in his imagination for a number of years after they separated. Indeed, one of Doris Lessing's multiple roles in Clancy Sigal's life was as his muse.

Chapter 6

Life in the Interior Zone

"I have never personally been mad or broken down, but I feel as if I have. The reason for my not having been personally mad or in breakdown is, I think—partly—that any inclination towards it has been staved off by writing about it." Doris Lessing (Walking in the Shade)

"Breakdown so indelibly marked me, I compare everything to it. It was what I always expected. And I have come to expect a repetition—almost wish for it." Clancy Sigal (unpublished journal)

Breaking Up

In June 1959, Doris Lessing sent Clancy Sigal an impassioned, pain-drenched letter, mentioning that she had destroyed several of her earlier attempts to explain why, in her words, "I don't want to see you just now" (5, postmarked June 23, 1959). She emphasized various points of contention: first, that she could tolerate almost anything except for his dishonesty about his liaisons with other women; second, that she had willingly served as his mother and psychiatrist even when she knew she should have declined these roles and that she was no longer willing to do so; and third, that he needed to see a psychiatrist to help him address his serious emotional issues. She expressed her genuine amazement that Sigal did not regard having sex with another woman as having an affair with her. What had finally compelled her to cool their relationship (as it turned out, they did not finally separate for another nine months) was the breach of trust resulting from Sigal's philandering and his habitual dissimulations about it—an especially grievous point, in Lessing's view, because she believed that they had reached a mutual agreement that he would no longer lie to her on that subject.

In her letter, Lessing refers to her three years of hard work in psychotherapy with a therapist who—despite her Jungian approach, which Lessing herself did not endorse—enabled her to grasp and master destructive patterns in her own behavior. as she phrased it,

> without my three years of going to the old lady (whose theories I didn't agree with) but who had a flair for human behaviour, I'd have cracked up long ago. Its [sic] necessary to you to think of me as stronger than I am, and for an easy reason—you needed my strength.
>
> Believe me, the hard work, and the pain that I put in to understanding some of my compulsive patterns, has made it possible for me to be happy now. And you know that I can be very happy, given half a chance.
>
> I'm saying this, because I'd like you really to understand that I too, have had to lock myself against emotion, had to run away from it, because it has been associated with pain. (Letter, 4)

Lessing begged Sigal to seek professional therapy for his destructive behavior and hoped that in time he would recognize not only the pain he had caused her but also the wisdom of her words. In closing, she advised him, "Look after yourself," and signed the letter simply, Doris. (Letter, 5). Many years later, Lessing, reflecting on that acutely painful stretch of her life, diminished Sigal's role in it: "Clancy and I were breaking up—had been for months or, you could say, from the moment we began. For one thing, we had so little in common. And then he had never made any secret of his wanting to live by himself and have girls.... With Clancy I hit the extremes in myself and had from the start, and this had nothing very much to do with Clancy the person. Partly it was because he was in 'breakdown...'" (*Walking in the Shade* 285).

Lessing elaborates that she was emotionally shattered by their breakup. As she describes it,

> I seemed to have no will; my intelligence watched what I did but was helpless. My surface behaviour accorded with: "Oh no, Clancy and I are good friends; that's all it is now." And we were good friends. But underneath I was all the betrayed woman, the abandoned one, I suffered and mourned and dragged myself about, with no more will than I needed to keep myself going and the fact that I despised myself made it all worse. (*Walking* 286)

Nonetheless, she apparently continued to pour herself into the task of completing *The Golden Notebook*, which was published in 1962. In the final segment of *Free Women*, Anna Wulf—who, by that point in the narrative, has been revealed as the author of the *Free Women* sections as well as of the four notebooks— describes an American Leftist writer named Milt who spends five days in her flat. Openly critical of her temporary lodger's sexual and emotional insecurities, she challenges him, "You don't think that there is something slightly extraordinary about a state of affairs where a man walks into a woman's flat and says: I've got to share your bed because I fall into space if I sleep alone, but I can't make love to you because if I do I'll hate you?" (*GN* 619) Later, when Anna's friend Molly asks her about, as she phrases it, "your American," Anna responds with a matter-of-fact statement that pointedly excludes all of the drama, disequilibrium, anger, jealousy, and emotional pain that saturate earlier pages of the narrative, "Well I had an affair with him" (*GN* 622). One can speculate that the objective, detached tone with which *The Golden Notebook* concludes reflects not only Anna Wulf's but also Doris Lessing's struggle to achieve emotional distance from the man who had deeply hurt and changed her.

Clancy Sigal similarly hit extremes in himself. Even before he and Lessing separated permanently in the spring of 1960—nearly nine months after Lessing sent her anguished letter—Sigal regarded their split as a "divorce" (1959–60 Journal, November 27, 1959). After he moved from Lessing's Warwick Road maisonette into his own flat, he wrote in his journal, "Moved in. Provoked quarrel w/ D. A big hole in my heart w/o her, can't bear being w/her w/o performing duty" (1959–60 Journal, March 13, 1960). During his first day in the new location, he confessed,

> I suddenly feel incompetent to take care of details of living—I've always seen myself as masterful & assertive, now I see I'm really a weakling out of English novel. Things are going to crash very shortly with Doris—she is flinging herself into art & work—I await symptoms. D. has known love & wants it again. I have never known it.... Breakdown so indelibly marked me, I compare everything to it. It was what I always expected. And I have come to expect a repetition—almost wish for it. (1959–60 Journal, March 14, 1960)

Yet, however distressed he may have been after he and Lessing separated, Sigal was planning to write about their relationship; the entry in his journal for his first day in his new flat concludes, "Subject of book." While he apparently also considered leaving England—he titled his journal for that period "Diary and Essay on Leaving England"—he remained in London for another three decades. Within a few months of his departure from Warwick Street, he assisted Lessing in her own move to a smaller flat in Langham Street, Soho. By then Sigal's own writing career had begun to take off with the publication of several pieces in British Leftist journals and newspapers and the approaching publication of *Weekend in Dinlock* and *Going Away*. However, for some months after he and Lessing separated, he continued to suffer from emotional distress and the effects of their "divorce." Nearly nine months after moving out of Lessing's flat, he wrote in his final journal entry for 1960 two terse phrases: "Can't cope. Crazy psychiatrists" (December 28, 1960).

* * *

Breaking Down

In her autobiography, Lessing comments that, while she wrote several novels featuring characters who are "mad, half mad, and in breakdown," she had "never personally been mad or broken down, but I feel as if I have. The reason for my not having been personally mad or in breakdown is I think—partly—that any inclination towards it has been staved off by writing about it" (*Walking* 267). She ruefully acknowledges that, with *The Golden Notebook*, she might have contributed unintentionally to a belief that circulated during the 1960s and early 1970s—to which she never subscribed—that "to go mad is to receive the ultimate in revelation.... I do not believe that ultimate truths come from being crazy" (267–8). Such thinking, promoted by the radical British psychiatrist R. D. Laing, whom Lessing knew, was central to Clancy Sigal's psychological and spiritual explorations during the period. One of the most controversial theories that Laing tested with actual schizophrenic patients was that psychotic breakdown, if permitted to run its course, provided a natural opportunity for mind-healing. The "inner space journey," as he termed it (*Politics of Experience* 104), was a therapeutic alternative to the traditional treatment of psychotic patients in mental hospitals, where they were typically and involuntarily administered powerful antipsychotic drugs to control their symptoms.

Like many others of their generation, both Doris Lessing and Clancy Sigal voluntarily experimented with drugs. During the 1960s, Lessing took mescaline once and also tried a drug that she later declared was "absolutely not to be recommended," ingesting "morning glory seeds, previously soaked in hot water to an acid jellyish state..." (*Under My Skin* 20). Under the influence of the drug, she induced for herself a therapeutic "good birth" (*Skin* 21) to cancel the negative story of her actual birth to a mother who yearned for a son and rejected her firstborn daughter virtually from birth. As Lessing reports, one of her strongest and most persistent memories from early childhood is that of her mother "telling [her] over and over again that she had not wanted a girl, she wanted a boy. I knew from the beginning she loved my little brother unconditionally, and she did not love me.... [M]y early childhood made me one of the walking wounded for years" (*Skin* 25).

For a time, Lessing was interested in R. D. Laing's path-breaking if controversial work in connection with her own interest in abnormal and unconventional modes of consciousness, including not only emotional illness and mental breakdown but also mystical experience. As she phrased it, she and Laing "were both exploring the phenomenon of the unclassifiable experience, the psychological 'breaking-through' that the conventional world judges as mad. I think Laing must have been very courageous, to question the basic assumptions of his profession from the inside..." ("One Keeps Going" 35, ellipsis in original). She may also have experimented with the psychotropic drug, LSD, with Laing, though the evidence is equivocal.[1] Five years later, by which time her enthusiasm for Laing's radical psychiatry had decidedly cooled, she remarked, "My view of Laing is that at an appropriate time in Britain, he challenged certain extreme rigidities in psychiatry with alternative viewpoints, and made other attitudes than the official ones possible. That is what he did. No more and no less" (Letter to the author dated March 28, 1977, qtd. in *The Novelistic Vision of Doris Lessing* 199 n30). Elsewhere Lessing suggested that Laing was a "peg" or authority figure at the time, to whom many people attached their own ideas about mental illness and schizophrenia (lecture at the New School of Social Research, qtd. by Nancy Shields Hardin in "Doris Lessing and the Sufi Way," 154–5). Nonetheless, apparently influenced by her knowledge of Laingian psychiatry as well as her own experience with psychotropic drugs, Lessing wrote *Briefing for a Descent into Hell* (1971), which she termed "inner space fiction" (frontispiece); her phrase, and the novel itself, closely accords with Laing's concept of the "inner space journey."

Among other ideas, *Briefing for a Descent into Hell* expresses in fictional form Lessing's condemnation of the conventional practices of the psychiatric profession for its insensitive and often punitive treatment of people suffering mental or emotional breakdown. The protagonist of the novel, a Cambridge professor of classics named Charles Watkins, is found wandering in London with an episode of amnesia so severe that he has literally forgotten his identity. Lessing acknowledged that she drew the character and this episode from a true experience, though not her own: a friend whom she visited in a psychiatric hospital explained to her that "[v]ery late one night...a man was brought in who had been found wandering on the Embankment. He had lost his memory. But so much 'together' was he that the doctors at first thought he was putting on an act.... He had no idea who he was, and it took something like six weeks before he remembered" ("Writing Autobiography," *Time Bites* 97). In *Briefing for a Descent into Hell*, during Charles Watkins's hospitalization for treatment of his amnesia, unnamed doctors, pointedly labeled "Doctor X" and "Doctor Y," strongly disagree over the appropriate treatment for the patient as they attempt to help him recover his identity. While they administer various therapies, beginning with drugs and proceeding to electroconvulsive therapy (shock treatment), Watkins is engaged in an interior journey that takes place in a series of vividly described alternate realities ranging from outer space to the Yugoslavian countryside during war and that is by turns illuminating, instructive, profound, discouraging, and even comic and parodic. When he experiences himself as most profoundly alert and alive to his experiences and his surroundings, he is, from a medical perspective, deeply asleep or unconscious. Though the alternating narratives concerning Watkins's experiences as psychiatric patient and inner-space traveler are mutually exclusive, the reader has access to both versions of his story.

Of note, given Doris Lessing's and Clancy Sigal's shared literary strategy of borrowing liberally from details in the lives of actual people for their fictional portraits, Lessing was criticized for seemingly appropriating details from the narrative of one of R. D. Laing's friends who recounted a remarkably similar experience. Charles Watkins's inner space journey contains a striking number of parallels with the ten-day psychotic/mystical journey described by a sculptor and friend of Laing's, Jesse Watkins, and included as the chapter, "A Ten-Day Voyage," in Laing's *The Politics of Experience* (120–37).[2] Asked about the numerous similarities between Charles and Jesse Watkins, Doris Lessing responded rather indignantly, dismissing as entirely coincidental the duplication of surname as well as multiple parallels in their inner journeys. In response to my questions on the subject, she remarked in a letter,

I had not taken Laing as my starting point. I had not read the piece in question by him, or the book *Politics of Experience*. My book was written out of my own thoughts, not other people's. ...It seems almost impossible for people to grasp that people can write from their own experience. As for the name Watkins, being used: I took the name out of the telephone book, which is my usual practice...[because of British libel laws]. I always use the commonest name I can find.... (Letter to the author dated November 17, 1972, qtd. in *The Novelistic Vision of Doris Lessing* 197 n7, my ellipses)

Lesley Hazleton observes that "Laing, Doris Lessing and...Clancy Sigal formed a circle of almost incestuous mutual influence, using one another as characters in their work and playing on the others' titles and characters' names" ("Doris Lessing on Feminism, Communism and 'Space Fiction'" 27).

The "interior journey" theorized by R. D. Laing and undertaken by Lessing's fictitious Charles Watkins was even more personally crucial for Clancy Sigal. In contrast to Lessing's indirect experience with the subject of mental illness, Sigal's familiarity was both immediate and firsthand. During his early thirties, he suffered night terrors, acute anxiety attacks, and other physical and psychosomatic symptoms of what he termed "It," a condition that more than once led him to the verge of mental breakdown. Following several unsatisfactory experiences with traditional therapists, he underwent psychotherapy with the radical psychiatrist whom he much later and more critically termed a "celebrity shrink" ("A Trip to the Far Side of Madness"). Laing, according to his own report, saw Sigal in therapy about once a week for two years (*Mad to be Normal* 303). At the time, Laing dared Sigal to "pass through his most private and cherished door: the door of perception known as the schizophrenic revolution." Although Sigal did not recognize it as a dare at the time, he accepted the opportunity. As he later quipped, "I'd no idea what he was talking about. But if it was a revolution I was all for it" ("Far side"). Further, "[Laing's] notions—that you actually might enjoy any part of your inner torment, and that misery if handled gently and with humour could yield profoundly self-therapeutic insights— threw [him] temporarily off balance" even as it deeply appealed to him (untitled reminiscence, "R. D. Laing," ed. Mullan 214).

Sigal was also closely involved on the other side of Laing's practice regarding schizophrenic breakdown and madness. He worked with Laing for seven years, including in his position as one of several cofounders of Kingsley Hall, a therapeutic community center located in the East End of London. For part of that time, he was chairman of the Philadelphia Association, the board that oversaw Laing's signature project, Villa 21—a safe place where patients diagnosed with schizophrenia were supported during their mental breakdowns and guided through a process of healing ("Working with Laing").[3] Beginning in 1964, Laing and several colleagues who were trained in psychiatry or social work "lived with a number of very disturbed 'psychotic' people who would otherwise have been in mental hospitals or psychiatric units and treated accordingly. Among us there were no staff, no patients, no locked doors, no psychiatric treatment to stop or change states of mind," as Laing himself described it (*Wisdom, Madness and Folly* xi). Sigal has explained that the project was "split-level": "to care for schizophrenics in a new, less authoritarian way, and to allow the carers full freedom to engage in their own 'schizophrenic voyage.' At the time this seemed no contradiction. Why should we not have some of the fun too?" (untitled reminiscence 214). Thus, while participating as a volunteer in the "brotherhood" of Laing's therapeutic community, Sigal underwent his own inner space journey under Laing's direct guidance. With Laing and others, Sigal also experimented with the psychotropic drug, LSD.

Sigal later fictionalized this dramatic period of his life in his third novel, *Zone of the Interior*, lampooning both himself and the unorthodox, even flaky, psychiatrist whose fictional name, Dr. Willie Last, perfectly captures the satiric tone of the narrative. Through his fictional double, Sid Bell, Sigal lightly disguises numerous details from his actual experience with Laing, Kingsley Hall, and mental breakdown. The novel was published to high praise in the United States in 1976. In the novel, Coral Brand—the name Sigal first used for his fictional transformation of Doris Lessing in his earliest unpublished disguised-autobiographical writings—makes a number of cameo appearances, usually negatively toned in ways that reflect Sigal's ambivalent feelings about her following their separation in 1960. Amusingly, one reviewer of the novel observed—whether innocently or not—that, "[A]t its best, *Zone of the Interior* reads like Doris Lessing's *Briefing for a Descent into Hell* as retold by the Marx Brothers" (Cheuse 6).

At the beginning of the novel, Sid Bell suffers from acute psychosomatic symptoms—stomachaches, vertigo, cold sweats, unexplained fevers, and rising anxiety. When the same symptoms had distressed Clancy Sigal/Sid Bell while he was living with Doris Lessing/Coral

Brand and attempting with difficulty to write a book, his lover had dismissed them as "writing pains" that would disappear once he achieved publication. A number of these symptoms are also ascribed to Saul Green in *The Golden Notebook*. In *Zone of the Interior*, Coral Brand recommends that Sid visit the Marxist psychiatrist, Dr. Willie Last. Despite his previous unsatisfactory encounters with therapists of various stripes, he decides in desperation to see the radical therapist. Fictionalizing Laing's convoluted diagnostic vocabulary to analyze what Sid describes as his "tortured relationship with Coral" (*Zone* 10), Sigal lampoons both Laing and Lessing. Affecting an exaggerated Scottish brogue that, Sigal elsewhere observes, Laing took on or put off at will ("Far side"), Willie Last pontificates that Sid is "engulfed by [Coral's] depersonalized fantasy of yir perception of her collusion wi' yir imploded false self system" (*Zone* 10). The therapist's prescription for Sid's recovery is an interior journey with heroic and mythical antecedents, one that will enable him to shed his "Oedipal conflicts with [his] human mother" (16) as he heals his damaged psyche. Sid is fascinated with Last's prescription for his recovery in part because it accords with his admittedly complicated feelings concerning the two most important women in his life. "What [Last] said dignified all those bloodcurdling quarrels with my mother and gave ritual value to experiences, such as the Coral fiasco, I was so ashamed of. (And hadn't Coral herself often told me that society's malaise was caused not by capitalism but because 'we're all so starved of ritual'?)" (16).

Still bruised by his separation from Coral, Sid comments acerbically on the way she had "gotten me out of her system by writing a play about us" and is now "busy with fresh raw material—her leading man..." (21). Later, reprising his outrage when he recognized the character closely modeled on himself as the antagonist of Lessing's *Play with a Tiger*, Sigal underscores this detail more rancorously: Sid remarks that Coral is "dating the Bronx method actor hired to impersonate me in her new play, *Scorpions in a Bottle*" (25). Nonetheless, he and Coral continue to see each other on occasion. Before surrendering himself to Willie Last's unconventional therapy, Sid scrubs his apartment, draws up a will, has a full physical checkup, and "[goes] around to Coral for a goodbye fuck..." (26). Coral is also involved in therapy, this time exploring a "'rational' mysticism in sessions with her Jungian shrink" (24).

Once Sid has completed his own Hero Journey, comically detailed in the narrative, he becomes one of Willie Last's acolytes, serving as a trainee in Conolly House, Dr. Last's safe house for schizophrenics, closely modeled on R. D. Laing's Villa 21 in London's East End. Sigal states elsewhere that he accepted Laing's invitation "to cease being a patient and became a...what? There was no name for it. Half-jokingly, I called myself a 'writer in residence' among schizophrenics and their fevered doctors.[...] I stopped taking notes at the Villas when the other patients insisted on seeing my obsessive scribbling as a symptom of craziness, which it was" (untitled reminiscence 215). While Willie Last regards this phase in Sid Bell's journey as his opportunity to "invent" himself, Sid sardonically terms it—in one of Sigal's sly comic self-references—"gathering material for a new novel'" (*Zone* 75). The inside joke is that Sid's "novel-journal," provisionally titled *Special File* (104) and based on Sigal's notes on his therapeutic experience with Laing, eventually became his actual novel, *Zone of the Interior*.

Having a bit of fun with such *roman à clef* asides, Sigal drops references to his former lover twice in the same sentence, once without disguise: Sid Bell, commenting on the rising British cultural establishment, offers a list of new talents that slyly combines actual and fictitious names: "Fred Bradshaw, John Osborne, Doris Lessing, Danny [Fior], Coral, me...." (22). Later, Sid composes a brief satiric verse in the manner of a poet named Herb Greaves: "Lessing's/No Blessing/Braine's/On the Wain" (109). The dig is a double jibe, for there is evidence that Lessing had a brief romantic affair with the novelist and poet John Wain.[4] Struggling to maintain his own writing career while pursuing his Laingian Hero Journey, Sid submits an article to *Vogue* magazine—"never printed"—that comically exaggerates his strained effort to bridge the utterly incompatible aspects of his life: "The Meaning of Meaninglessness in Fashion and Mental Illness" (109).

Still licking his wounds from his "bustup" [*sic*] with Coral (97), Sid cannot get her off his mind. At one point he recalls a girl with a German accent who had virtually thrown herself at him, slipping into his sleeping bag during a pause in one of the Aldermaston marches against nuclear armament in Britain. He had resisted her enticements for several reasons, including both her obvious youth and his fear of "Coral's jealous rages" (91). He still covets and wears a "black wool, floor-length cowled monk's robe Coral had sewn for [him during his] first English winter" (105). As he becomes more involved with Willie Last's mental–spiritual health project, Sid makes a final attempt to purge Coral from his life by junking the parting gift she had given

Life in the Interior Zone ❦ 141

to him when he moved to his own flat, "the secondhand king-size bed she and I'd slept in. 'From now on you'll probably need this more than I will,' she had predicted with a kind of sour triumph. Well, I'd show her that two could play at the game of sexual disillusionment. Henceforth I'd use the floor as a pallet, just like a real monk" (106).

As Sid's spiritual journey progresses, his creator ratchets up his satirical treatment of R. D. Laing, including the would-be soul-doctor's prescription for spiritual nirvana. Sigal enjoys skewering the Laingian posturings of mystical profundity as his fictional alter ego, optimistic about the progress of his interior voyage, sees even such chance and insignificant events as "the route a dust speck took settling to the floor" as "parts of a Universal Jigsaw Puzzle I was on the verge of solving. For the first time in England I felt my life to be in complete control. Before had been Coral years. Many of my English friends and contacts had sprung from knowing her. How would I have made out without her?... Never again would I be owned" (*Zone* 109). To define his new position in Willie Last's venture, "Urban Shamanism" (113), Sid fashions an amalgam of medical and spiritual approaches to his "rebirth" script, into which he liberally splices cinematic plot lines concerning the conquest of literal germs and microbes. Later, Sigal provides one of a number of laugh-out-loud observations in the novel as Willie Last soberly observes to Sid Bell in his affected Scots brogue, "We are th' disease we're tryin' tae cure" (141).

As Sid tries without success to recruit "cultural big-shots" to Willie Last's controversial venture, Sigal gets in another jab at Doris Lessing and her turn to speculative fiction during the same time period. Sid has learned from Coral that, in her words, her next novel is "all about how the world nearly ends and is saved by the mentally ill. From what I'm told, if I met your dotty Scots boyfriend I might have to change the last chapter and it's already written" (146). The comment alludes to the ending of Lessing's *The Four-Gated City* (1969), the final volume of *Children of Violence*. The apocalyptic Appendix describes a small group of survivors, including Lessing's own literary alter ego, Martha Quest, 25 years after an unspecified but probably nuclear catastrophe in Britain during the 1960s. In his final dig at Lessing in *Zone of the Interior*—this time a lampoon of her embrace of Sufism and Eastern spiritual practices—Sigal describes a chat between Sid Bell and Boris Petkin, a fictitious therapist in Laing's therapeutic brotherhood, possibly modeled in part on an actual social worker in Laing's Villa 21, Sid Briskin. "I found out that we actually shared an experience: Coral Brand, whom he had briefly psychoanalyzed on her rebound from Jung to Subud.... 'Pretty promiscuous, analytically speaking'" (147), Petkin snidely comments.[5]

Ultimately, Sid Bell progresses through his Laingian Hero Journey, by turns skeptical and optimistic that he is on the very verge of achieving not simply emotional healing but spiritual illumination. However, skepticism ultimately triumphs over credulity. Emerging from a state of inner chaos in which he is reduced to speaking pseudo-mystical gibberish, the spiritual wanderer is ultimately stripped not only of his worldly misconceptions but of his otherworldly illusions as well. Sigal's sustained comic trip through inner space is a brilliant send-up of Laing and his dubious proselytizing for schizophrenic breakdown as a pathway to psychological healing and spiritual nirvana.[6] Sigal's own ostensibly guided but actually out-of-control mental "trip" was an important turning point in his adulation of Laing. Describing the process of going crazy in the company of supportive "witnesses" at Kingsley Hall, he writes that the episode culminated when he

> [l]eaped and danced on the communal supper table, and with an imaginary prayer shawl around my shoulders skipped around wailing an authentic, or gobbledegook, Hebrew prayer. And then it came, the vision I'd been working and longing for. I had to laugh. God, in the shape of (I swear) a railway union organiser, sat me on His knee for some stern advice. Stop being so crazy, He commanded. It's self-indulgent. Go back to your writing and live normally like other folks. ("Far side")

In hindsight, Sigal concluded that he and Laing had "sealed a devil's bargain. Although we set out to 'cure' schizophrenia, we became schizophrenic in our attitudes to ourselves and to the outside world" ("Far side"). His psychotic episode at Kingsley Hall on Rosh Hashonah was, he later wrote, "the site of my apotheosis from which it took me years to recover. But I never blamed Laing or his co-workers because we all understood at the time what the risks were: nothing less than our lives" (untitled reminiscence 215). In retrospect he could see that "[t]here was no single R. D. Laing. His self was as divided as any I've seen. This, [Laing] told me, was his main healing credential" (untitled reminiscence 214).[7] From 40 years' distance, Sigal could regard more dispassionately the stretch of his life at the edge of mental chaos, observing, "One of things I most liked about England was that half the people I knew had broken down and they treated it like any other domestic chore, without drama or self-pity, just something that happens" (*A Woman of Uncertain Character* 263).

Because British libel laws are more stringent than those in the United States, *Zone of the Interior* did not appear in print in England for nearly 30 years after its US publication. Sigal is convinced that Laing "block[ed] publication of the novel in the United Kingdom because he was furious with its descriptions of his activities" (Klein 200).[8] His assumption foregrounds the vexed relationships among the method of disguised autobiography, the genre of *roman à clef*, and literary and legal ethics. As Sean Latham explains, "unlike a criminal trial...in which a defendant is presumed innocent, in a libel suit he or she is instead presumed guilty and must assume the full burden of proof. That is, it must be conclusively demonstrated to a jury that the defendant's comment were, in fact, true and that they were not published in a malicious attempt to damage the plaintiff's business or personal reputation" (*The Art of Scandal* 77). A libel suit pivots on the matter of defamation of character and assumes that the ambiguities of a literary text can be reduced to unambiguous categories: as either fact or fiction. Rather, Latham argues, the "destabilizing interruption" (81) of these categories points precisely to the irreducible boundary-straddling and unruly nature of *roman à clef*.

Regarding Sigal's *Zone of the Interior* as a *roman à clef*, one may well ask: Who may claim the ethical high ground—its author, whose book could not be published in England because of concerns about defamation of character, or the "originals" who were the sources or "keys" to his characters and his story? Quite apart from the tit-for-tat aspect of the matter, one might ask the same ethical question of Doris Lessing, who breached Sigal's privacy and trust to create the characters of Saul Green in *The Golden Notebook* and Dave Miller in *Play with a Tiger*. Ironically, Sigal suspects that Lessing herself had a role in blocking the publication of *Zone of the Interior* in Great Britain "because of its alleged portrayed of her personal life" (Klein 200). Lessing refused to read the novels by Sigal in which fictionalized versions of her appear because, as she explained, "I knew I'd fly into a rage and say, how can you tell all these wicked untruths?...He's perfectly entitled to put me in a novel. But I'm not going to read it..." (Innes, "A Life of Doing It Her Way").

Regarding the ethical considerations discussed earlier in this study, psychological pain, which may include a sense of betrayal or a feeling of having been exploited, may result when a person discovers a version—particularly an unflattering version—of himself or herself rendered in the pages of fiction (Mills 197). Doris Lessing categorically denied any actual resemblance between the fictitious Charles Watkins, whose interior journey unfolds in *Briefing for a Descent into Hell*, and Jesse Watkins, whose remarkably similar interior journey is recorded in R. D. Laing's *The Politics of Experience*; it is not known whether Jesse Watkins read or expressed an opinion on Lessing's fictional treatment of the subject. Moreover, while Lessing's Charles Watkins is seriously depicted, Sigal's characters in *Zone of the Interior* are exaggerated for comic effect. As a literary method, caricature significantly embellishes and even ridicules the models upon whom it is based, so much so that parallels between "original" and "copy" are more obviously distorted or skewed than is the case in disguised autobiography. Since *Zone of the Interior* was ultimately published in Great Britain—albeit not until 2005, 16 years after the death of R. D. Laing and 29 years after the novel's US publication—the differences of opinion between author and subject were apparently resolved literarily rather than legally. It may be little or no solace for admirers of Doris Lessing and R. D. Laing that, among the "originals" whom Sigal lampoons in *Zone of the Interior*, his narrative alter ego, Sid Bell, is no less mercilessly skewered than are Coral Brand and Willie Last. As the *roman à clef* form demonstrates, one writer's truth cannot easily be disentangled from another writer's fiction.

Chapter 7

Poetic License and Poetic Justice

"I was Rose's subject. But what was mine?" Clancy Sigal (The Secret Defector)

Getting Even

Although it took him nearly three decades, Clancy Sigal ultimately got his own back in the game of literary cross-reference between himself and Doris Lessing. Beginning sometime during the 1960s, he drafted major chunks of an autobiographical narrative that focused almost microscopically on his early years in England, including the four years during which he and Lessing lived together. The work-in-progress evolved through several unfinished drafts with different titles, including *The Ceiling and the Spike*, *Picking up where I left off*, and *In England*, and culminated in *The Secret Defector*, published in 1992. While working on the novel, Sigal reread the novel by Lessing that features a fictionalized version of himself as Saul Green. In his journal, he noted that, "to break out of the thrall (Golden Notebook etc)...I read Lessing, after working on my draft of my early days in London. I want to tell my story my way. She 'wants' me to tell it hers" (1968–9 Journal, June 2, 1968). Several weeks later, he added, "Reading 'GN' again. I try to read Doris' book w/the cold eye of an editor. Hard" (July 1, 1968). A few days later, he wrote, "Reading over 1st draft of 'Ceiling & the Spike.' I'm now even using Doris' handwriting" (July 6, 1968, Sigal's underscoring). Clearly, Sigal had not yet broken out of Lessing's—and *The Golden Notebook*'s—"thrall." With the publication of *The Secret Defector* nearly 25 years later, he finally returned the favor, so to speak, of Lessing's use of aspects of his character and personality as sources for Saul Green in *The Golden Notebook* and Dave Miller in *Play with a Tiger*, transforming his former lover into fiction with, one might almost say, a vengeance. Through the cracked mirror reflection of her as Rose O'Malley, one may discern the exaggerated but recognizable outline of Doris Lessing. In fairness, it must be said that Sigal also mocks the tortured soul, Clancy/Gus.

The picaresque narrative traces the odyssey of an American Leftist and aspiring writer whose adventures in London, loosely fictionalized, closely track Clancy Sigal's own. Thus, many portions of the novel have nothing to do with Doris Lessing and will not be summarized here. However, Lessing's exaggerated fictional double is present frequently enough in the pages of *The Secret Defector* to qualify as a central character, appearing as Gus Black's lover and adversary, literary supporter and friend/critic, sublime cook, mother of a preadolescent son, and inner voice. By this point in his literary career, Sigal had achieved sufficient distance from his subject to approach with humor matters that had caused him consternation in earlier years. Rose O'Malley is Doris Lessing not simply writ large but in caricature, the embodiment of personal qualities and literary achievements that Sigal exaggerates and at times ridicules or parodies for comic effect.

The novel's six "books" or chapters begin with thinly disguised variations on Clancy Sigal's earliest days in London and his relationship with Doris Lessing during the late 1950s; retrace—with some overlap with his earlier novel, *Zone of the Interior*—his sojourn with radical psychiatry and R. D. Laing during the 1960s; describe his convoluted path through marriage to and divorce from an Australian feminist during the 1970s and 1980s; and follow his struggle to maintain his Leftist idealism during the later 1980s while Britain under the conservative leadership of Margaret Thatcher, and America under the equally conservative direction of Ronald Reagan, shifted decisively to the right around him. By the end of the novel, Sigal's bemused alter ego, Gus Black, has lost both his political and sexual innocence but has—perhaps—found himself.

The first chapter of *The Secret Defector*, "Going Away"—the title explicitly echoes that of Sigal's second book, also a picaresque novel featuring a thinly disguised version of the author—focuses on the period during which Clancy Sigal and Doris Lessing lived together in London. The stage is set with the first sentence, which describes an altercation in "the London maisonette of Rose O'Malley, an African born white writer" (*The Secret Defector* 3), during the summer of 1958. Gus Black, returning to Rose's apartment after a visit to the Yorkshire coal-mining area that is the subject of his research for a documentary novel in progress—a transparent reference to Sigal's documentary novel, *Weekend in Dinlock*—announces his arrival with "H'lo, Maggie" (*Defector* 3). For the reader's benefit, he adds, "Though it was before dawn, I knew Rose would be standing at the top of the hall stairs, an invisible rolling pin tucked in her angrily folded arms" (3). The image clarifies Sigal's verbal allusion to a cartoon strip of his youth, "Bringing up Father" (not identified as such in the novel), traditionally referred to by the names of its principal characters, Maggie and Jiggs. Jiggs is a browbeaten husband whose late-night returns from poker with the boys—not from "screwing" women, as Rose accuses Gus—perennially aggravates his domineering, no-nonsense wife. The jealous Rose, not letting Gus get away with what she regards as yet another in a series of sexual betrayals, accuses him of lying to her about the circumstances of his absence. Following several more exchanges in a verbal duel that has become almost ritualized—at least, in Sigal's literary iterations of it—Gus and Rose, erotically stimulated by their quarrel, proceed to tear each other's clothes off. Just in time, Gus notices Rose's ten-year-old son Aly (Alastair) peering down from the second-floor balcony with puzzled concern regarding the couple's gyrations. As the lovers hastily separate, Gus initiates a game with Aly to distract him from what he has witnessed. Hoisting the boy on his shoulders and pretending he is a horse, he warns Aly's mother, "Keep this out of your novel, Rose" (6).

In the fictionalized version of his life with Doris Lessing, Sigal gives Rose a colorful background—loosely embroidered from the facts of Lessing's actual life—including a brief marriage to a coffee planter in her native South Africa and her conversion to Marxist socialism. After the marriage dissolved, Rose came to London to pursue her writing career. Later, she, like Lessing, left the British Communist Party in protest of the brutal Soviet suppression of the 1956 Hungarian uprising. Although Rose and Gus share political values, they differ on intimate matters. As Gus describes their imperfect compatibility, "[t]he big thing was, we spoke the same language—of love and politics if not sex" (6). However, he adds with tongue in cheek, "God...I sure don't want to fall in love with this woman. That would ruin everything" (7).

Filling in his own backstory, Gus Black describes his Chicago childhood as the son of Jewish labor union organizers. Of note, in this fictionalized version of Sigal's life, the father who abandoned him is named Jake, a name Sigal reassigns from one of his earliest attempts at disguised autobiography, "The Sexual History of Jake Blue." Hewing closely to facts from his own life, his literary alter ego explains that his budding career as a Hollywood agent was short-circuited by the McCarthy-era Red-hunt during the 1950s. Following his blacklisting, he had taken off cross-country by car, pursued by a pair of FBI trackers who resemble characters in "Mutt and Jeff," another cartoon strip dating from Sigal's childhood. The trackers are, in Gus's sardonic judgment, "the only Americans who took my Marxism seriously enough to want to put me in jail" (10). Like Sigal, Gus later discovers—courtesy of the Freedom of Information Act—their characterization of him in his FBI file: "Subject explains persistent abscondings by stating he is writing a novel about the Bureau and needs more raw material" (9). Recently, Sigal confirmed that these details are close to fact, explaining, "It's true FBI chased me all this time. I had 2 favorite agents. But I left America only when things eased up and I could go 'with honor'" (e-mail message to author dated February 29, 2012). By way of Paris, Gus Black eventually arrives in London and Rose O'Malley's flat as Sigal condenses yet another rendition of the fateful story that began when he arrived at Doris Lessing's Warwick Street flat in the spring of 1957. Many of the details that follow ring changes on incidents and themes that figure in Sigal's earlier published and unpublished stories, sketches, plays, and novels.

To shape the fictionalized episodic narrative of his life to that date, Sigal draws significantly on his experience as a Hollywood film agent and a cinephile, alluding not only to classic films and stars but also to technical elements such as scene-setting, dissolves, and other devices borrowed from the cinematic form. In the draft of an unfinished precursor to *The Secret Defector* titled "In England: The Political, Sexual, and Medical History of Sidney Bell," cinematic elements figure even more centrally, with a number of scenes written as brief script-like dialogues that are cast with appropriate Hollywood stars and reference classic films. In *The Secret Defector*, the protagonist, Gus Black, links his pursuit of an elusive political and emotional equilibrium to the exploits and complications encountered by his film heroes. Moreover, Gus takes Rose and her son Aly to films at the local Odeon, their enjoyment enhanced by Gus's first-hand experience in the film industry and his lively anecdotes about his encounters—"some true" (11)—with celebrated stars and well-known directors.

Rose, already a successful writer, encourages Gus's fledgling literary ambitions, remarking that he has "all a writer's equipment except self-confidence" (18). Suffering from a severe writer's block, Gus marvels that living with Rose is "like signing up for the Creative

Writing course I'd avoided at UCLA" (18). Among other things, Rose generously introduces him to a number of her writer friends. However, Gus regards with disdain the "five Johns"—"Wain, Braine, Mortimer, Osborne, and Berger" (29)—because he regards them as much less interesting than his macho Hemingway/Mailer ideal of a writer; he is convinced that he has something more "virile" to say than do these up-and-coming but, in his view, dull British writers. Years later, Sigal described with humility the "lesson" he learned from his initial misunderstanding of contemporary British writers whom he had disparaged during his early years in London, including not only the "five Johns" who had elicited such a sneering dismissal from his fictitious alter ego Gus Black but also others whose talents he had failed to appreciate. Just before he returned permanently to the United States in 1989, he apologized,

> The first writers I met [in England] were, at first glance, astonishingly normal people. Alan Sillitoe, John Wain, Angus Wilson, Doris Lessing, Mervyn Jones, John Osborne, V.S. Pritchett, Colin MacInnes, Bernard Kops, Robert Bolt, Laurie Lee seemed incredibly gray and downbeat compared to boisterous types I admired like Jack Kerouac and Norman Mailer. You had to be "interesting" to write good prose, surely.... I thought I was a hell of a lot more "interesting" than the writers I met, but they had the trick while I was still knocking about the country getting into fights, combatively squaring off against writers who seemed deeply bored by my posturing. Damn their eyes, I'd show 'em. ("Goodbye Little England")[1]

In *The Secret Defector*, Sigal creates his most scathing fictional representation of his former lover through an authorial perspective that is simultaneously sharpened by satire and mellowed by time. Early in the narrative, he revisits the decisive moments in his relationship with Doris Lessing, further embellishing what had by then become a series of literary set pieces. Again, he highlights his discovery, early in their relationship, of Lessing's appropriation of information from his private journal and her use in *The Golden Notebook* and *Play with a Tiger* of details based on elements of his character and personality as well as their intimate relationship. Reprising and burnishing the first primal scene for comic effect, Sigal creates the verbal equivalent of infinite regress. In the voice of Gus Black, he explains,

> After one of our quarrels, usually over "other women," I'd flee upstairs to the tiny but cozy room Rose had rented me, and for relief scribble

in my ledger-sized journal.... Then, meticulously, I'd deposit the diary in the middle drawer of my bureau, carefully tying a nearly invisible black thread between the knobs of the bottom and top drawers. Anyone breaking in would have to snap the thread—a trick I learned from [...] spy movies.[...] Then, with a loud banging of doors, I'd slam out of Rose's pad...whereupon Rose would sneak upstairs, read my journal, and rush back down to her old Royal typewriter to use my self-exonerating arguments in her own manuscript...parts of which [...] she'd oh, sort of accidentally on purpose, drop around the house, in glaringly obvious places like the kitchen table or even on my bed...for me to read and, like Pavlov's dog, dash upstairs to respond in my diary, which she'd break into, read, and then run back to her typewriter, which she left untended for me to scan its pages. [...] (*Defector* 18, Sigal's ellipses unless bracketed)

With regard to this scene in *The Secret Defector*, an unidentified reviewer of the novel aligned himself with its author, employing an incriminating term to characterize Doris Lessing's method of literary appropriation, as filtered through Clancy Sigal's transformation of the incident. Summarizing this part of the plot line, the reviewer writes,

[Sigal] tells about his earliest days as an apprentice writing lusting to break loose with his first book but immured in writer's block. The problem: as Gus Black, he's living with Rose O'Malley (read Doris Lessing), a novelist from South Africa now in London...who is writing *Loose Leaves from a Random Life* (read *The Golden Notebook*, in which Sigal is Saul Green), with daily installments about their love affair and Rose's cannibalizing Gus's notes about that affair. (unsigned review, *Kirkus Reviews*)

Sigal plays for humor Rose O'Malley/Doris Lessing's difficulty settling on the best name for the character based on her lodger/lover for her novel then in progress; fictionalizing the artistic problem, Gus slyly credits himself for its solution. As he phrases it, "I could see her struggle with the American figure named Teddy Blue. Teddy? I was no toy bear. Neatly I crossed out the first name and inserted 'Jim.' More manly. Next day she crossed that out and wrote 'Jonas.' We compromised on 'Paul.' All without exchanging a single word about this strange silent collaboration" (*Defector* 19). In the hall of mirrors in which Sigal and Lessing riffed on their invented images of each other, Sigal had, years before, chosen Paul Blue as one of several names for himself as the fictitious Saul Green.

Though initially Gus Black is more flattered than offended by Rose O'Malley's transparent adaptations of intimate details from his journal and their relationship for her own fictional purposes, his indulgence soon gives way to outrage. In the second set piece in the Sigal/Lessing primal drama, Gus—like Clancy Sigal—discovers on a page resting in Rose's typewriter roller a character sketch of himself featuring details so close to the bone that he is incensed. In this latest fictional iteration of the indelible moment of discovery, Sigal significantly condenses the details and sharpens the point, transforming Lessing's penchant for critical analysis of his unresolved emotional problems into his own self-analysis:

> "THE CASE OF G.B. [Gus Black]: Ex American Red comes to London. Finds woman on her own who takes him in. Thinks he's escaping FBI but in reality running from unresolved attachment to mother. Disguises his Oedipal terror as randiness. Born exploiter of vulnerable women who can't help nursing this crippled cat disguised as romantic hero. Hates women he fucks because they give him temporary refuge. Everywhere he turns, especially in bed, comes face to face with mother he's terrified of."
>
> ...It sucker-punched me in the stomach. (*Defector* 19, upper case in original)

The interval of three decades apparently provided both emotional and aesthetic distance from the unnerving discovery and enabled Sigal to turn the tables: amusingly, it is not Gus but Rose who takes umbrage at her lover's surreptitious incursions into *her* private writing. Over the one of the "magnificent breakfasts" she has prepared for the two of them, she accuses, "How dare you go through my private papers?... Don't lie to me again. You've been reading my novel!" (20). Gus protests that it is unclear what else he can be expected to do when she leaves pages of it in plain sight. For the reader's benefit only, he adds, "Uh-oh, she must be near finishing her novel" (21). Temporarily escaping the emotional tensions between himself and Rose, he leaves London to visit coal miners in Thurlock, a Yorkshire colliery town fictionalized as Dinlock in Sigal's documentary novel, *Weekend in Dinlock*. His contact, a Communist miner and writer named Len Doherty, whose name and village are presented without disguise in *The Secret Defector* (24),[2] is not only a friend of Rose's but, Gus suspects, one of her former lovers.

As in his earlier fictionalized versions of Doris Lessing, Sigal takes sharp satiric aim at both Rose O'Malley's feminism and her protestations against it. Rose remarks to Gus, "You'll never understand, will you? A woman on her own is a free woman despite herself.... We never say 'free man.' A woman alone is more vulnerable, less protected, than a man alone. Each man she meets isn't a scalp on her belt, as a woman is for a man, but an exploration of her contingent freedom" (*Defector* 24–5). With the last sentence in particular, Sigal satirizes academic feminism, with Rose speaking theoretical jargon that neither Doris Lessing nor the fictitious Anna Wulf would use. Ironically, according to Lessing herself, the first readers to "approve" *The Golden Notebook* were not female but male. Later, the novel was embraced by feminists, who, to Lessing's eternal irritation, adopted it as "the 'Bible of the Women's Movement'" (*Walking in the Shade* 342). As she complained, "A book that had been planned so coolly was read, I thought, hysterically.... [W]omen were claiming me as their own, seeing nothing in the book but their own agendas..." (342–3). In *The Secret Defector*, Sigal further lampoons feminism by emphasizing Rose O'Malley's traditionally feminine culinary skills. She "practically threw a side dish of buttered asparagus, lightly sprinkled with Romano cheese, in my face.... 'When,' [she] shouted, ladling out the gravy as if she wished it were molten lead, 'will you stop using your penis for a reporter's pencil?'" (*Defector* 25).

As was true in the actual relationship between Clancy Sigal and Doris Lessing, there was indeed a third party, though the lovers disagreed on the identity of the person who triangulated their relationship. From Lessing's perspective, it was whichever other woman Sigal happened to be sleeping with when he left her flat—or, alternatively, his mother—while, from Sigal's perspective, it was Lessing's preadolescent son, Peter. In *The Secret Defector*, Rose's son, pointedly nicknamed Aly, is Gus's ally, with whom he "share[s] the problem of Rose" (33). But Aly is also his mother's ally, defending her against the men who "haven't been specially good to her." Gus, discerning the clear outlines of an Oedipal script underlying their triangular relationship, admits that it is getting difficult to determine whether "I was Aly's dad or he mine" (34).[3]

While Gus waits impatiently for his muse to visit, he dabbles in politics, both the street variety and Marxism in its more abstract form. Having concluded that the England where he lives does not match the England of his fantasies, he nonetheless attempts to inhabit a political space where his socialist principles and actions matter. The place he wittily terms "Marxshire," where much of the action of *The Secret Defector* occurs, does not appear on any map of

Great Britain but nonetheless has "its own language, customs, and special culture" (45). Gus and Rose argue frequently about politics because Rose, "an anti-apartheid militant who'd been expelled from South Africa for her activities" (47)—like Doris Lessing, who was prohibited from returning to Southern Rhodesia for 25 years because of her Leftist political activities and associations (*African Laughter* 11–12)—maintains unexamined contradictions of her own, including the gap between Marxist theory and practice. As Sigal satirizes the complex intersections and impasses between Gus and Rose concerning politics, sex, and writing, the disagreements typically end in the kitchen, with Gus continuing to relish the leftovers of Rose's cuisine, such as "delicious lamb stew cooked in fennel and lightly braised with ginger" (*Defector* 48) before they end up in bed together.

In *The Secret Defector,* Sigal expresses intimate matters in print in a manner that undermines his objections to Lessing having similarly done so years before. Early in the intimate relationship between Gus Black and Rose O'Malley, Gus commits the faux pas of criticizing Rose's behavior in bed; in turn, Rose faults Gus's "terrible sexual etiquette" (52) and his cavalier dismissal of her "soul-center" during lovemaking (70). Through Gus's pleas in defense of his amorous technique, Sigal humorously skewers both partners in the complicated juncture of sexual and literary aspirations: "'But Rose...I'm always thinking of ways to please you too. And I'm not the one who gets out of bed in the middle of the night to transcribe on my typewriter what my lover has just gasped on the pillow.' (I waited till next morning and wrote in longhand.)" (52). Suffering from his tenacious writer's block, Gus directs his anger toward not only Rose but her literary friends. In a scene that appears frequently enough in Sigal's fictionalizations of this period of his life to make one wonder whether it actually occurred, his fictional alter ego Gus "lashed out in rage and envy, and even took a punch at the playwright John Osborne backstage at the Royal Court Theater...where Rose was rehearsing a play" (54). Rose's obvious productivity and success compound Gus's feelings of literary impotence and insignificance. At one point, he frets, "I was Rose's subject. But what was mine?" (57). While Gus may not yet have found his subject, Clancy Sigal had: himself—with a helping (and the help) of Doris Lessing.

Although Gus initially assumes that his relationship with Rose will culminate in marriage, the growing fissures between them increasingly dictate against that eventuality. Among other things, Rose persists in dispensing armchair psychoanalysis, attributing his emotional problems to unresolved issues concerning his overpowering mother. As Gus phrases it, "Rose kept prying under the Oedipal rock to show me my darkest secrets..." (57). When he objects to psychotherapy—his lover's all-purpose solution for his creative impasse as well as for the difficulties in their relationship—Rose accuses him of avoiding the unconscious issues that adversely affect both aspects of his life. However, circumstances catapult him out of his comfort zone. Ironically, a belated visit from his muse prompts him to write what becomes a successful published piece about Yorkshire miners for British *Vogue* magazine. Tracking quite closely Clancy Sigal's own birth as a writer, that moment marks the end of Gus Black's writer's block and the beginning of the next phase of his odyssey.

Although the character Rose O'Malley appears less frequently in the succeeding chapters of *The Secret Defector*, she remains a commanding presence throughout the novel and continues to affect Gus Black's emotional and literary lives. Clancy Sigal, with greater distance from what he had once regarded as a violation of the private/public boundaries between two complicated people who are also writers, continues to mine—this time, for comic effect—the third set piece of their intimate relationship: the ego-bruising episode of Lessing's literary identity theft for her *Play with a Tiger*. Gus Black, accompanied by Aly, attends the premier of Rose's new play, caustically and punningly titled *Sol and Me and the Rest of Us*, opening at the Royal Court Theatre. The drama concerns "a London lady writer, her absurdly macho American lover, and her young son" (*Defector* 67). Afterward, Aly, by now 15 and still too smart by a mile, offers the critical judgment that his mother's play "wasn't bad" (67). As he clarifies for Gus, "she's having this affair with the actor bloke who's you. So now she's got three of you in her life—the real you, what she wrote about you, and this guy pretending to be you.... Frankly, I don't know how she keeps track" (67). The boy adds that he is accustomed to such literary appropriations by his mother, having discovered that he appears as a character in "three of Ma's short stories, two novels, and now this [play]. I reckon I'm owed danger money, don't you?" (68).[4]

While Aly "keep[s] his cool," Gus himself is "boiling" (67) after he sees Rose's play, wondering whether he is "as crazy in real life as the actor who played me" (68). When he returns to Rose's flat later that evening, his anger takes the form of physical aggression: "I whacked her" (69). In a reversal of the accusations of infidelity that usually spring from Rose's lips, Gus rails at her, "You let me make love to you after you'd been with that crummy hack poet who hasn't written an original line in his life?" (69). Although the ruffled feathers are temporarily smoothed on both sides, the incident is a turning point in the relationship. As Gus explains, "After that, Rose never mentioned my slugging her and I didn't raise the subject of her play. Gradually, while still sleeping together, we censored out the painful parts, which grew in number as our separate careers prospered" (69).

What signals the end of the Gus/Rose (and Sigal/Lessing) affair, however, is less the impasses in their intimate relationship than a legal decision in America that had significant consequence for Clancy Sigal. The Supreme Court's 1958 landmark decision in the Paul Robeson case, pronouncing that "no U. S. citizen could be denied a passport merely for his or her beliefs" (*Defector* 71), means that Gus need no longer hide out in London with an expired American passport. Both he and Rose know that, now that he is free to leave her, he will. Over time, they have become "like two boxers who'd gone the full fifteen rounds and were too exhausted to slug it out anymore. The fight was over" (72). Their amicable parting is sealed by an apparently final act of congenial lovemaking—though Gus privately wonders if even that bittersweet moment will show up as a scene in one of Rose's novels. Nonetheless, he remains in contact with Rose while he enjoys the fruits and bemoans the brickbats that come with his emerging success as a writer and journalist.

Concurrently, Rose has become involved with a man for whom Gus has scant regard—another of Sigal's caricatures of Idries Shah, Doris Lessing's real-life teacher and guru and popularizer of Sufi mysticism in the West. Gus disdains the "oily beauty in a white turban and knee-length Nehru jacket who claimed to be a wise man from Kabul" and who "fed Rose morning glory seeds and tracts on Subud to help her explore 'new psychic frontiers'..." (87).[5] Rose O'Malley's interest in mysticism is a symptom of dramatic changes underway not only in her personally but also in the larger culture movements of the 1960s. However, as Clancy Sigal concluded in hindsight, "the sixties was a lie" [*sic*] (87). According to his narrative alter ego, the iconic images of the period were pure media inventions, composed of an amalgam of celebrations of the Beatles, Woodstock, and other cultural expressions of radical social change. The dark underside of the period's feel-good vibes was expressed in race riots, high unemployment in Britain and America, the Cuban missile crisis, and other troubling political and social disturbances that seemed less significant at the time than they were understood to be in historical hindsight.

More personally, "the sixties" also encompassed Clancy Sigal's experiments with LSD and his temporary infatuation with the radical psychiatry of R. D. Laing, events to which he had already given literary expression 16 years earlier in *Zone of the Interior*.[6] Reprising in much-condensed form the saga of his descent into craziness with an assist from the illimitable Dr. Willie Last, his caricature of Laing, Sigal briefly reprises his foray into madness and others' concern over his risky psychiatric odyssey. Rose O'Malley frets that Gus is "losing too much weight on a diet of cabbage hearts and distilled water" (90). When Gus refuses her culinary creations that were once irresistible to him, Rose knows that he is not only serious about his psycho-spiritual journey but probably also in emotional distress. In actuality, Sigal recalls Doris Lessing being deeply concerned about his precarious mental state at the time. As he phrases it, "I was totally nuts...and I remember her saying to me very clearly, 'You be very careful of what you're doing, because I think you're getting caught in something so dark and so powerful that you want to be extremely careful'" (qtd. by Klein 198).

In the final chapters of *The Secret Defector*, Sigal extends Gus Black's picaresque journey into the 1970s and 1980s, with diversions through the Women's Movement, marriage, divorce, health complications, and aging. Even more than a decade after his separation from Rose O'Malley, Gus still finds himself comparing other women to his most significant lover. One woman in particular, whom he meets at a feminist conference at Oxford that he attends out of political curiosity, draws his attention. Accordingly, as a romantic relationship develops between Gus and Helen Hadley—who appears to be based on Sigal's first wife, Margaret Walters—he learns that Helen, "a professional macroeconomist in a government department" (129), reveres Rose O'Malley for her groundbreaking feminist novel, (still titled) *Loose Leaves from a Random Life*. When Helen learns of Gus's previous history, she presses him—with an authorial wink from Sigal concerning the porous boundary between fact and fiction—"Did you really do all those things Rose says in her book?" (116)

Deflecting his new partner's prurient curiosity, Gus congratulates himself on having found a woman of the younger generation who, manifestly unlike Rose O'Malley, offers the possibility of a different kind of intimate relationship, even inspiring him to lend a hand in the kitchen. Gus and Helen live together for several years during the mid-1970s and eventually marry. But tensions present in the relationship from the beginning deepen. Despite their adaptations to the changing gender roles spurred by the Women's Movement, Helen agonizes that marriage and domesticity are at odds with her bedrock feminist principles. Gus, recognizing his own political compromises, struggles to locate himself somewhere along the feminist spectrum that is so central to his wife's identity. As he later observes in one of the italicized authorial asides that intermittently punctuate the narrative, "*The 1970s was no time for a Marxshire marriage*" (*Defector* 135, italics in original). As the Women's Movement loses momentum and most of Helen's friends choose childbearing over consciousness-raising, the marriage starts—in an appropriately domestic image—"coming apart at the seams" (137). Eventually Gus and Helen, like Clancy Sigal and Margaret Walters, divorce. As Gus acerbically phrases it, "she got The House, I got The Depression, and we shared The Mortgage" (131).

However, during the early years of their relationship, Gus's wife is eager to meet his famous ex-lover. Gus, aware that Rose O'Malley and feminism have long since parted (if they were ever joined), frets that a meeting between the two most important women in his life will be awkward, which indeed proves to be the case. When they meet for lunch, each woman makes an apparently innocuous statement about the man they have in common that puts the other on the defensive. Before long, their polite words deteriorate into sharp-edged insults that recall the biting dramatic dialogues between Rose O'Malley and Shirley Barker in Sigal's 1983 radio play, "A Visit with Rose." As Helen slyly queries both of them, "Who's going to write about this lunch first?" Rose rejoins with a coded dig at Gus's often-blocked creative process, "It's not...who writes it first but who publishes it" (127).

In *The Secret Defector*, as in *Zone of the Interior*, Sigal explicitly smudges the boundary line between fact and fiction in a brief passage a move that signals the *roman à clef* "key" for those in the know: he name-drops in the same sentence the names of both Doris Lessing and his invented literary version of her. Describing feminists of different generations, he observes that Rose O'Malley is more closely aligned than is his wife with the "Victorian toughies" of an older generation— "rather old-fashioned, risk-all bohemians" such as "Annie Besant, Margaret Sanger, Marie Lloyd, Florence Nightingale, the Pankhursts, Rebecca West, Doris Lessing" (128). Rose, whose preferred model of literary path-breakers is not the Victorian elders whom Gus names but Virginia Woolf, once told Gus that she "would have killed herself in adolescence if she had not happened on Virginia Woolf's essay 'A Room of One's Own.' 'Those last words of Woolf's..., "She will be born," I was sure were addressed to me personally'" (129). Judith

Shakespeare is Woolf's invention, the playwright's imaginary sister who aspired to be a writer and who, because of her gender, was profoundly handicapped by the obstacles facing women with literary talent and ambition during the sixteenth century. At the end of *A Room of One's Own*, Woolf affirms that, "Drawing her life from the lives of the unknown who were her forerunners, as her brother did before her, [Judith Shakespeare] will be born" (*A Room of One's Own* 114). Glossing Woolf's phrasing, Sigal writes that Rose O'Malley had, in her words, "*willed* myself to be born, again" (*Defector* 129, Sigal's italics). In 2007, when Lessing learned that she had been awarded the Nobel Prize in Literature, she remarked, "I've been on the shortlist for 40 years. It is good to be the 11th woman on the list, I'm only sorry that one of the first or fourth or the fifth wasn't Virginia Woolf" (Allardice and Jones, "It's Me? I've Won after All These Years?"). Her choice of surname for the protagonist of *The Golden Notebook*, Anna Wulf, may have been the author's way of paying homage to her literary idol.

By the time Clancy Sigal published *The Secret Defector* in 1992, he had considerable practice with the technique of disguised autobiography and the form of *roman à clef*. Adding still another set of reflections to the hall of mirrors of overlapping lives and fictions between himself and Doris Lessing, he lampoons the "self-cannibalizing" dynamic of their shared literary method, a major example of which is *The Secret Defector* itself. Alluding to the neurotic relationship between Anna Wulf and Saul Green in *The Golden Notebook*, Sigal's Gus Black observes that his wife's respect for the author of *Loose Leaves from a Random Life* "was based on an instinctive understanding that Rose had genuinely flayed herself to become who she was" (*Defector* 128). With tongue firmly in cheek, Sigal has Helen Hadley marvel, "Who in our right minds would be so masochistic as to love a man like Paul Blue?" Gus drolly replies, "Books aren't life, exactly" (128). In his most expansive view of his involuntary role as raw material for two of Lessing's key literary characters, Sigal offers through his fictional alter ego the generous insight that "What Rose put into her writing was one thing; what she left out was also important but harder to identify. I wanted to tell Helen, Look, Rose splits herself into all sorts of people in order to write, and some of those people have to be strangled for the survivors to live. The 'creative process' itself was a lie we agreed on" (128).

Tracing the progress of his fictional double through the 1980s and his permanent departure from England, Sigal describes Gus's serendipitous escape from deepening marital tensions. He accepts a short-term appointment as a "Visiting Distinguished Teacher" in the

Cinema Studies Department at "San Andreas State," Los Angeles (*Defector* 142). Encouraged by Helen, he sees the lucrative academic position as an opportunity to salvage their marriage. Ironically, Gus is, apparently for the first time since they married, sexually tempted by another woman—one whose "fierce inner heat" and "indignation" (150) remind him of Rose O'Malley. The name Doris also appears in a minor role, not as a love interest but as the name of a computer clerk at the university where Gus teaches.

Eventually, Gus returns to England to discover not only that his wife has found a lover of her own but that, with Thatcherism in the ascendant, Great Britain has changed as well. After he and Helen divorce, he muses wryly, "You never stop being married. You just act single. Would Rose O'Malley's curse never lift?" (189) Ironically, his first visitor after he moves to a bachelor flat in tony suburb of London is none other than Rose herself, who comes for tea. "Rekindle my fire, Rose, I thought, but only said, 'Lemon or milk?'" (192). Sigal lampoons Lessing's literary success, taking her down several pegs through Gus Black's private observation that Rose, recently named a "Dame Commander of the British Empire" in the Queen's Royal Honors list, is, at 68, "a picture of greedy, sedate fame" (192). Exploring the literary and professional implications of this honorific British designation, Susan Watkins has explored the ambiguous implications of Lessing's position as the "'grande dame' of contemporary British writing," noting that "the title of 'Dame' is that conferred on women members of the Order of the British Empire, carrying with it ideas about seniority and public recognition" (*Doris Lessing* 164). However, Lessing, characteristically resistant to "becoming a part of the establishment ... actually refused the title when it was offered her..." (Watkins, "'Grande Dame' or 'New Woman'" 244). In *The Secret Defector*, Sigal also inserts a poison-pen jab at Lessing by giving her rather than the usual suspect, himself, the star position in a history of promiscuous intimate relationships that began after their own liaison ended (193).

Although the ensuing banter between Gus Black and Rose O'Malley initially suggests that they will end up in bed for old time's sake, Gus is deterred by the changes he finds in his former lover. Rose currently subscribes to an assortment of ideas that prompt either his skepticism or his incredulity, including "imminent Apocalypse, ruined civilizations, global suicide, the tragic limits of human intelligence.... Clearly, Rose's stray into the Other Zone had been more profound than mine" (194). The latter phrase is a sly gloss on the title and substance of Sigal's own earlier novel, *Zone of the Interior*.

Still, Gus cannot help but admire his now-aging former lover. Despite her ailing body, she is, in her late sixties, "a wonder...fuller of life than two of me. I'd bet she still made a juice-oozing meatloaf" (194). In turn, Rose is mildly amused by Gus's apparently unquenchable ardor. Fumbling with her sari—apparel that may signal her preoccupation with esoteric religions—he privately complains, "Why didn't these goddamn things have buttons?" (194). Rose, resisting Gus's almost laughable amorous overture, pushes him away both physically and verbally. As she exits his flat, she offers a condescending parting "zinger" through which Sigal directs acerbic humor at both Doris Lessing and himself. Gus realizes with chagrin that Rose has "waited thirty years" to deliver her final cut: "Just before leaving, she patted my arm maternally. 'My little Red Peter Pan'" (195).

Sigal's fictional alter ego can never entirely escape Rose's shadow. She has become an aspect of himself—so much a part of him that, even after all of the intervening years since they separated, she returns at times as an arch, critical internalized voice: "'Still at it, old friend? You'll do anything to avoid the writing desk. Why waste your energy on puerile activism? Grow up!' I wished I could" (*Defector* 203). What finally convinces Gus to follow her advice is the limits of his own aging body. But first, a few more symbolic rounds remain between him and the invincible Rose O'Malley, whose fictionalization of him as Jake Blue in *Loose Leaves from a Random Life* "had bestowed [him] a mild notoriety" (204) that he—like Clancy Sigal vis-à-vis Saul Green— cannot escape. At San Andreas State, his new colleague and office mate—a "distinguished" feminist who promotes her bona fides as "Betty Friedan's collaborator and Gloria Steinem's mentor" (203)—gushes, "If you're anything remotely like O'Malley's portrait of you, oh boy, kid, are we going to have fun together!" (204). To his chagrin, Gus soon finds himself in an updated version of his erstwhile "male geisha" role: as a "male bimbo" (204).

The concluding chapter of *The Secret Defector* chronicles Gus's struggle over where he really belongs, both geographically and politically: can Marxshire survive in Margaret Thatcher's England or should he decamp permanently to Los Angeles? Politically disillusioned, he decides—as did Clancy Sigal—to leave an economically, racially, and class-stratified England that no longer feels like home; Sigal relocated to California in 1989. Before his alter ego, Gus Black, returns to America, he pays a parting visit to Rose O'Malley at her country house in the seaside town of Rye, where she continues to "pound out novels about human monsters and visions of the present dressed up as futuristic prophecy..." (271). The observation alludes to Lessing's *The Fifth Child*, published in 1988, which traces the collapse of an ordinary British family following the birth of a genetic throwback. Lessing's five-volume intergalactic series, *Canopus at Argos: Archives*, was published during the 1980s.

In *The Secret Defector*, the Rose O'Malley of the 1980s lives alone, her son, Aly, having relocated to central Africa as an agronomist.[7] Noticing that Rose still types on her now-ancient Royal portable typewriter, Gus almost expects to see "a sheet of paper in it, 'THE CASE OF G. B...'" (271, Sigal's caps and ellipsis). He regards his former lover as neither quite friend nor enemy. Rather, the two of them are "alley cats with a respect for each other's claws" (271)—perhaps a sly allusion to the tiger image that Lessing had used years before to characterize Sigal in both *The Golden Notebook* and *Play with a Tiger*. Gus also recognizes that Rose "had used my body to break her block. And she had been my best friend in a bad time" (271). When the culinarily accomplished Rose offers store-bought scones to accompany their tea, Gus realizes just how dramatically things have changed in her and between them. *The Secret Defector* concludes with the prodigal son returning home with a renewed optimism as he undertakes the next phase of his life's journey.

More than Clancy Sigal's previous fictionalizations of Doris Lessing, *The Secret Defector* demonstrates how the passage of time, the achievement of emotional distance, and the refinement of Sigal's characteristic literary method combine to transform, one more time and most successfully, the raw material of his intimate relationship with Lessing and its afterlife. Autobiography—both transparent and disguised—and fiction blend and cross-reference each other in a continual dance across the fluid borders of *roman à clef*. The Rose O'Malley of *The Secret Defector* is Sigal's most fictitious—and fanciful—version of Doris Lessing, elements of whose "character" are exaggerated for comic and satirical effect. At times these embellishments are at Lessing's expense; at other times, they are at Sigal's, for Gus Black himself is hardly a virtuous character.

"You Can't Do It!"

No doubt anticipating the criticism that *The Secret Defector* might prompt because of his caricature of Doris Lessing—unmistakable to those with the "key"—Clancy Sigal published a piece in the *New York Times Book Review* shortly after the novel was published in 1992. In it, he describes the long saga of his role as "raw material" in other people's—notably, Lessing's—literary works and defends his privilege to write likewise. For readers of the piece who may have been unaware of his earlier liaison with Lessing, he explains how he met her in the 1950s, first as a "rent-paying boarder, then as her lover" ("'You Can't Do It!'" 13–4). As readers of this study know through Sigal's repeated variations on several themes, early in their affair when he discovered that Lessing was secretly reading his private journal, he colluded in the process by "speaking" to her through it. As he explains in the *New York Times* version, "at that time I had the moral upper hand—although she was reading my diary I was not yet reading hers" ("'You Can't Do It!'" 13). Lessing's appropriation for her literary purposes of details from his journal and their intimate relationship remained a sore spot for Sigal, as evidenced by his multiple literary reprises and variations on those decisive incidents. At the time, Sigal had demanded that Lessing cease writing about him,

> or rather "Saul Green," the macho American she had extracted from my rib. It wasn't right for her to use our moments of intimacy in her book.
> "You can't do it!" I shouted.
> "Oh, can't I?" she shouted back. "Why not—it's my work, isn't it?" ("'You Can't Do It!'" 13).

This time around, Sigal judges Lessing's method more leniently, observing, "I began to see my sentences or sentiments echoed in Mrs. Lessing's manuscript—but, of course, with an imaginative flourish I could not then give to my own apprentice work" ("'You Can't Do It!'" 13).

Lessing insisted that she did not read Sigal's novel(s) in which she is caricatured (*Walking* 172). In general, she explained, to read and respond to such portraits would simply perpetuate a pointless "he said/she said" argument. In support of her position, she offered a hypothetical dialogue, as if between two quarreling children or as if between herself and Sigal—that expresses their mutually exclusive perspectives; the exchange eerily mirrors Sigal's *New York Times* version of their quarrels:

> "But I didn't say that." "Oh yes, you did!"
> "I didn't, I tell you." "But I tell you you did."
> "Didn't." "Did." "Didn't." "Did."

"That never happened." "I know it did."
"I know it didn't." "It did." "Didn't." "Did." "Didn't." "Did." (*Walking in the Shade* 172)

In defense of his side of their protracted literary/amatory quarrel, offered from a distance of more than 30 years and with a self-interested eye to his own similar literary method, Sigal strategically endorses the point that Lessing had made years earlier: artistic license trumps personal privacy. Indeed, "[i]n the end, we helped each other unblock. She published 'The Golden Notebook' and I wrote my first novel, 'Weekend in Dinlock.' Rage, pain, tumult, quarrels, lies, cross-martyrdoms, infidelities—God knows we earned our way through the dry hell-gate. But, of course, we could not survive our separate successes..." ("'You Can't Do It!'" 13). For years after they parted company, Sigal found it impossible to "disentangle [his] feelings about being written about from the complicated heat of [his] feelings toward the author" ("'You Can't Do It!'" 13–14). As suggested in his almost obsessive attempts to fictionalize the subject from his initially aggrieved and eventually bemused and amused perspective, a contributing factor in their breakup was what Claudia Mills and other ethicists of the subject term "psychological pain" ("Appropriating Others' Stories" 197). Adding insult to injury from Sigal's perspective was the fact that, in *Play with a Tiger*, "the actor playing me was, well, a wee bit too effeminate for my taste. Can we negotiate this? I asked [Doris]. You get rid of him and I'll rewrite some of his dialogue and— End of affair" ("'You Can't Do It!'" 13).

Moreover, as his own literary career began to flourish, Sigal resented Lessing's patronizing habit of taking credit for having "invented" him. Only much later, when he had achieved his own literary success, did Sigal come to appreciate his former lover's skill in transforming their romantic liaison into fiction.

> [A]s I fiddled with characters in my own books, I began to see that perhaps she was right. It really is hard to make a fiction come alive and breathe. Saul Green, I know, is seen as real by lots of people I have meet. Men tend to dismiss him. But women often take Saul very seriously and confuse me with him. It's been tricky living up to his brawling, explosively neurotic reputation so I have not tried too strenuously. But that seems to get Mrs. Lessing's fans upset, as if somehow I am patronizing her work. You can't win. ("'You Can't Do It!'" 14)

Perhaps to head off criticism of his often scathing caricature of Lessing in *The Secret Defector*, Sigal defends the imaginative process that he learned in part from his intimate partner and literary mentor. As he phrases it, unlike Lessing "who stuck me hot and steaming into her prose like a still-struggling lobster, I have had years to think about what sort of woman I want my Rose to be" ("'You Can't Do It!'" 14). He is at pains to point out several significant differences between his presumed model and the character he invented: not only is Rose O'Malley a "proto-feminist, which Mrs. Lessing has always denied she is or was" but she lacks the sense of humor "that Lessing privately always had." Moreover, Rose is "a woman who would endure her lover's beatings, which I cannot imagine Mrs. Lessing doing for a single moment" (14). While perhaps Sigal protests too much, he underscores his attachment to his literary creation, a character that, while clearly inspired by his former lover, is by no means identical to her—just as Saul Green is not identical to Clancy Sigal. With a closing statement that is garnished with both affection and a sprig of belated poetic justice, he adds the flourish, "It was fun to invent and not just report Rose O'Malley. She is almost as dear to me as Doris Lessing once was" (14).

CHAPTER 8

VARIATIONS ON A THEME

"[N]o fact has any truth unless it is placed in its true context." Simone de Beauvoir (Force of Circumstance)

"Beauvoir and Sartre without the garlic." Clancy Sigal (The Secret Defector)

French Connections

Several years before Doris Lessing and Clancy Sigal reciprocally purloined details of their intimate liaison for their respective literary purposes, another romantic relationship with uncanny parallels to theirs unfolded between a European woman writer in her late thirties and a Leftist Jewish writer from Chicago. The relationship lasted for four years, its "half-life" for many years afterward. Soon after the actual relationship ended, the female partner established herself as a pioneer of feminism, publishing a landmark book concerning, among other subjects, female sexuality, the vexed relations between the sexes, and the difficulty of autonomy for women in patriarchy. In 1947, several years before her major reputation was secured by her groundbreaking work, *The Second Sex*, the French writer and philosopher, Simone de Beauvoir, visited the United States for the first time. While in Chicago, she met (through a friend's reference) and fell passionately in love with Nelson Algren, a writer who had published two novels and a volume of short stories but not yet his own breakthrough and award-winning novel, *The Man with the Golden Arm* (1949).[1] Although de Beauvoir, then approaching 40, had been Jean-Paul Sartre's intellectual and intimate partner for nearly two decades without benefit of marriage, her acquaintance with Algren rapidly developed into a full-fledged romantic affair that lasted until 1950. After the two confirmed their passionate love for each other during the winter of 1947, de Beauvoir returned to France. During the lovers' time apart, they maintained a prolific correspondence; apparently, only de Beauvoir's side has been preserved (*A Transatlantic Love Affair*: *Letters to Nelson Algren*). De Beauvoir visited Algren in the United States several more times; in turn, he visited her in Paris in 1949, staying with her in a flat near the Notre Dame (Donohue 182). They also traveled together in Mexico, Central America, France, and elsewhere in Europe. Algren gave de Beauvoir a silver ring and begged her to marry him. She refused his proposal because she felt that she could not leave Sartre, France, or her work; however, she wore the ring for the rest of her life (Carole Seymour-Jones 345). When Algren finally concluded that there was no future in their relationship, given de Beauvoir's unwillingness to leave Sartre, he signaled to her that he no longer loved her. As Mim Udovitch concludes from the love letters that de Beauvoir penned to Algren, their relationship,

> which lasted in one form or another for almost two decades, began its long, episodic disintegration a little more than a year after it began. Misled, perhaps, by her habit of addressing him as "beloved husband" and describing herself as "your loving wife" (and on one occasion, "your naked moaning wife"), Algren asked Beauvoir to marry him. And while it is only fair to note that he was no more willing to move to France, or even to learn French, than she was to move to Chicago, it is also clear that although in the end she was technically the rejectee, she wanted only courtship where he wanted marriage.... [I]n touch from 1947 to 1964, they spent less than a year and a half in each other's physical presence, mostly in holiday pursuits, with much of that time, according to Beauvoir's other autobiographical writings, filled with anxiety, frustration and petty dissatisfaction. ("Hot and Epistolary")

Although de Beauvoir was heartbroken when she knew that the love affair was over, her relationship with Algren lived on in her writing in two forms. First, her passionate sexual relationship with the man with whom she apparently experienced her "first complete orgasm" (Bair 333) gave her further insight into female sexuality and influenced her pioneering work on the female condition, a project that began with notes she wrote for an essay while traveling for the first time in the United States. According to one of her biographers, "it was [de Beauvoir's] passionate relationship with Nelson [Algren] that provided the energy and stimulus which brought *The Second Sex* into being..." (Seymour-Jones 376). Moreover, de Beauvoir gave her affair with Algren literary immortality. In her most celebrated novel, *The Mandarins*, published in French in 1954 and in English translation two years later, she drew specifically on the details of their love affair. Making only slight alterations in the particulars of their relationship, she dedicated the book to Algren.

In three chapters of the *roman à clef* that also includes several other characters drawn from life,[2] de Beauvoir traces the course of a passionate relationship between a French psychiatrist—who, much like the author, had lived for some time in an intellectually close but apparently sexless relationship with her intimate partner—and a promising American writer. In coincidental parallels with the romantic liaison between Doris Lessing/Anna Wulf and Clancy Sigal/Saul Green, as the romantic affair between Simone de Beauvoir/Anne Dubreuilh and Nelson Algren/Lewis Brogan of *The Mandarins* begins to collapse during the summer of 1949, Anne accuses her lover of lying to her. In return, Lewis accuses Anne of secretly reading his correspondence (*Mandarins* 470). They quarrel over the terms of their relationship, with Lewis complaining that Anne wants things only on her conditions. Anne, recognizing that their relationship has lost its center, muses, "I was too old for pledges of eternal love; I lived too far away. I asked only that our love live long enough so that it would die out gently, leaving untarnished memories in our hearts and a friendship that would never end" (*Mandarins* 477).

Sometime after the affair ends, Anne explains to her friend Paule that she "didn't feel [her]self capable of living solely for love" (*Mandarins* 527). Retrospectively minimizing the degree of her happiness in the relationship, she adds, "Lewis was merely an episode in my existence.... After years of abstinence, I had been hoping for a new love, and I had very deliberately brought this one about. I had magnified it out of all proportion because I knew my life as a woman was drawing to a close" (529). Anne's words uncannily suggest those written by the coincidentally named Anna of Doris Lessing's *The Golden Notebook*. In Lessing's novel, it is the woman rather than the man who feels and suffers more deeply. However, in the culminating *Free Women* section of the novel, Anna Wulf—like de Beauvoir's Anne Dubreuilh regarding Lewis Brogan—reduces her complicated romantic and sexual relationship with Saul Green to a much less emotionally intense encounter. Even before she meets the American writer named Milt, she determines that "the remedy for her condition was a man" and "prescribed this for herself like a medicine" (*The Golden Notebook* 606).

Beauvoir both acknowledged and prevaricated on the similarities between Nelson Algren and the fictitious Lewis Brogan of *The*

Mandarins as well as on the ethical implications of transforming into a fictional character a man with whom she was so intimately connected. Of her literary appropriation of details of her relationship with Algren, she later attempted to establish a clearer demarcation between life and fiction than was accepted by her real-life model. She observed in a rather circular defense of her method,

> I wrote it because it gave me pleasure to transpose into a fictional world a real occurrence that meant so much to me.... Of all my characters, Lewis is the one who approaches closest to a living model...[.] It so happened—a rare coincidence—that Algren, in his reality, was very representative of what I wanted to represent; but I did not content myself with a mere anecdotal fidelity: I used Algren to invent a character who would exist without reference to the world of real people. (*The Force of Circumstance* 267)

Her words recall Doris Lessing's similar insistence that in *The Golden Notebook* she attempted to "take the story out of the strictly personal, to generalise personal and private experience..." (*Walking in the Shade* 337).

Speaking more generally, de Beauvoir, though a philosopher, saw no ethical breach in her literary practice. Indeed, she explicitly defended the *roman à clef* form while cautioning that it was fruitless for readers to try to tease out correspondences between actual people and their fictional counterparts. Rather, she argued, "[t]he extent and the manner of the fiction's dependence upon real life is of small importance; the fiction is built only by pulverizing all these sources and then allowing a new existence to be reborn from them. The gossips who poke about among the ashes let the work that is offered them escape, and the shards they rout out are worth nothing; no fact has any truth unless it is placed in its true context" (*Circumstance* 268). Yet her disclaimer is belied by the facts: in *The Mandarins*, de Beauvoir appropriated numerous specific details of her relationship with Algren, including, in one case, words identical to those the couple exchanged just before de Beauvoir's departure for Paris after their breakup.[3]

Like Clancy Sigal, who was initially shocked and angered when he discovered characters who closely resembled him in Lessing's *The Golden Notebook* and *Play with a Tiger*, Nelson Algren was furious when he read *The Mandarins* in English translation in 1956. To people who knew him, Lewis Brogan could not be mistaken for anyone another than himself (*A Dangerous Liaison* 406). As mentioned earlier in this study, the philosopher Claudia Mills, considering disguised autobiography from an ethical perspective, observes that the model for a writer's appropriation of details from people in his or her actual life may suffer not only "psychological pain" from such transformations but a sense of "betrayal" and/or "exploitation" ("Appropriating Others' Stories" 197), all of which Algren indeed suffered. According to Carole Seymour-Jones, he "vented some of his spleen" in *Who Lost an American?* (1963), a series of sketches of his travels in America and Europe during the decade after his relationship with de Beauvoir ended. In the chapter on Paris, he skewers de Beauvoir's feminism through sarcasm and exaggeration, writing that she

> disposed of all sewing of buttons, all washing of dishes, all sweeping of all floors, all shopping, all cooking, all childbearing—she not only did not know one end of a broom from the other, but was actively opposed to other women differentiating between either end.... I worried a bit about how the human race was going to perpetuate itself once Castor [de Beauvoir's nickname] took over. She struck me as a bit preposterous. (96–7)

Despite his anger, Algren felt compelled to credit his former lover for her existentialist philosophy, understood as "a means of living in the world with freedom and joy" (*Who Lost* 98). And, in a conciliatory note, he repaid her favor of dedicating *The Mandarins* to him by dedicating *Who Lost an American?* to her. Unlike Algren, who was hurt and angered by his former lover's exploitation of their private relationship for her literary purposes, de Beauvoir regarded her fictionalization of their love affair as (in Mills's more general terms) "a way of paying homage ... a uniquely moving tribute" (199) to a person in her life and was taken aback by Algren's outrage. In an interview with her biographer, Deirdre Bair, she commented—"with an element of genuine surprise in her voice"—"'when I started to write *The Mandarins*, all I had in mind was to pay homage to Nelson Algren by writing our love story!'" (Bair 411). Her exclamatory remark, whether disingenuous or not, highlights the discrepancy of ethical perspectives that obtains between a writer and the object of her literary appropriations.

In Algren's eyes, de Beauvoir's memoir, *Force of Circumstance*, the second volume of her autobiography, which appeared in English translation during the same year as his *Who Lost an American?*, further compounded his sense of personal injury and psychological pain. In the book, he discovered for the first time that de Beauvoir had a pact with Sartre that long predated her relationship with Algren (Bair 158; Seymour-Jones 458–9). The French couple had pledged fidelity to each other regardless of their other sexual liaisons, of which there were many, mostly on Sartre's side, over the years. Indeed, they maintained an "open marriage" in every sense except legally; they agreed to maintain fidelity in a sense that did not depend on or assume sexual monogamy. However, as Lisa Appignanesi contends,

> in this lifelong relationship of supposed equals, [Sartre], it turned out, was far more equal than [de Beauvoir] was. It was he who engaged in countless affairs, to which she responded on only a few occasions with longer-lasting passions of her own. Between the lines of her fiction and what are in effect six volumes of autobiography, it is also evident that de Beauvoir suffered deeply from jealousy. ("'Our Relationship Was the Greatest Achievement of My Life'")

For his part, Nelson Algren, in retaliation for what he regarded as de Beauvoir's betrayals of him—both intimate and literary—"spent the next few years castigating her in reviews and articles, and the rest of his life denouncing her to anyone who would listen. 'Autobiography—shit!' he roared several weeks before his death in May 1981. 'Autofiction, that's what she wrote'" (Bair 500). His prolonged sense of injury may explain, though not justify, two of his own ethical breaches. Not only did he review *Force of Circumstance* for two different publications, a violation of journalistic ethics; further, it was a fundamental conflict of interest for him to review de Beauvoir's book in any case, given his far from neutral position as her former lover, still smarting from having been dumped by her, to say nothing of his pique at knowing he was the involuntary model for a major character in *The Mandarins*. In his review of *Force of Circumstance* for *Harper's*, Algren snarled at length,

> No chronicler of our lives since Theodore Dreiser has combined so steadfast a passion for human justice with a dullness so asphyxiating as Mme. de Beauvoir. While other writers reproach the reader gently, she flattens his nose against the blackboard, gooses him with a twelve-inch ruler, and warns him if he doesn't start acting grown-up she's going to hold her breath till he does.... Mme. de Beauvoir's world [...] is a reflected vision; no one ever lived behind that looking-glass. Which is why all the characters of her novels, although drawn directly from life, have no life on the printed page.... Anybody who can experience love contingently has a mind that has recently snapped.

How can love be *contingent*? Contingent upon *what*? ("The Question of Simone de Beauvoir," *Harper's*, May 1965, qtd. by Hazel Rowley, *Tête-à-Tête* 303; italics and ellipses in original unless bracketed)

* * *

Cross-connections

The relationship between Simone de Beauvoir and Nelson Algren, immortalized in de Beauvoir's fictional transformation of Algren into Lewis Brogan in *The Mandarins*, and Algren's aggrieved response to that fact, might merit only a footnote in this discussion if it were not for the multiple intersections among the lives and writings of de Beauvoir, Algren, Doris Lessing, and Clancy Sigal. If Sigal's fictional representations of events are to be trusted—and, since this study has suggested the impossibility of establishing the "true" version of many events in his life, I must speak advisedly—he met de Beauvoir at least once while he lived in Paris. In an early version of his unpublished sketch with the exaggeratedly long title, "How to Live with a Lady Writer: First Lesson, Don't call her a Lady Writer—A Kiss and Tell Story," Sigal amusingly embellishes the anecdote, opening his sketch with the observation, "If Simone de Beauvoir had slept with me, my life would have been much simpler. I'd come to France to make love to her.... Ever since I read Beauvoir's *Les Mandarins*—among other things, about her affair with Nelson Algren—I'd itched to show her what a younger Chicago boy could do with a powerful intellectual lady..." ("How to Live with a Lady Writer" 1).

As it turned out, Sigal did have an affair with a French woman, Riva Boren Lanzmann, a visual artist of Polish descent who happened to have a close connection to de Beauvoir: through her marriage to Jacques Lanzmann, she was the sister-in-law of Jacques's older brother, Claude Lanzmann, de Beauvoir's much-younger lover by 17 years and later an important film director.[4] Riva Lanzmann, whom Sigal identifies as de Beauvoir's "foster daughter," introduced him to the "Great Couple" ("Lady Writer" 1); Sigal was convinced that de Beauvoir disdained him because of his execrable French accent. Sartre apparently tried to persuade Sigal to end his affair with Riva, who, in any case, soon returned to her husband. Consistent with the de facto "open marriage" arrangement practiced by Sartre and de Beauvoir, the Lanzmann siblings appear to have conducted themselves similarly in their intimate relationships. In a French version of the hall of mirrors image I have used to frame the lives and writings of Doris Lessing and Clancy Sigal, several years before Sigal's brief liaison with Riva Lanzmann, the Lanzmann brothers' younger sister, Evelyne, was involved in a celebrated affair with Sartre. Clancy Sigal—or, rather, his fictionalized and at times comic double in his "Lady Writer" sketch—comments that he "fled France regretting only that I hadn't been aggressive enough to push Beauvoir's lover, Claude Lanzman [sic] out of the way. Thus I arrived in England with an unassuaged appetite to link up with any small sexy European lady writer" ("Lady Writer" 1–2). Enter Doris Lessing—or, as Sigal later wittily described their relationship, "Beauvoir and Sartre without the garlic" (*Secret Defector* 108). Given Sigal's frequent literary paeans to Doris Lessing's culinary skills, one may wonder why he omitted the garlic.

In another instance of the coincidental overlappings among the four writers' lives, while Clancy Sigal lived in Paris in 1956 and 1957, he rented a flat on a lower floor of the same building on the Rue Boucherie in which Nelson Algren and Simone de Beauvoir lived together for a time in 1949 (Donohue 183). Sigal had met Algren in Hollywood several years before he left for France, when he worked at the Jaffe Agency, a Hollywood film agency that represented many screen talents. He recalls listening as Algren "told his tale to incredulous moguls" ("Recalling the Kindness of Algren"). During the evenings they chatted over drinks at the "Red Log bar, in Westwood," as Sigal, an aspiring but not yet published writer, confessed as much to Algren. While the older writer "kept a straight face," Sigal boasted—in what may be an apocryphal embellishment—that he "was going to quit [his] job, sail to France, write a big novel and have an affair with Simone de Beauvoir." As he adds, Algren "didn't blink an eye. 'That's a pretty good idea,' he drawled. 'But you don't want to mess with her boyfriend, Sartre. If *she* doesn't talk you to death, *he* certainly will'" ("Kindness," Sigal's italics).

Sigal recognized several affinities between himself and Algren: both were Leftist Jewish writers who grew up in working-class Chicago neighborhoods. Algren's background influenced his literary subject matter, resulting in what Sigal terms his "immortal short stories about America's dispossessed," written by a man who "sided unequivocally with the scum of the earth" ("Pre-War Tough Guy from Chicago"). When Algren died in 1981, Sigal wrote an appreciation of the man he generously credited with "[making him] into a writer" ("Kindness") and regrets that he failed to express his appreciation directly to his mentor during his lifetime.[5] With chagrin and the benefit of hindsight, Sigal adds, "In my ignorance, I did not realize until I read Beauvoir's *The Mandarins* just how close she and Algren were" ("Kindness"). In an amusing embellishment that was cut from his published tribute to Algren, he mentions that the older writer tactfully "never mentioned this faux pas of mine—except years later, when I introduced him to my English version of Beauvoir [Doris Lessing]. All he said afterwards was, 'Nice lady. Were you too lazy to learn French?'" (Tribute to Nelson Algren).

To further complicate the connections among these four writers, Doris Lessing not only knew Nelson Algren but was introduced to him by Clancy Sigal. In the second volume of her autobiography, she mentions a visit from algren, who, "[a]ccording to the newspapers and general report...was bitter about having been put into *The Mandarins*...as the evasive American lover—straight from life" (*Walking* 305). Surely Lessing knew a thing or two about such matters. Although the two writers didn't "fancy" each other romantically, "we did like each other and spent several agreeable days together..." (305). Moreover, Algren regarded himself as an admirer of Lessing's fiction. In a letter to Clancy Sigal dated June 28, 1962, he wrote, "Tell Doris Lessing I received her GOLDEN NOTEBOOK the day I was leaving and it was too big to pack. I was irritated about that because I would have liked to review it."[6] The freighter on which Algren was a passenger, *American Mail*, was literally setting sail that evening, bound for Hokkaido, Japan, and other Asian ports. Algren added, "I also had your idol de Beauvoir's latest, 'Prime of Life' [the second volume of her autobiography], and was supposed to review it, but decided against it." Algren apparently couldn't resist adding a disparaging comment concerning his former lover. He wryly remarked, "You have to be a true-believer to finish a book that prolix. And I'm not that great a believer." Closing his letter to Sigal with the written equivalent of a wink, Algren advised his friend, "Drop by when you learn French." [signed] Nelson (Algren letter 2).

Clancy Sigal affirms his connection to and admiration of Nelson Algren in several places in his fiction and elsewhere in his writing. In *The Secret Defector*, his alter ego, Gus Black, struggling to write his first book, "experiment[s] with trying to copy Nelson Algren, but it kept coming out all wrong, like Norman Mailer with a hernia"

(*Defector* 20). Later, defending in his own voice his fictionalized version of Doris Lessing as Rose O'Malley in *The Secret Defector*, he remarks,

> My friend, Chicago-born Nelson Algren, immortalized (or whatever the verb is) by *his* former love Simone de Beauvoir as "Lewis Brogan" in "The Mandarins," had given me fair warning before I left America for Europe. "Women over there," he had said, "don't play by Chicago rules. They're not used to men like us. They'll break your heart while talking you to death about how you've broken their heart." Algren never used de Beauvoir in his fiction. ("'You Can't Do It!'" 14, Sigal's italics)

Further, in "In Pursuit of Saul Green," Sigal's unpublished story about a graduate student in American Studies who successfully tracks down and interviews the "true" Saul Green of Lessing's *The Golden Notebook*, Abner Briskin also struggles to complete a book, in this case a doctoral thesis on *roman à clef* that, naturally, includes attention to de Beauvoir's *The Mandarins*.

When a selection of the 350 love letters that de Beauvoir penned to Algren was published in 1998 as *A Transatlantic Love Affair: Letters to Nelson Algren*, Sigal favorably reviewed the volume for the *Los Angeles Times*. In his judgment, the Beauvoir–Algren affair was "a spectacular affirmation—at first—of two great hearts and minds struggling past language, personal and cultural incongruities. The 'failure' of their relationship was in many ways a function of the competing claims of Paris or Chicago" ("The Torrid Affair between Nelson Algren and Simone de Beauvoir," October 18, 1998). It is tempting to read Sigal's praise from the perspective of his own grand passion with Doris Lessing nearly four decades earlier. With telling understatement, he adds, "Writers in love can be hell on each other" ("Torrid Affair"). Moreover, in an unmistakable parallel with his own relationship with Lessing that emphasizes his gratitude for her literary mentorship, Sigal proposes that de Beauvoir and Algren

> owed each other a tremendous untraceable debt. He opened her up to an emotional freedom she had never before experienced. His thumbprints are all over de Beauvoir's now-classic "The Second Sex".... On Algren's work, de Beauvoir's impact is less evident—until we recall that the main female character in "The Man With the Golden Arm"... might easily have jumped off the pages of "The Second Sex." ("Torrid Affair")

Sigal argues that, despite Algren's dismay when he found himself the involuntary model for the fictional Lewis Brogan in *The Mandarins*, he and de Beauvoir remained "in love... for the rest of their lives" ("Torrid Affair"). Indeed, Sigal felt strongly enough on this point to pen a letter to *New York Times Book Review* expressing his objections to the condescending tone and "careless inaccuracies" he found in the reviewer Mim Udovitch's patronizing characterization of the transatlantic love affair. As he phrased it, "Somebody else's love letters are easy to make fun of. The fact is, de Beauvoir and Algren were deeply, sexually—and lastingly—in love. It was no simple affair. On her death she was buried alongside her lifelong companion, Jean-Paul Sartre, while wearing Nelson Algren's wedding ring" (Letter, *New York Times Books* December 27, 1998)

Coincidentally, the de Beauvoir–Algren love story also has several links with Doris Lessing. There is no evidence that Lessing and de Beauvoir ever met. What a fascinating meeting it would have been if these two pioneer writers on the subject of female experience, whether in the mid-twentieth century or throughout history, had exchanged views on topics of mutual interest, including female sexuality, social conditioning of gender roles, patriarchal social structures, and other matters—possibly even including disgruntled former lovers and the merits and ethics of *roman à clef*. Describing these two indisputably major figures of the "cultural landscape of 1960," Elizabeth Wilson labels de Beauvoir and Lessing "Cassandras of women's experience, an experience that was everywhere silenced, concealed and denied" ("Yesterday's heroines" 57).

Whether or not Doris Lessing had read *The Second Sex*, published in English translation in 1952, by the time she began to write *The Golden Notebook* during the mid-1950s, a number of de Beauvoir's philosophical claims concerning historical gender arrangements and the situation of women dovetail with Lessing's literary representation of a woman living—or attempting to live—as a "free woman" in Britain during the mid-twentieth century. Paralleling de Beauvoir's revolutionary assertion at the conclusion of *The Second Sex* that "[t]he free woman is just being born" (714), Anna Wulf explains to her therapist her belief that "there are whole areas of me made by the kind of experience women haven't had before.... I believe I'm living the kind of life women never lived before" (*GN* 441). Yet Anna's discouraging and even emotionally shattering experiences illustrate, among other ideas, the obstacles that independent heterosexual women faced in their relations with men at that time. Most of the male characters in *The Golden Notebook*—as in Lessing's *Play with a Tiger*—whether married or single, major or minor, expect women to accept male sexual promiscuity rather than monogamy as the norm. As has been documented earlier in this study, a central bone of contention between Doris Lessing and Clancy Sigal was their incompatible convictions regarding emotional and sexual fidelity. Saul Green remarks in response to Anna Wulf's jealousy over his dalliances with other women—behavior that he regards as unremarkable, insignificant, and therefore of no consequence for their relationship—"The trouble is, when we took each other on, you took fidelity for granted and I didn't. I've never been faithful to anyone. It didn't arise" (*GN* 538).

Circumstantial connections between Simone de Beauvoir and Doris Lessing also appear in two other contexts. When, several decades after the publication of *The Golden Notebook*, Lessing prepared to write the first volume of her autobiography and was pondering the second—which encompasses, among other major periods of her life, her relationship with Clancy Sigal—she invoked de Beauvoir as a reference point for her consideration of how much of the truth to divulge in one's autobiography. She wondered whether she should

> follow the example of Simone de Beauvoir who said that about some things she had no intention of telling the truth. (Then why bother?—the reader must be expected to ask.)... And why all this emphasis on kissing and telling? Kisses are the least of it.... Some of the most noisy... scandals or affairs of our time, that have had a searchlight on them for years, are reflected wrongly in the public mind because the actual participants keep their counsel, and watch, ironically, from the shadows. (*Under My Skin* 11–12)

A decade later, when the fiftieth-anniversary edition of *The Mandarins* was published in 2005, the preface was written by none other than Doris Lessing. In her brief introduction, she explained why, half a century after its original date of publication, de Beauvoir's novel was still worth reading. In her judgment, it was not for its Leftist politics—which, given the collapse and dissolution of the Soviet Union in 1991, came to have (like the political dimension of *The Golden Notebook*) "something of the flavour of ancient religious squabbles"—but for what she calls "an ironical reason: its brilliant portraits of women" ("Simone de Beauvoir," *Time Bites* 209). With respect to the correspondences and divergences among historical and disguised autobiography, fiction, and "truth" that are so central to her own literary endeavors, Lessing also comments on the fictionalized version of the celebrated love affair between de Beauvoir and Algren that appears in *The Mandarins*. Of Algren, she remarks that the writer was famous, if not at the time of his liaison with de Beauvoir then soon afterward, for "cult novels" that "romanticis[ed] the drug and crime cultures of big American cities"; his characters, "dying of drugs, or in prison for selling drugs, or with lives wasted by poverty[,] were in every way preferable, full of poetry and adventure that cocked a snook at capitalism and the middle class" ("Simone de Beauvoir" 208). In Lessing's judgment, the affair between two writers shaped by vastly different cultures and worldviews inevitably acquired a significance beyond their personal lives through the "symbolical mating of worlds apparently opposite but linked by a contempt for the established order, and a need to destroy it" (208). As with Sigal's comments on the de Beauvoir–Algren love affair, Lessing's observation might be applied to her own complicated romantic relationship with Clancy Sigal. Moreover, her concluding observation on *The Mandarins* also describes her own now-classic *The Golden Notebook*: the novel "chronicles its time, but with all the advantages and disadvantages of immediacy, for large parts of it are like the hot, quick impatience of reporting" (209).

The multiple coincidental cross-connections among the lives and writings of Doris Lessing, Clancy Sigal, Simone de Beauvoir, and Nelson Algren—and between life and art—continue to unfold. Recently, Clancy Sigal and his wife, actress Janice Tidwell, collaborated on the screenplay for a film treatment of the de Beauvoir–Algren affair, provisionally titled *My American Lover*.[7]

CHAPTER 9

OF PARENT AND CHILD

"*Do children feel their parents' emotions? Yes, we do, and it is a legacy I could have done without.*" Doris Lessing (Alfred and Emily)

"*Now that I am a father and tempted to veil from my son certain facts of my own life, I see where family mystery gets us: Nowhere.*" Clancy Sigal (A Woman of Uncertain Character)

Reconciliations

Relatively late in their careers—many years after their association with each other had ended—Doris Lessing and Clancy Sigal each returned once again to the genre of autobiography, this time not to mine the details of their intimate relationship with each other or with any other living person but to compose memoirs of their deceased parents and, in the process, to give literary form to key elements of their own literal and literary origins and formative years. Strictly speaking, neither Sigal's *A Woman of Uncertain Character: The Amorous and Radical Adventures of My Mother Jennie* (2006) nor Lessing's *Alfred and Emily* (2008) is disguised autobiography or *roman à clef*, since there is no attempt on the authors' parts to disguise their subjects. However, the memoirs are noteworthy in the context of this study because of both writers' interest in the borderlines between fact and fiction. Lessing's book is of particular note because of her unorthodox approach to the boundaries of literary genre.

Although Clancy Sigal's mother died in 1959, it took him nearly 50 years to reach a position from which he could write honestly about their complicated relationship during his childhood and youth. Until writing *A Woman of Uncertain Character*, he excluded her from mention in his fiction and other writing. He alludes to her only indirectly in the context of his quarrels with Doris Lessing, who felt that their intimate relationship was compromised by Sigal's unacknowledged and unresolved mother-problems. As Sigal phrases it in the opening paragraph of his memoir, "Like Dr. Frankenstein, I, Jennie's son, bring the dead back to life. In Hollywood, where I write movies, I helped raise Frida Kahlo from her grave, gave the kiss of life to Sandra Bullock as the wartime nurse who was Hemingway's first love, and resurrected Maria Callas and Simone de Beauvoir. The only woman who has resisted my touch is my own mother" (*A Woman of Uncertain Character* 1).[1] He acknowledges that for many years a significant obstacle to his writing about his mother was a "conspiracy of silence" (*Woman* 2), based on Jennie's radical political activism, that was an article of faith between them during his early years. Later in life, Sigal's wish to provide his own young son (then ten years old), with understanding of his grandmother prompted him to break the code of silence to tell his mother's story as candidly and honestly as he could. As he phrases it, "Now that I am a father and tempted to veil from my son certain facts of my own life, I see where family mystery gets us: Nowhere" (2). Jennie Persily's story is inseparable from Sigal's own biography, several details concerning which he reveals for the first time in his memoir of his mother.

Jennie Persily was born to Jewish parents in what is now Ukraine and immigrated with her parents and, over time, nine siblings; the family settled in New York's Lower East Side. Growing up as the "bohemian" radical of her large family, she became passionately involved at the age of 24 with a radical union organizer who—as Clancy Sigal learned only many years later—was already married to another woman. Following Leo Sigal to Chicago against the advice of her family, Jennie joined him in his union-organizing activities. When she was 31, she gave birth to her only child, a son she named Kalman (Clarence). Often she and Leo—or she alone—dragged the boy along with her to raucous union meetings. During his boyhood, Sigal regarded his father's unpredictable appearances and disappearances as a kind of mystery. Leo Sigal was "in and out of our lives when the mood was on him according to cosmic laws of motion I never understood.... When, without warning, he'd drop by, Jennie was transformed into a young girl, flushed and excited, flashing legs and full of sparkle. I, too, came alive, heady with male love, eager to impress Dad, aiming to be the perfect son" (37–8).

Sigal and his mother lived on South Kedzie Avenue, a "95 percent Jewish and 115 percent Democrat" neighborhood in the Lawndale area of Chicago (*Woman* 64). Despite the neighborhood's ethnic purity, he grew up without strong ties to his religious tradition. Instead, he hung out with a closely bonded group of boys who called themselves the Rockets (60). When, intermittently, Sigal's father was around, his parents managed the Family Hand Laundry; the elder Sigal was a "skilled craftsman in a trade that no longer exists: quality shirt ironing and finishing" (91). Leo continued to come and go "according to the laws of his own nature and how badly our business was doing..." (84). However, even when absent, he was "present" for Sigal as "a living force, as I ascended a scale of delinquency that was sure to impress him. Shoplifting, hubcap-stealing, reasonless fistfights, baseball card scams, I was a one-man riot of petty crimes that *had* to get Dad's attention, even if from afar. One way or another, he'd be so proud of his son" (84, Sigal's italics).

From his mother, an "emotional policeman" (*Woman* 126), Sigal learned early on that he should keep his feelings in check. "Grief, sorrow, or anger" were acceptable only up to a point, after which they were regarded as self-indulgences. Sometime during his adolescence, Sigal figured out that he was a "bastard" (148). In his memoir of his mother, he attempts to untangle the oedipal aspect of their relationship that, years before, Doris Lessing had recognized and repeatedly pressed him to do. Benefiting from mature hindsight, Sigal recalls the mother of his childhood. However, as he reconstructs his physical memory of her, he figuratively and almost voyeuristically strips her down to her undergarments, more than hinting at the sexual tensions that colored their relationship during his formative years:

> Ma's flesh communicates a more immediate language than words, a language I spend my childhood deciphering. Rich, abundant, cascading, engulfing flesh, product of a fast-developing puberty, its physical mass caged and trapped in the mandatory undergarments of her time. The hospital-pink, iron-buckled corset, with its thousand hooks and straps, the strangulating scar-leaving girdle, the D-cup brassiere laying siege to her nipples, the shroud-like Belgian silk slip, the thigh-length silk stockings held in place by snap-ons attached to bloomer-like panties, and a flowered dress from Lane Bryant's "styles for the stout," defined, dignified, and garroted Jennie's "form-fitting" figure. A warrior queen. (34)

Once Sigal entered puberty, his mother began to loom even more disconcertingly in his eyes as a provocative sexual presence. "Ma and I were like two erotic locomotives heading toward each other on a collision course. I was sixteen and inventing myself as a man, she was forty-seven and struggling to liberate herself from the trauma, just setting in, of Dad's exit. Sparks flew whenever we were in the same room.... [M]y pubescent body, with a will of its own, seemed to involuntarily lean into hers at the slightest opportunity" (197). Eventually, Jennie, recognizing the improper sexual attraction between them, shipped her academically slow son off to what he soon discovered was a high school for girls; as Sigal phrases it, "Being a boy in a girls' school is no fun except in theory" (206). After he graduated, he got a job, his first, as a junior mail clerk. Flexing his radical political muscles in a different direction from his mother's while awaiting induction papers for the US Army, he stumbled into a meeting of the Young Communist League and soon became a member of the "Corpuscle Quartet," a musical foursome with a radical spin.

In 1944, at the age of 18, Sigal was inducted into the infantry of the US Army, serving in Germany for two years and rising to the rank of Sergeant Major. The army appealed to something in him. As he writes, "Long before I joined an actual army I was a boy-soldier-in-my-head, in perpetual training for a final conflict between good and evil.... Soldierness was a perfectly rational technique for organizing one's fears about the outside world's chronic war fever" (224–5). In fact, he found military life so satisfying that at the end of his stint he "almost 'reupped'" (e-mail message to author dated March 10, 2012). Instead, he returned to the United States and briefly lived again with his mother, who by then had relocated to Los Angeles. "She badly wanted a grandchild but I was already mentally zipping my bags to get out of the country before somebody nailed me for something" (257). What followed—Sigal's escape to Europe, including his brief sojourn in Paris followed by his fateful arrival at Doris Lessing's London flat in the spring of 1957—is repeatedly reprised in his diverse literary transformations of that critical phase of his life.

While Sigal was living in England, his mother died of a heart attack in 1959. Because "her apron strings stretched all the way across the Atlantic" (*Woman* 261), when she died, their enduring but difficult bond complicated Sigal's grieving process. Looking back nearly 50 years later, he understood that, whatever else Jennie's death had meant for him, it had marked the end of his protracted "life as a boy" (263). Of note, Sigal's biographical account introduces a significant discrepancy concerning his living arrangements at the time of his mother's death. As is articulated in multiple autobiographical and fictionalized accounts of his early years in London, when Jennie Persily died in September 1959, he was living with Doris Lessing in her Warwick Road apartment—though, on the precise date that he learned the news of his mother's death, he was indeed not at that location because he was in Yorkshire. In *A Woman of Uncertain Character*, he describes living in a "Swiss Cottage [London] basement bedsit" (263). As the result of the vagaries of memory or intention, he omits Lessing from his account of the circumstances that ultimately prompted his decisive literary breakthrough. Rather, he highlights his mother's death as the event that sprung him free of a tenacious writer's block; indeed, he even credits her as a trigger for his career as a writer.

Although Sigal had not previously been a practicing Jew, following his mother's death he underwent a period of grieving during which, to his surprise, he found himself performing traditional Jewish mourning rituals—fasting, shaving his head, and uttering the traditional prayer for the dead. Then, with a characteristic dash of hyperbole, Sigal explains:

> as if awakened by a pistol shot, I straightened up, dry-eyed, got dressed, and went to my typewriter on a table in the corner. Fasting, or Jennie's ghost, had unjammed the memory machine and my fingers flew over the keys.... The piece that rattled off the roll of yellow copy paper... had nothing to do with Jennie but came easily and fast, a short story out of nowhere. I copyedited it and slipped it into an envelope... and mailed it to the magazine *New Statesman and Nation*. A day later, such was the efficiency of the British postal system then, the editor rang with an acceptance.... And I was on my way.
>
> Jennie's death, which even today I have a hard time believing in, took a weight off me that I hadn't even known was there and gave me a sense that I was now and forevermore alone in the world and therefore had to make something of myself. I owed her that. (264)

In earlier autobiographical and fictional versions of Sigal's "origin story" as a writer, it is not Jennie Persily but Doris Lessing who nurtured him through his protracted writer's block and mentored his literary talent. In his revisionist version of that formative period of his writing career, Sigal selectively edits Lessing out of the story and gives his mother significant credit, if only for the character traits that ultimately made his chosen vocation possible.

> For all [Jennie's] life she had maintained, at great cost, her steely self-control. Now, it seemed as if all that anger, resentment, and pent up fury she could never articulate, for fear of being consumed by it, shot straight into my veins.... Insofar as I have a "personality" as a writer it is, at least partly, something I borrowed from her. All this time she was teaching me how to be a writer.... I chose my mother wisely. Her hands are on these keys. (266)

On a more recent occasion, during which he recalled the decisive moment of breaking through the writer's block that had dogged him so relentlessly as he attempted to launch his writing career during the 1950s, Sigal assigned the honor neither to Doris Lessing nor to his mother but to his—and Lessing's—good friend, Joan Rodker. In his obituary of Rodker, who died in December 2010 at the age of 95, Sigal remarks, "Joan opened her home to exiles of any persuasion. I was one of them, a fugitive, passportless American illegal alien in need of family warmth and protection. My first two or three years in Britain are linked irrevocably to Joan's amazing, open-hearted house in Kensington. For me it was a safe haven, a second home, a dazzling salon of the international left and a creative springboard where her soul-filling cooking dissolved my 'block' and released me to produce my first book" ("Joan Rodker" [obituary]).

The resolution of Sigal's writer's block thus seems to have had multiple sources—or, more likely, his inconsistent attributions at different moments in his own life demonstrate that the process of recollection and the interpretation of the details of one's experience shift over time, compounding the difficulty of capturing autobiographical "truth." Given the constantly shifting ground between fact and fiction that is the subject of this study, one may legitimately conclude that the slippage of attribution offered at different times and under different circumstances is a function of both the vagaries of memory and the application of artistic license. Yet psychologically, all versions are true: over time, Sigal credits not only his biological mother but two other important women in his life who "mothered" him, whether emotionally, artistically, gastronomically, or in various combinations of these contexts. In different ways and to different degrees, Doris Lessing—who, during the years of her relationship with Clancy Sigal, protested against his unconscious casting of her in the maternal role—and Joan Rodker both provided important forms of sustenance. Sigal's celebration of both women's culinary skills attests to the literal aspect of their nurturance. Not only literally but psychologically, all three women—Jennie Persily, Doris Lessing, and Joan Rodker—were instrumental to Clancy Sigal's personal development and his birth as a writer.

A Woman of Uncertain Character is Sigal's late-life attempt to achieve reconciliation not only with his mother but with both parents. Although the principal focus is his complex relationship with Jennie, a doting and overly close single parent during his childhood and youth, he also accomplishes if not a reconciliation, at least a reunion with his unapologetically absent father. More than two decades after

Of Parent and Child ⬧ 185

Leo disowned him during his adolescence, Sigal tracked his father down in the New York borough of the Bronx through a telephone directory search. Although he had known for many years that he was an illegitimate child, it was only during the belated reunion with his father in 1962 that he discovered the other crucial part of the story: from the beginning of Leo Sigal's relationship with Jennie Persily and during the years of his childhood when Clancy knew Leo as his father, he was married to a woman named Lena and had a son and a daughter, half-siblings of whose existence Sigal was entirely unaware. By the time Clancy met his father again in adulthood, Leo was divorced from his first wife and married to a woman named Sarah.

Throughout their meeting, Leo Sigal kept addressing his son as Percy rather than Clancy, despite Sigal's efforts to correct his father's wince-inducing mistake. In what may be an apocryphal embellishment, Sigal writes that his shrewd father knew of his then-recently ended relationship with Doris Lessing. One wonders how he could have known such privileged information, since *The Golden Notebook* was published during the same year as the meeting between son and father, when it was not yet known to outsiders who lacked the "key" that Sigal was the model for the fictitious Saul Green. Leo Sigal, "a Jack Dempsey of evasion... fended off all my personal questions by constantly changing the subject to the British cultural scene..." (271), at which point Sigal, channeling his father's voice and idiom, delivers a verbal jab—whether fact or fiction—aimed at his former lover. His father calculatingly remarks, "That South African dame, the one who put you in her book, she really hooked it to you, didn't she?... How did you let yourself get sucker punched like that, Percy?" (271–2). Leo Sigal also casually states that his "bad luck" began on the day his son was born. In his parting remark to "Percy," his father offered a kind of apology laced with belated advice: "we [Sigal's parents] did not intend a rough deal for you.... Don't be a sorehead. It won't get you anywhere. Be a man. What choice do you have?" (276). Leo Sigal died in 1963, a year after the reunion between Clancy Sigal and the father who had erased himself from his son's life.

* * *

Dream Parents

By contrast with Clancy Sigal, whose parents are largely absent from his writing before *A Woman of Uncertain Character*, Doris Lessing wrote about her mother and father on several occasions, in both fictional and overtly autobiographical forms. As she phrased it in "My Father," her earliest nonfictional account to focus on either of her parents, "We use our parents like recurring dreams, to be entered into when needed; they are always there for love or for hate…" (*A Small Personal Voice* 83). However, like Sigal, Lessing struggled for years to achieve reconciliation with her mother, with whom she had had an emotionally fraught and contentious relationship virtually from early childhood, when the young Doris recognized Emily Maude Tayler's profound disaffection for her. Lessing first attempted to express her view of their antagonistic relationship in fictional form through her characterizations of May Quest, Martha Quest's meddling, critical, hide-bound mother and *bête noir* in the five volumes of *Children of Violence*. Mrs. Quest's profound inability to understand Martha, her irritating intrusions into her daughter's life, and her relentless hypercriticism constitute the emotional ground—indeed, the battleground—of their combative and static relationship. In the final volume of the series, *The Four-Gated City*, Lessing gives her fictionalized mother a voice of her own, narrating an entire section from May Quest's point of view (*The Four-Gated City* 236–74). However, her story is inevitably colored by Martha's/Doris' negative view of her. Mrs. Quest, traveling by ship from Africa to England, reviews her entire unhappy personal history, bringing it up-to-date when she arrives in London and begins to express her disapproval of every aspect of her daughter's life, beginning with Martha's unorthodox living arrangement and her communist politics. Every dialogue between mother and daughter conveys their colliding values and intractable differences.

What Martha Quest profoundly wishes for—a wish that can never be granted—is that her mother would simply try to accept her as she is.. Before Mrs. Quest leaves London, feeling herself unwanted and unloved by her daughter (the feeling is mutual), she visits a doctor at Martha's insistence, at which point "out of her flooded years and years and years of resentment, all focused on Martha" (*Four-Gated City* 273). Lessing's barely disguised portrayal of Emily Maude Tayler was, she later speculated, "the first no-holds-barred [literary] account of a mother-and-daughter battle" (*Alfred & Emily* 178). She acknowledges that, for much of her life, "I hated my mother" and describes their frequent clashes as "titanic" (179, 183). Their contentious relationship affected her emotional life for many years, during which she was "always in flight," her mother "always in pursuit." (267).

Six years after the final volume of *Children of Violence* was published, Lessing attempted another fictional version of her mother in a narrative that she terms her own "imaginative biography" ("The Habit of Observing" 148), although *The Memoirs of a Survivor* (1975) was not understood in that way when it was first published. Once again, Lessing blurred the boundary between actual and fictionalized memoir to explore deeply personal experiences. An important element of the narrative is a series of dreamlike scenes that feature pertinent details concerning the nameless elder narrator's childhood, apparently based on the emotional circumstances of both Doris Lessing's mother's childhood and her own. Elsewhere Lessing has explained that *The Memoirs of a Survivor* developed out of her idea to write a novel composed entirely of dreams. Though ultimately she did not write such a novel, she incorporated the idea into *Memoirs*: "what the narrator believes that she is seeing behind the wall, that apparent dream world, actually represents her own life, her own childhood" ("Observing" 148). Of the dream-like scenes that unexpectedly open to her on the far side of the wall of her apartment, one strand of her explorations suggests potentiality and transformation while the other conveys static scenes of utter misery.

In the latter emotionally claustrophobic realm, the narrator witnesses scenes that include an unloved, neglected child—a composite of Lessing herself as the daughter who keenly felt the absence of her mother's love, and her mother, Emily Maude, whose own mother died when she was three years old and whose early life was shaped by a similar experience of maternal absence and emotional neediness. The young Emily in the scenes beyond the wall is alternately ignored and shamed but never cuddled, while her younger brother receives the lion's share of their mother's affection and attention. Concurrent with the narrator's multiple visits to the far side of the wall, in the external realm of the narrative, the "real" world outside the narrator's flat is in a state of escalating social collapse. Early on, a preadolescent girl—who, significantly, is named Emily—arrives and becomes the narrator's "responsibility" for the duration of the narrative.

A decade after she wrote *The Memoirs of a Survivor*, Lessing endeavored to articulate more straightforwardly her complicated feelings about her mother, publishing a two-part memoir in two issues of the journal *Granta* that featured autobiography, as "Impertinent Daughters" (1984) and "My Mother's Life (Part II)" (1985). In the first portion, she admitted, "it has taken me a lifetime to understand my parents..." (*Granta 14: Autobiography* 52). She emphasized that her memories of her mother were "all of antagonism, and fighting, and feeling shut out.... She didn't like me.... She paralysed me as a child by the anger and pity I felt. Now only pity is left, but it still makes it hard to write about her" ("Impertinent" 61, 68).

As is demonstrated in the first volume of Lessing's autobiography, published in 1994—a decade after the two pieces in *Granta*—in her seventies, she still had not resolved her complicated feelings about her mother. Indeed, in both volumes of her autobiography she struggled with guilt as she recalled their life-long mutual antagonism. She wrote, "I was in nervous flight from [my mother] ever since I can remember anything, and from the age of fourteen I set myself obdurately against her in a kind of inner emigration from everything she represented.... Now I see her as a tragic figure, living out her disappointing years with courage and with dignity. I saw her then as tragic, certainly, but was not able to be kind" (*Under My Skin* 15). When Maude Tayler—who dropped the name Emily early in her married life—died in 1957, Lessing suffered from "a chilly grey semi-frozen condition" that she accurately named "occluded grief" (*Walking in the Shade* 223), one of the features of which is a profound sense of guilt. She asked herself,

> At what point during this long miserable story of my mother and myself could I have behaved differently? [...] But I had to conclude that nothing could have been different.... So what use grief? Pain? Sorrow? Regret? [...] There are deaths that are not blows but bruises, spreading darkly, out of sight, not ever really fading. [...] Suppose she were to walk in now, an old woman, and here I am an old woman...how would we be? [...] [M]ost of all I think that I would simply put my arms around her.... Around who? Little Emily, whose mother died when she was three, leaving her to the servants, a cold unloving stepmother, a cold dutiful father. (*Walking* 223-4, Lessing's ellipses unless bracketed)

As Lessing observed with gratitude, Clancy Sigal supported her through her complicated grieving over her mother's passing. "His feelings for his mother, whom he pitied and feared, enabled him to understand mine" (*Walking* 223). Sigal's mother died in 1959, two years after Lessing's mother died.

Lessing's father, more preoccupied with medical and economic difficulties than with his daughter, did not loom as threateningly as did her mother in the young Doris's emotional life. Accordingly, Alfred Tayler is a less vexed subject in her autobiographical and imaginative writing. Though she pitied him, apparently she did not fear him or feel suffocated by stultifying prescriptions for her life. A fictionalized version of a man who may be partially based on Alfred Tayler appears in the hall of mirrors of *The Golden Notebook* as the father of Ella, Anna Wulf's fictionalized alter ego. Ella's father is "a military man turned some sort of mystic. Or had always been a mystic?" (*GN* 432). Although Lessing's father was seriously injured in World War I, the fictional Ella's father is quite different from Lessing's. Not only did he outlive his wife—rather than the reverse, as was true for Lessing's actual parents—but his character contains facets that apparently were not true of Lessing's father, including his mystical side and a hidden literary impulse to write poetry. The fictional portrait suggests a wish on the author's part to have had a father with hidden virtues that she could have discovered and admired.

Perhaps the imaginary father in Ella's story in *The Golden Notebook* was the seed for Lessing's much later and final attempt to imagine an alternate version of her father's life. In what proved to be her final attempt to give literary form to her feelings about her parents, *Alfred and Emily* pivots directly on transformations from fact to fiction. Moreover, even her reconstructions of fact are more revisionist in literary terms than is Clancy Sigal's memoir of his mother's life in *A Woman of Uncertain Character*: *Alfred and Emily* features two complementary and mutually exclusive narratives of Lessing's parents' lives. The first part is a novella that departs admittedly and dramatically from the facts. The second is a factual, albeit occasionally speculative, reconstruction of her parents' actual lives in Banket, Southern Rhodesia, through which Lessing interweaves memories of her own childhood, adolescence, and early adulthood and life in the bush country of southern Africa.

Lessing believed that World War I decisively influenced the choices and emotional lives of her parents both before and after they met and married: "The First World War did them both in. Shrapnel shattered my father's leg, and thereafter he had to wear a wooden one. He never recovered from the trenches.... On the death certificate should have been written, as cause of death, the Great War. My mother's great love, a doctor, drowned in the Channel. She did not recover from that loss" (*Alfred* vii). Moreover, the decisive formative event of Alfred Tayler's and Emily Maude McVeigh's lives was also a defining one for Lessing: the war—"The Great Unmentionable," in her father's phrase ("My Father" 89)—"squatted over" her childhood, its toxic residue poisoning her own early years. Even late in her life, she felt, "here I still am, trying to get out from under that monstrous legacy, trying to get free" (*Alfred* viii). Lessing underscores the irony that her father's survival was the result of his absence, twice, from events that nonetheless altered the course of his destiny: "[his] appendix burst just before the battle of the Somme, saving him from being killed with the rest of his company. He was sent back to the trenches where shrapnel in his right leg saved him from the battle of Passchendaele" (*Alfred* 31). The severity of his war injuries necessitated his transfer to a British hospital, where his severely damaged leg required amputation; he nearly died during surgery. During his year-long hospitalization and a slow recovery protracted by shell-shock and depression ("My Father" 88), he met and fell in love with his nurse, Emily Maude McVeigh, whom he married soon after he was discharged from the hospital. Emily, who had struggled to become a nurse against her father's strong objections—he wanted her to attend university instead—was so competent in her vocation that she was offered a senior staff position at the hospital. With difficulty, she declined that promising career path to marry Alfred and accompany him to Kermanshah, Persia (now Iran), where he managed the Imperial Bank of Persia. Doris and her brother Harry were born during their parents' stay in Persia. When Lessing was five and her brother was two-and-a-half, the family relocated to Southern Rhodesia, where Alfred Tayler, who had always wanted to be a farmer, hoped to realize his ambition by growing maize in the British colony. In *Alfred and Emily*, Lessing captures the collision of her parents' different styles and ambitions through a particularly striking visual image: the Taylers' primitive mud and thatch domicile in the bush country of Southern Rhodesia was stylishly if incongruously furnished with Persian rugs, copper wash stands, and curtains fashioned from Liberty of London fabrics (*Alfred* 220).

However, the version of Lessing's parents' lives that readers encounter first in *Alfred and Emily* is not the factual one but the fictitious one, in which Lessing took significant imaginative liberties by altering key details of their histories. As she explains at the outset, she tried to imagine the lives her parents might have had "if there had been no World War One" (*Alfred* vii). It is a daring idea: to erase from history the Great War that so warped the lives of her parents, along with so many others' lives. She gives Alfred Tayler, who would "rather die than be a bank clerk" (14), the vocation of farming to which he aspired—accomplished not in Southern Rhodesia but on the less recalcitrant farmland of England. Although the paths of

Alfred and Emily occasionally cross in Lessing's fictitious version of their young adult lives, each is otherwise involved and they do not end up with each other. Rather, Alfred marries a different nurse—Emily's good friend and genial soul, Betsy—while the cooler Emily pursues her nursing career, disowned by her father because she did not abide by his strong preference for her to attend college. She marries a successful cardiologist, Dr. William Martin-White, but the relationship is devoid of warmth and passion and she finds no pleasure in the marriage. Providing insight into the conditions that produced her malaise, the narrator of the fictional portion of *Alfred and Emily* observes that she was

> brought up by an authoritarian father, in a strict cold house where everything went along by rule and rote. From that she escaped to the hospital, with its hierarchies, its disciplines, its order. She had lived her entire life bounded by rules and regulations and discipline. And now—there was nothing, and she did not know what it was she missed.... [S]he felt cast out on to a sea of possibility with no chart.... Her husband was not a loving man and there was certainly no fun in bed.... If she could have put a name to the dark pit, she would have felt better. (*Alfred* 54–5)

Indeed, Emily suffers from a version of the malady that, several decades later and in a different country, Betty Friedan would term "the problem that has no name."[2]

When Emily's husband dies of a heart attack ten years into the marriage, she is more relieved than grieved. Fortuitously, the doctor leaves a small fortune to his wife, a legacy significant enough for her to apply to the establishment of charitable schools for poor children in London's East End. At one point, she meets and feels romantically attracted to a Scottish storyteller who returns her affection. However, incapable of acting on her feelings, she realizes only after his death five years later how much she had cared for him. She dies of a heart attack at the age of 73, the age at which Maude Tayler actually died. Thus does Lessing extrapolate a life of public reward and private loneliness based on her mother's demonstrable administrative skills, philanthropic feelings, and lack of success in intimate relationships—the last a failure stemming from Emily's own emotional and sexual inhibitions. Of the promising but repressed intimate relationship between Emily and Alistair, the Scottish storyteller, Lessing explains that the idea grew out of her and her brother's encouragement of their mother to marry again after their father died. "It was partly selfish: we made no excuses about wanting that formidable energy directed away from us. But there was also concern for her" (*Alfred* 141). However, Emily Maude Tayler dismissed the idea out of hand, as if her children were crazy to propose such a prospect.

In the imaginary alternative script that that Lessing wrote for her father, Alfred Tayler has a satisfying marriage, becomes a successful farmer, raises twin sons, and lives to a ripe old age. In reality, Lessing's father "died at sixty-two, an old man" (*Alfred* vii) and a failed farmer. As Lessing remarks at the conclusion of the novella portion of *Alfred and Emily*, she "enjoyed giving [her father] someone warm and loving" as a mate (140) and no doubt also enjoyed substituting good health and longevity for the much less rewarding conditions of his actual life as a man with a missing leg and serious health problems.

In the second portion of *Alfred and Emily*, Lessing changes narrative gears to examine, apparently without embellishment or invention, the facts of her parents' lives as she came to understand them. She speculates that her father suffered from what would now be diagnosed as post-traumatic stress disorder and depression, conditions that in more recent years might have been more effectively managed through appropriate therapy and medication. In addition, he developed diabetes, a condition that was quite difficult to manage in the Southern Rhodesian bush and which significantly eroded the quality of his life. Her mother's story was far more difficult to plumb; Lessing found it almost impossible to reconcile the enormous discrepancy between the woman who was known as a lively "social butterfly" (*Alfred* 174) in Persia before Doris was born and the stern, resolutely conventional woman who attempted to stifle her daughter's need for independence while the family struggled to survive on a farm in the bush.

For the first time in her fictional and autobiographical renderings of her mother's life, Lessing speculates in *Alfred and Emily* on the circumstances that might have accounted for such a dramatic personality transformation. Not long after her family arrived in Southern Rhodesia, Emily Tayler suffered from an illness that lasted for a year, during which she spent most of her time in bed. Lessing concludes that the illness was a nervous breakdown, precipitated not simply by a likely case of malaria but by her mother's realization that she was inescapably trapped in a life that she found suffocating. Perhaps Lessing first began to draw on her mother's unidentified malaise as early as her first novel, *The Grass Is Singing* (1950), the story of the childless Mary Turner, who is married to an ineffectual white South

African farmer. As she struggles not only against life in the bush but against her husband's emotional and economic inadequacies, her only satisfaction in life becomes her cruel power over her African houseboy, who ultimately rises up to murder her. Less dramatic but almost as emotionally destructive, the extended period of malaise suffered by Lessing's mother was, in the daughter's interpretation, a response to the collapse of "everything she had been and was" (*Alfred* 159). Although she had no visible scars or wounds like those of her husband, she too was a victim of war: "[T]he real Emily...died in the breakdown she had soon after she landed on the farm. For a long time I knew I had never known my father, as he really was, before the war, but it took me years to see that I had not known my mother, as she really was, either" (192).

Like Clancy Sigal's *A Woman of Uncertain Character*, Doris Lessing's *Alfred and Emily* is the author's attempt, late in life, to understand as well as to subdue and transform the powerful parental figures of childhood. In doing so, she gives literary form to a life task that continues to be undertaken, often with difficulty, by many adult children, including a number of writers. One thinks of Virginia Woolf's masterpiece, *To the Lighthouse*, in part a *roman à clef* in which the author immortalized her parents, Leslie and Julia Stephen; their fictional stand-ins, Mr. and Mrs. Ramsay, are so universalized as the archetypal Victorian couple that they even lack first names. As Woolf later phrased it, "I wrote the book very quickly; and when it was written, I ceased to be obsessed by my mother. I no longer hear her voice; I do not see her. I suppose that I did for myself what psycho-analysts do for their patients. I expressed some very long felt and deeply felt emotion. And in expressing it I explained it and laid it to rest" ("A Sketch of the Past" 81). In this emotionally demanding endeavor, the writer attempts to resolve conflicted feelings about his or her parents. In *Alfred and Emily*, Doris Lessing rhetorically asks, "Do children feel their parents' emotions?" and answers, "Yes, we do, and it is a legacy I could have done without" (*Alfred* 258). To master that heavy legacy, she appends two unique chapters to the process of filial reconciliation, speculating not only on what her parents might have been like before she entered their lives but also what they might have been like if given entirely different scripts that better matched their personalities, ambitions, and capabilities.

In the spirit of reconciliation, Lessing attempts to understand Emily Maude Tayler apart from her own admittedly biased filial view of her, acknowledging with greater sympathy the limiting circumstances of her mother's life. From that perspective she discerns that, despite her mother's emotional repression, neurotic behavior, and regrettably stifled talents, she had at least one major positive influence on Lessing: through her storytelling skills and love of literature, the mother bequeathed to her daughter a lifelong love of books and reading. Thus, Lessing revises—perhaps slightly embellishing—her view of her mother, determining that "The real Emily McVeagh was an educator, who told stories and brought me books. That is how I want to remember her" (192). Like Clancy Sigal, Lessing both examines and revises the parent-child story, in this instance to offer a more charitable view of the mother who had for many years existed for her entirely in the negative.

What is both noteworthy and moving about Doris Lessing's complementary reconstructions of the lives of her parent is her attempt not only to explain but to forgive their respective shortcomings. In recreating their lives in both fictitious and autobiographical forms, she acknowledges the regrettable fact that, given their personalities and the significant obstacles that blocked their chance at happiness, they could not have been or acted otherwise. In this final attempt to give literary expression to her parents' stories, Lessing, a writer who frequently blurred the boundaries between fact and fiction, once again challenges generic conventions. However, in *Alfred and Emily*, as she improvises and extrapolates from the biographical details of her parents' lives both before and after she was born, she draws an unmistakably clear line between fact and invention. In the fictitious version, she gives each parent a gift that only a daughter who is also an accomplished writer can bestow: imaginary but richer and more fulfilling lives than the ones they actually lived. As she phrases it almost deferentially in the Forward to the complementary narratives, "If I could meet Alfred Tayler and Emily McVeigh now, as I have written them, as they might have been had the Great War not happened, I hope they would approve the lives I have given them" (*Alfred* viii). In effect, Lessing's mutually exclusive versions of her parents' life stories embody a liberating dialogue within herself.[3] What is startling about her imaginary and imaginative filial reconstruction is its implication for her own biography. Though the fictional version of Alfred fathers several children with his wife, Betsy, there is no daughter—or any offspring—of Alfred and Emily Tayler. Through this literary sleight of hand, Doris Lessing released herself from a damaging emotional legacy that it took her most of her lifetime to shed.

Conclusion

His, Hers, Theirs

"*Every novel is a story, but a life isn't one, more of a sprawl of incidents.*" Doris Lessing (Under My Skin)

"*But if the novel is not the literal truth, then it is true in atmosphere, feeling, more 'true' than this record [autobiography], which is trying to be factual.*" Doris Lessing (Under My Skin)

"*It was fun to invent and not just report Rose O'Malley. She is almost as dear to me as Doris Lessing once was.*" Clancy Sigal ("'You Can't Do It!'")

As Doris Lessing has expressed in so many words—a phrase that may be understood in more than one sense—there is no privileged position from which to articulate the "true" version of any experience. Not only do degrees of aesthetic and emotional distance influence the way even the most ostensibly neutral facts are reported but the passage of time inevitably introduces further alterations. The fictitious Anna Wulf's multiple notebooks and the pseudo-omniscient *Free Women* sections of *The Golden Notebook* together demonstrate that experience is not singular but multiple. What can be said depends on who expresses it, when it is expressed, and how and from whose perspective it is aesthetically shaped. Each iteration of the "same" event is a new expression that introduces a slightly different angle, if for no other reason than that one cannot step into the same river twice. The very act of giving literary form to experiences inevitably alters them even as it fixes them in time. Indeed, one result—to our good fortune as readers—is fiction.

As Lessing began to write her autobiography during the 1990s, she observed, "[Y]ou see your life differently at different stages, like climbing a mountain while the landscape changes with every turn in the path.... Besides, the landscape itself is a tricky thing. As you start to write at once the question begins to insist: Why do you remember this and not that.... *How do you know that what you remember is more important than what you don't?*" (*Under My Skin* 12, Lessing's italics).

Moreover, she stressed the difference between fictional and autobiographical "truth": "if the novel [*Martha Quest*] is not the literal truth, then it is true in atmosphere, feeling more 'true' than ... [this autobiography], which is trying to be factual" (*Under My Skin* 162). From a somewhat different perspective, Clancy Sigal, regarding his earlier published work, addresses a related aspect of the subject, acknowledging that

> Once you write a book what you've said in it tends to set in concrete. You've invested so much—a life—in it that it tends to keep you in one place. This inertia struggles with a horror of repeating yourself: the only solution is to shut up or write better, or at least differently. The writing, with its own logic, takes over and you may even find yourself betraying what you previously said. ("Going Away," *San Francisco Review of Books* 15)

In both their overtly and, as it were, covertly autobiographical writings, some of which falls within the genre of *roman à clef*, Doris Lessing and Clancy Sigal have given fictional and dramatic expression to different versions of their overlapping experiences, making creative choices that have affected both the essence and the "truth" of their fictions. Circumstances brought the two together for four years in a complex romantic relationship in which, despite their frictions and their eventual recognition of incompatibility, they shared politics, writing, and a number of other interests. Moreover, since both were writers—or, for Sigal at the time he met Lessing, an aspiring writer—their relationship became the raw material for their fictions, resulting in a kind of unnegotiated joint ownership of their literary half-lives for years afterward, particularly for Sigal. Through their creative "use" of each other—without agreement or consent— as models for literary discovery, improvisation, and transformation, both writers developed or perfected their craft.

On the one hand, the boundary line between fact and fiction is revealed to be a capacious one, permitting multiple transformations of the raw material on which writers necessarily draw. On the other, it is a contested one. The ethical question has yet to be and likely will never be satisfactorily answered: to what degree, if any, are writers responsible for the pain and distress that may result when they appropriate and disguise—perhaps sometimes only thinly—details from the lives of relatives, friends, acquaintances, or intimate partners for works of the imagination? Writers typically feel no responsibility to take into account the potential consequences, including psychological pain, of "appropriating others' stories" for their literary projects (Mills, "Appropriating Others' Stories" 197). As the memoirist Dorothy Gallagher instructively phrases it with regard to the genre of memoir—but as I apply her observation to fiction—"The writer's business is to find the shape in unruly life and to serve her story. Not...to serve her family, or to serve the truth, but to serve the story.... A writer serves the story without apology to competing claims" ("Recognizing the Book that Needs to be Written").

But there *are* competing claims. If Clancy Sigal's and Nelson Algren's reactions are any guide, the subject (or object) of what in its extreme form might be called literary identity theft feels betrayed by the person who breached his (or her) trust, appropriating details of their intimate relationship for literary purposes. In each instance, the pain was compounded by feelings ranging from a sense of injustice at the violation of privacy to feelings of exploitation or betrayal. For her part, Doris Lessing, like Simone de Beauvoir, was unapologetic about her literary purloinings, not least because she believed that fictionalizations (or dramatizations) based on her lovers and other acquaintances reflected not unmediated fact but "emotional truth" (*Walking in the Shade* 172). In defense of the fictionality of *The Golden Notebook*, she insisted that, "Strange as it may seem, I made it up..." (*Walking* 344, Lessing's ellipsis). As I have demonstrated in this study: not entirely, and not without reference to real life models—and to Clancy Sigal's private journals. Indeed, the ellipsis in Lessing's otherwise-emphatic statement invited scholarly exploration. Similarly—perhaps sincerely, perhaps disingenuously—Simone de Beauvoir expressed surprise that her former lover took such umbrage upon discovering a recognizable version of himself as the character Lewis Brogan in *The Mandarins*, since her noble intention, as she professed it with exclamatory emphasis, was only "to pay homage to Nelson Algren by writing our love story!" (Bair 411).

Whether or not Lessing and de Beauvoir *should* have been apologetic for their fictionalizations of their romantic liaisons depends on whether one privileges the aesthetic (artistic license) or ethical (psychological pain) side of the argument concerning authors' mining for literary purposes details from the lives of people they know. Nelson Algren got his own back with Simone de Beauvoir, not by fictionalizing his own view of their love affair but by attacking his former lover without disguise in nonfictional form. For years after publication of *The Mandarins*, he found opportunities to castigate de Beauvoir concerning what he regarded as her literary exploitation of their liaison and her public betrayal of him. Clancy Sigal, implementing an arguably more effective form of payback, perfected the same method of mining personal experience that Lessing regularly employed. Many years after the fact, he softened his view of Lessing's borrowings, objecting to what he regarded as my construction of him and Lessing as "practiced predators circling each other waiting for a chance to use the other person in a book" (Sigal's language, not mine). Rather, he countered, "it was a love affair where, all thunder aside, we helped each other's writing. She encouraged my ambition, I protected her from—as she felt it—the wolves of envy and sex yipping at her heels. I was the Guy, she was my Woman. It doesn't get more basic than that" (e-mail message to the author dated April 29, 2012).

Yes—and no. As Sigal's comment suggests, Doris Lessing—his "Woman" for a time—was, among her several roles in their relationship, his literary midwife, supporting him at the beginning of his literary and journalistic career as he struggled through the labor pains of a protracted writer's block. Over the course of a long and successful writing career that began in Lessing's flat, Sigal adapted and embellished experiences drawn from his life (and Lessing's and others' lives). Indeed, in the judgment of one of his critics, Sigal does not, strictly speaking, write *romans à clef.* According to Daniel Stern in his review of *The Secret Defector*, "A novel worth its salt will weave its themes and characters together to make a texture of revelation that is more than the sum of its parts. Not true here. *The Secret Defector* is an autobiography with the names changed, which is quite another thing" ("Surviving the Revolution" 28). I would argue, on the contrary, that, although Sigal indeed began by writing "autobiography with the names changed," his fiction evolved beyond that transparent method. While his earliest unpublished fictionalizations of Doris Lessing as Coral Brand and Sophie Ravenscroft are closer to disguised autobiography than to invention, as he began to transform his source material more freely, his characters came to depend less on factual resemblance. Concerning Doris Lessing and R. D. Laing, he shaped his characterizations, by way of exaggeration and humor, into comic satire and caricature.

It must be stressed that such literary appropriations and transformations are a matter of degree as well as kind, involving tonal variations that reflect different stages of emotional, aesthetic, and temporal distance on the authors' part. Characters in Doris Lessing's work that are recognizably modeled on Clancy Sigal—recognizable, at least, to those with the key—appear only in *The Golden Notebook* and *Play with a Tiger*, both composed while Lessing and Sigal lived together. After creating Saul Green and Dave Miller, Lessing was essentially "finished" with Sigal as a source of literary raw material. At about the same time that she and Sigal separated, she began to move away from autobiography as a source for her fiction. Much later in her life, she turned to the form of historical autobiography to revisit her earlier experiences, presumably without introducing fictional transformations of them. For Clancy Sigal, the autobiographical method and the raw—in more than one sense—material of his relationship with Doris Lessing remained central for far longer.

Taking a page from Lessing's most recent fictional experiment in *Alfred and Emily*—her unorthodox erasure of the Great War from history in order to imagine and fashion more satisfying lives for her parents—I would like to reconsider the subject of this study by performing a similar, albeit far smaller, act of historical erasure. If Clancy Sigal had not entered Doris Lessing's life in the spring of 1957, just as she was composing *The Golden Notebook*, she might very well not be remembered now for her pioneering account of a writer pushed to her emotional limits by forces both within and outside of her, including those imposed by the then-patriarchal norms concerning heterosexual intimate relationships. Nor might she be celebrated for her success in expressing in a complex metafictional novel, whose innovative form is now appreciated at least as much as its themes and ideas, difficult literary/aesthetic questions concerning the possibility—or impossibility—of capturing experience truthfully in language and the effects of time and memory on autobiographical writing. And, of course, there would have been no Saul Green. Similarly, if Doris Lessing had not rented a room in her London flat to Clancy Sigal at a critical juncture in his life, he might not have found his starting point as a writer—or, if so, certainly not in the manner he found it. The circumstances that led to the love affair between him and Doris Lessing also led him to spring himself free of a writer's block and to perfect his own form of disguised autobiography, increasingly leavened with the generous yeast of humor. And of course there would have been no Rose O'Malley.

As Doris Lessing acknowledged in an interview, writing *The Golden Notebook* "completely changed me" ("Writing as Time Runs Out" 89). Similarly, as Sigal expressed it through his narrative stand-in in "Lunch with Rose," Rose O'Malley became "an indelible part of my bloodstream" ("Lunch with Rose" 44). These recognitions signify what one might term the literary residue of the relationship between

Doris Lessing and Clancy Sigal. Whatever the mutual purloinings that transpired between the two lovers/writers and the distress that resulted from each mining the details of the relationship for his/her respective literary purposes, both also benefited creatively from their association. The love affair that caused Doris Lessing "as severe a dislocation of my picture of myself as ever in my life" (*Walking* 173) also decisively influenced the characters, ideas, and shape of *The Golden Notebook* and *Play with a Tiger*—"[n]ot necessarily facts, but emotional truth is all there" (172). In turn, Sigal, who acknowledged that "perhaps [Lessing] was right. It really is hard to make a fiction come alive and breathe" ("'You Can't Do It!'" 14), got his start as a novelist in part by transforming elements of his relationship with her into fiction. As I have argued in these pages, one of Lessing's several roles in Sigal's life was as his literary muse. As he comically phrased it in his send-up of the "real" Saul Green, who asks the naïve graduate student who has tracked him down, "[Doris] didn't put me, not the real me, into her stuff. But you're going to, right?" ("In Pursuit of Saul Green" 16).

Quite apart from the actual complex relationship between Doris Lessing and Clancy Sigal, their literary half-lives endure in their reciprocal creations—particularly Saul Green and Rose O'Malley, but also other characters and events that they bring to life in the not-so-gray (green, perhaps? or rose-colored?) area where life and art eternally intermingle.

Notes

Introduction   Where the Story Begins

1. The *New York Times* obituary of Sam Jaffe, founder and head of the Jaffe Agency from 1935 to 1959, states that the agency "suffered during the McCarthy era, when many of its clients were singled out by the House Un-American Activities Committee." "Sam Jaffe, 98, Hollywood Agent" [obituary].
2. Sigal began writing *Going Away: A Report, a Memoir* before he left the United States for Europe in 1956 and completed it in London. As a result of publication delays, it did not appear in print in the United States under the Houghton Mifflin imprint until 1962, the year after his later-written book, *Weekend in Dinlock*, was published in London by Secker and Warburg.
3. *Zone of the Interior* (New York: Crowell, 1976) was first published in Britain in 2005 (Hebden Bridge, West Yorkshire: Pomona Press, 2005).
4. In Lessing's view, her mother let it be known virtually from her birth that she was "not wanted in the first place; that to have a girl was a disappointment that nearly did her in altogether, after that long labour;...that I was an impossibly difficult baby, and then a tiresome child, quite unlike my little brother Harry who was always so good.... [M]y memories of her are all of antagonism, and fighting, and feeling shut out; of pain because the baby born two-and-a-half years after me was so much loved when I was not" ("Impertinent Daughters" 61).

1   Hall of Mirrors

1. See Introduction, p. 10, for a list of the eight books.
2. Subsequent references to the novel in this chapter and throughout the text are to the 1981 paperback edition (New York: Harper Perennial/Bantam Windstone, 1981), abbreviated as *GN*.
3. I am especially grateful to Clancy Sigal and to the Harry Ransom Center, The University of Texas at Austin, for permission to quote from unpublished materials in the Clancy Sigal Archive.
4. Riva Boren Lanzmann (1926–95) was a visual artist of Polish descent whom Sigal later described as a "Communist militant" ("Going

Away" 14). While she and Clancy Sigal were lovers, she was married to Jacques Lanzmann (1927–2006), later a literary critic, publisher, editor, journalist, scriptwriter, and lyric composer. For more about the Lanzmann family, see chapter 8 below.

5. This typescript draft (in Boxes 50.9 and 50.10, Clancy Sigal Archive, Harry Ransom Center, University of Texas) is included in folders labeled "CS writing about DL." Subsequent references in the text will appear as "CS writing about DL." Coral typescript or "Coral typescript."

6. Carole Klein, Lessing's unauthorized biographer, speculates that Jane Bond is based on Anne Edwards, a friend of Sigal's in Hollywood who "moved to London about a year after he did" and whose home "became sort of a refuge for Sigal.... Edwards remembers Sigal informing her that she had been turned into a character in *The Golden Notebook*. Presumably he was referring to the interloping Jane Bond" (*Doris Lessing* 176). In her autobiography, Anne Edwards describes her friendship with Sigal, "a former Hollywood agent (and Beverly Hills neighbor, and coworker of my ex-husband)." She notes that Sigal "hinted that Doris was the jealous type. If so, she had no reason to be jealous of me as Clancy was a good friend, nothing more" (*Leaving Home* 42).

7. Sigal categorically denies my claim that Lessing's literary method influenced his. As he objected, "IN FULL CAPS. I do NOT credit Doris as a major influence.... If there was any immediate influence, it was Simone de Beauvoir's *The Mandarins* and Sartre's *Roads to Freedom* series. Remember, I'd first gone to Paris and hung out on the fringe of the Flore café" (e-mail to the author dated March 10, 2012, Sigal's caps). When asked further about the influence of *The Mandarins* on his writing, he revised his earlier statement, elaborating, "'Influences' tricky. I'd read Mandarins but, on reflection, it didn't make that big an impact. Friendship with Algren more important and 'influential.' The more important immediate influences Hemingway, Dos Passos, Irwin Shaw, radio plays put on by Welles's *Mercury Theatre of the Air*, a Hungarian writer named John Pen, Thomas Wolfe (*Look Homeward Angel*), Salinger, certain comic strips like *Terry & The Pirates* and *Prince Valiant* for their narrative skills" (e-mail message to the author dated April 28, 2012).

8. Undated letter from Doris Lessing to Joan Rodker, headed "July" [from internal evidence: 1957], Box 2.6. Joan Rodker Archive, Harry Ransom Center. Subsequent references in the text will be abbreviated as "letter headed 'July.'" I am grateful to Ernest Rodker and the Harry Ransom Center for permission to quote from unpublished materials.

9. Undated letter to Joan Rodker, headed "Friday" [from internal evidence: summer 1958], Box 2.6. Joan Rodker Archive, Harry Ransom Center. Subsequent references in the text will be abbreviated as "letter headed 'Friday.'"

10. Undated letter to Joan Rodker headed "Sunday" [from internal evidence, 1958], Rodker Archive, HRC.
11. Letter to Joan Rodker dated December 4 [postmarked 1957], Rodker Archive, HRC.
12. Concerning Saul's description of Anna as "two women," Claire Sprague observes that "Molly is revealed as a part of Anna that has been temporarily given a separate, objective existence" (*Rereading Doris Lessing* 61). In this context, Beth A. Boehm contends that readers are invited to read the novel in mutually exclusive ways, as "realistic" and as metafiction: "Suddenly Molly's existence as a character in some fictional 'real' world—the world we believed was being created by 'Free Women'—is challenged; we must ask if she is merely a projection of Anna's split personality, and if she is, we then must ask what her appearance in the blue and red notebooks, the most 'factual' of the notebooks, tells us about the ontological relationship of those texts to some fictional 'real' world."("Reeducating Readers" 92–3).
13. FLN is the acronym for the Algerian National Liberation Front—in French, the *Front de Libération Nationale*—the revolutionary group that fought against France in the Algerian War of Independence during the 1950s. Web.
14. Over many years of critical analysis of *The Golden Notebook*, numerous scholars, including myself, have pondered the problematic fictional status of the character Saul Green. See my earlier analysis of Saul's ontological status as a character in *The Novelistic Vision of Doris Lessing* 102–7. See also Molly Hite, *The Other Side of the Story*, esp. 55–102; and Suzette Henke, "Doris Lessing's *Golden Notebook*" 159–87.

2   Truth Values and Mining Claims

1. As Beth A. Boehm observes, "Lessing bitterly complained about the many misreadings produced by critics of her novel and about the fact that no one noticed that her major aim was indeed metafictional, although she does not, of course, use that word" ("Reeducating Readers" 89). An early scholar of the novel, John Carey, concurs with Lessing's objection, observing that "[m]any of the early reviewers of *The Golden Notebook* treated it as important chiefly as disguised autobiography or as a statement of principle rather than as a novel." Carey cites half a dozen reviews that reflect this bias ("Art and Reality in *The Golden Notebook*" 439–40, n5). In a letter to Paul Schlueter, Lessing further objected that readers failed to read her fiction "in the right way. The right way to read a novel is as if its [*sic*] a thing by itself, with its own laws, with due attention to its shape, not with reference back to possible autobiographical incidents" (Letter dated July 24, 1965, qtd. in Schlueter 80–1). Schlueter proposes that readers regard

The Golden Notebook less as an autobiographical or confessional novel than as "a highly detailed examination of the forces which have gone into the complicated life of a real person who has some parallel characteristics with her fictional protagonist" (81).
2. The same phrase, "Anything processed by memory is fiction," was also stated by Wright Morris in a lecture at Princeton University on December 2, 1971, cited by Paul Fussell in *The Great War and Modern Memory* 205.
3. Susan Watkins observes that Lessing experimented with these constraints elsewhere in her fiction. In the pseudonymous *Diaries of Jane Somers*, the diary that the protagonist Jane Somers keeps "demonstrate[s] the 'fictive' or 'self-conscious' artfulness of life-writing (rather than its transparent reflection of reality)…in order to question how we define realism in literature and highlight its inevitable exclusions" ("The 'Jane Somers' Hoax" 84).
4. See Draine's full analysis of Rhys's *Quartet* in relation to the facts of her relationship with Ford and to his novel, *The Good Soldier* (Draine 318–37). See also Latham 160–1.
5. I am grateful to Ernest Rodker, executor, and the Harry Ransom Center, The University of Texas at Austin, for permission to quote from the Joan Rodker Archive.
6. Doris Lessing's brother, Harry Tayler, apparently objected to her transformation into fiction of factual events and biographical details from their earlier years. According to Dee Seligman, who interviewed Tayler during her trip to Southern Rhodesia in 1973, he found Lessing's "The Story of Two Dogs" "very much distorted." Seligman speculated that Tayler's "displeasure with his sister's work apparently stemmed more from personal disapproval of her use of autobiographical material than from any literary criticism" ("Four-faced Novelist" 6). "The Story of Two Dogs"—the final story in Lessing's collected *African Stories*—focuses on the 14-year-old first-person narrator who traces a series of events involving her brother, herself, and the family's two dogs (*African Stories* 616–36).

3 Plays and Power Plays

1. In answer to my query regarding the composition dates of his plays, Clancy Sigal responded, "Didn't write plays till we separated" (e-mail to the author dated April 29, 2012).
2. The BBC contract with Sigal for the play is dated 1983 (Box 53.3. Sigal Archive, HRC). According to Sigal, Irene Worth starred as Rose (e-mail from Clancy Sigal to author dated April 28, 2012). The specific date of the airing and the cast could not be further verified in BBC Archives or in the performance biography of Irene Worth.

3. For scholarly analyses of Lessing's fictional treatment of the subject of aging, see Claire Sprague, "Mothers and Daughters/Aging and Dying," *Rereading Doris Lessing* 108–28; Roberta Rubenstein, "Feminism, Eros, and the Coming of Age" *Frontiers* 22.2 (2001): 1–19; Ruth Saxton, "Sex over Sixty? From *love, again* to *The Sweetest Dream*," in *Doris Lessing Studies*, spec. issue: "Coming to Age" 24.1–2 (2004): 44–7; Virginia Tiger, "'Sleepers Wake': The Surfacing of Buried Grief in Doris Lessing's *love, again*, Paule Marshall's *Praisesong for the Widow*, and Margaret Drabble's *The Seven Sisters*," *Adventures of the Spirit*, ed. Perrakis 27–46; Phyllis Perrakis, "Navigating the Spiritual Cycle in *Memoirs of a Survivor* and *Shikasta*," *Adventures of the Spirit* 47–82; and Jeanette King, *Discourses of Ageing in Fiction and Feminism* 73–100 and 146–71.

4 Will the Real Saul Green Please Stand Up?

1. See Clancy Sigal's journal entry for March 3, 1958, qtd. in Chapter 1 above, p. 41.
2. For a fuller discussion of the overlapping connections among Clancy Sigal, the Lanzmann siblings, Simone de Beauvoir, and Jean-Paul Sartre, see chapter 8.
3. Years later, in a piece published just before he left England permanently in 1989, Sigal explained, "I was lucky enough to meet a miner named Len Doherty, also a writer, who understood my hunger because he too was famished for escape. We collaborated on my first book, *Weekend in Dinlock*, though only my name appeared on it. I wrote it but he opened his village, his pit, and himself to me. When I showed him my final manuscript, he shoved it back across the pub table and said: 'It'll make thy reputation, lad. But it won't solve thy problems. God Almighty couldn't help the likes of us.'" "Goodbye Little England," *Partisan Review* 59.1 (1992): 131.
4. For an analysis of "A Visit with Rose," see chapter 3.
5. Sigal does not recall the significance of either term in these similar titles (e-mail message to the author dated April 8, 2011).
6. I have borrowed Sean Latham's useful phrase, "narrative double," to describe a character in a *roman à clef* that is a fictionalized version of an actual person (*The Art of Scandal* 134).
7. For a fuller discussion of Simone de Beauvoir, Nelson Algren, and de Beauvoir's *The Mandarins* as *roman à clef*, see chapter 8.

5 A Rose by Any Other Name

1. "The Corpuscle Quartet" was the name of a singing group to which Sigal belonged during his adolescent years in Chicago (*A Woman of Uncertain Character* 242).

2. *North American Review* 268.3 (September 1983): 41. I am grateful to the *North American Review* for permission to quote passages from this story.
3. Jake Kerridge refers to a letter Lessing wrote in 1992 in which she provided her reason for "declining John Major's offer to make her a Dame Commander of the British Empire. She explained that she could not accept an offer made in the name of an Empire that she once campaigned against as a young woman in Southern Rhodesia.... [T]he reason she gave on another occasion seems just as valid: that being called Dame Doris would make her sound like something out of a pantomime" ("Doris Lessing and the Honours Pantomime," *The Telegraph* October 23, 2008. Web).
4. In her obituary of Shah following his death in 1996, Lessing described him as "a good friend to me, and my teacher. It is not easy to sum up 30 odd years of learning under a Sufi teacher, for it has been a journey with surprises all the way, a process of shedding illusions and preconceptions" ("On the Death of Idries Shah," *The Daily Telegraph* December 7, 1996. Rpt. (slightly revised) as "Summing Up: When Idries Shah Died," *Time Bites* 357).
5. For further discussion of the influence of Sufism on Lessing's fiction, see Nancy Shields Hardin, "Doris Lessing and the Sufi Way," *Doris Lessing*, ed. Annis Pratt and L. S. Dembo, 154–5; Roberta Rubenstein, *The Novelistic Vision of Doris Lessing*; and Müge Galin, *Between East and West*.
6. Sigal has indicated that the similarity between the names and the "Aztec queen" image are entirely coincidental. The script for *Frida* was based on "previous screenplays by multiple previous authors" and was "a 50–50 collaboration between Janice Tidwell (my wife) and me" (e-mail message to the author dated April 28, 2012). In another coincidence, a character in Doris Lessing's story, "Each Other" is also named Freda. The story, which Lessing identified as one of her "personal favorites," features an incestuous sibling relationship. See Lessing, *Stories* 345–53, cited by Judith Kegan Gardiner in "No Climax: The Rhetoric of Incest and Short Story Form in Lessing's 'Each Other,'" *Doris Lessing Studies* 9–14.

6 Life in the Interior Zone

1. According to Carole Klein, Lessing's unauthorized biographer, Lessing took LSD under Laing's supervision during the same period in which Clancy Sigal experimented with the drug: "Laing told Dr. Bob Mullan, a friend who has edited several books about the Scottish analyst, in addition to a 1999 biography, that he had given the drug to Doris Lessing over a series of six visits, but she fell into

the category of client who received no visible benefit from the experience.... Lessing... never publicly acknowledged such treatments, or any use of LSD" (*Doris Lessing* 197). In one of a number of conversations between Mullan and Laing published as a book in 1995, Mullan asked Laing specifically about his associations with Lessing and Sigal. Laing indicated that he had met Lessing only "on one occasion" (*Mad to be Normal* 303).
2. Elsewhere, I have examined in detail the parallels between Charles Watkins's and Jesse Watkins's interior journeys. See Rubenstein, "Briefing on Inner Space: Doris Lessing and R. D. Laing," *Psychoanalytic Review* 63.1 (1976): 83–93. See also my analysis of *Briefing for a Descent into Hell* in *The Novelistic Vision of Doris Lessing* (175–99). Marion Vlastos discusses similar and additional parallels in her analysis of the correspondences between Lessing's and Laing's views of madness and the psychotic experience ("Doris Lessing and R. D. Laing: Psychopolitics and Prophecy," *PMLA* 91. 2 [1976]: 245–58).
3. See also Mullan, *Mad to be Normal* 176, 303.
4. In an undated letter to Joan Rodker written in November 1957 (based on internal evidence), Lessing wrote, "I got fed up [with Clancy], started an affair with John Wain.... However, what it amounted to as things turned out [was] that I seemed to be committed to two men at once and this was a bit too much of a good thing." (Letter [November 1957], Rodker Archive). Wain was a poet, novelist, and critic, best known for his comic novel, *Hurry on Down* (1953). John Braine, a novelist associated with the "Angry Young Men" of the 1950s in Britain, is best known for his novel, *Room at the Top* (1957). Sid Bell's satiric couplets in the manner of the fictitious "Herb Greaves" may allude to the poet Christopher Logue, who wrote terse verses and with whom Lessing had a brief liaison in 1958 (letter from Doris Lessing to Joan Rodker dated "Friday" [1958], Rodker Archive).
5. Elsewhere, Sigal identifies "a clear-headed social worker named Sid Briskin" as one of the "real makers" of Kingsley Hall because "by then Laing... and I were walking on the other side of madness" (untitled reminiscence 215). Briskin was among the original founders of Philadelphia Association and Kingsley Hall, along with Laing, Sigal, and several others. Subud is an international spiritual movement that began in Indonesia during the 1920s.
6. A number of years before I began the current project that became this book or knew who Clancy Sigal was or knew of his association with Doris Lessing, I reviewed *Zone of the Interior* for the *New Republic*. I described the novel as "a marvel of verbal pyrotechnics," with Sigal taking his readers "through the psychic guerrilla warfare of the counter-culture, mercilessly exposing the rhetoric underlying the links between the 'fascism of irrationalism,' drugs, leftist

politics, and the politics of madness itself. If some of the resident schizophrenics occasionally seem more like caricatures than objects of sympathy, it is to remind us by exaggeration of the excesses committed in the appropriation of schizophrenia into the consciousness movement. Sigal's witty amalgam of mystical, military and political metaphors may skirt slapstick at times, but it never loses sight of its satirical target. *Zone of the Interior* is a comic verbal feast, with a fortune cookie at the end. Madness will never be the same" (*The New Republic* September 18, 1976: 31). Sigal wrote to me personally to express his enthusiasm for the review (Letter to the author dated November 24, 1976).

7. Thomas Szasz, author of the classic *The Myth of Mental Illness: Foundations of a Theory of Personal Conduct* (1961), lambasts R. D. Laing at length for his controversial theory of mental illness and his treatment of schizophrenic breakdown. In Szasz's judgment, Laing, a self-identified "antipsychiatrist" whose misuse of that term caused "great mischief" in the mental health profession, endeavored to heal patients suffering from schizophrenia and mental breakdown through techniques that were ethically irresponsible and fraudulent to the point of medical quackery (*Anti-Psychiatry: Quackery Squared* 59, 29). Szasz specifically mentions Laing's "violence toward his patient-friend-colleague Clancy Sigal...documented in Sigal's roman à clef, *Zone of the Interior*" (59). However. Szasz also criticizes Sigal and Doris Lessing for their naïve endorsement of Laing's theories and practices (60–5; see also chapter 3, "The Doctor of Irresponsibility," 59–85).

8. Szasz bluntly accuses Laing of "us[ing]...British libel laws to stop Sigal from publishing his book in the United Kingdom" (*Antipsychiatry* 71). The British edition of *Zone of the Interior* was published in 2005 by Pomona Press (Hebden Bridge, West Yorkshire).

7 Poetic License and Poetic Justice

1. Rpt. (slightly revised) in *Partisan Review* 59.1 (1992): 129–37, qtd. passage is on 130. In the original version, Sigal wrote, "The first writers I met here were astonishingly *dull* people" (my italics).
2. See chapter 4, n3.
3. Sigal's unpublished play, "Little Big Horn, N.W. 6," features the same Oedipal triangle. See chapter 3.
4. According to Carol Klein, Peter Lessing was "so troubled about being associated with Lessing[']s characters that he objected to having her later novel *Landlocked* (1965) dedicated to him." Lessing instructed her publishers to remove the dedication (*Doris Lessing* 177).
5. For fuller discussion of Lessing's association with Idries Shah and her turn to Sufism, see chapter 5.
6. For a full analysis of the novel, see chapter 6.

7. His profession more closely resembles that of Doris Lessing's older son, John Wisdom, who for a time pursued a career in forestry in Canada (Lessing, *Walking in the Shade* 247–8).

8 Variations on a Theme

1. Algren received the 1950 National Book Award for fiction for *The Man with the Golden Arm*, which was also made into a successful film directed by Otto Preminger and released in 1955. Web.
2. As Eric Alterman observes in an essay on twentieth-century *romans à clef*, *The Mandarins* is, in addition to its fictionalization of the love story between de Beauvoir and Algren, "a kind of intellectual cluster bomb. De Beauvoir idealizes her weird relationship with Sartre and bloodies virtually everyone in Paris who deviated from their ever-changing political line. She is particularly vicious toward her former friend and comrade Camus, thinly disguised as Henri Perron, to whom she attributes some of Sartre's most egregious real-life moral shortcomings" ("Inspiring Eggheads," *New York Times Books* July 26, 1998. Web).
3. "The night of my departure, I [Anne] said, 'Lewis, I don't know if I'll ever stop loving you; but I do know that all my life you'll be in my heart.' He held me against him. 'And you in mine, all my life'" (*The Mandarins* 708; cited in Bair 422).
4. Claude Lanzmann directed *Shoah* (1985), a celebrated and controversial nine-and-a-half hour long documentary film about the Holocaust. The late esteemed film critic, Roger Ebert, wrote of the film, "There is no proper response to this film. It is an enormous fact, a 550-minute howl of pain and anger in the face of genocide. It is one of the noblest films ever made." Web.
5. See also Sigal's comment regarding his literary influences: "Friendship with Algren more important and 'influential' [than *The Mandarins*]" (chapter 1, n7).
6. Letter to Clancy Sigal from Nelson Algren dated June 28 [1962]. Box 32.6. Clancy Sigal Archive, HRC; hereafter cited in the text as "Algren letter."
7. The film was in development in 2011, with Lasse Hallström as its director and Johnny Depp and Valerie Paradis—then married to each other—cast as Nelson Algren and Simone de Beauvoir. "Update on *My American Lover*...," Johnny Depp-Zone.com. Part-Time Poet blog post February 22, 2011. Web. The couple's subsequent separation seems to have put the film project on hold.

9 Of Parent and Child

1. Sigal's film script credits include *Frida* (rewrite), Miramax (2002), based on the love story of Frida Kahlo and Diego Rivera; *In Love*

and War (credited), based on *Hemingway in Love and War* by Henry Villard and James Nagel; New Line (1996); and *Maria/Callas*, based on Arianna Stassinopoulos's biography: *Maria Callas: The Woman behind the Legend* (New Line [n.d.]. Curriculum vitae [1990s], Sigal Archive).

2. As Betty Friedan introduced her now-classic study of women's emotional malaise within the patriarchal structures of marriage and society, *The Feminine Mystique*, "[t]he problem lay buried, unspoken, for many years in the minds of American women. It was a strange stirring, a sense of dissatisfaction, a yearning that women suffered in the middle of the twentieth century in the United States. Each suburban wife struggled with it alone. As she made the beds, shopped for groceries, matched slipcover material, ate peanut butter sandwiches with her children, chauffeured Cub Scouts and Brownies, lay beside her husband at night—she was afraid to ask even of herself the silent question—'Is this all?'" (*The Feminine Mystique* [1963] 11).

3. Pertinently, Susan Watkins queries, "Is the 'fictionalised' part of the book liberating because it moves away from the restrictions of fact, allowing [Lessing] to play fast and loose with the truth? Or is the memoir liberating because it generates a 'talking/writing cure' for the author, confronting the truth directly?" She concludes that "it is the creative interplay between both parts of the book," including the fact that "both and neither represent the 'truth', that allows Lessing to negotiate her 'monstrous legacy'" (*Doris Lessing* 162).

WORKS CITED

Doris Lessing

Books

African Laughter: Four Visits to Zimbabwe. New York: HarperCollins, 1992. Print.
African Stories. New York: Simon & Schuster, 1965. Print.
Alfred and Emily. London: Fourth Estate, 2008. Print.
Briefing for a Descent into Hell. New York: Knopf, 1971. Print.
The Diary of a Good Neighbor [writing as Jane Somers]. New York: Knopf, 1983. Print.
Each His Own Wilderness. New English Dramatists: Three Plays. Ed. and intro. E. Martin Browne. Harmondsworth, UK: Penguin, 1959. Print.
The Fifth Child. New York: Knopf, 1998. Print.
Five: Short Novels. London: Michael Joseph, 1953. Print.
The Four-Gated City. [*Children of Violence*, vol. 5]. New York: Knopf, 1969. Print.
The Golden Notebook. 1962. New York: Harper Perennial/Bantam Windstone, 1981. Print.
The Grass Is Singing. London: Michael Joseph, 1950. Print.
The Habit of Loving. New York: Thomas Y. Crowell, 1957. Print.
Landlocked. [*Children of Violence*, vol. 4]. 1965. New York: Simon and Schuster, 1966. Print.
love, again. New York: HarperCollins, 1996. Print.
The Marriages Between Zones Three, Four, and Five. [*Canopus in Argos: Archives*]. New York: Knopf, 1980. Print.
Martha Quest. [*Children of Violence*, vol. 1]. 1952. New York: Simon and Schuster, 1964. Print.
The Memoirs of a Survivor. New York: Knopf, 1975. Print.
Play with a Tiger. London: Michael Joseph, 1962. Print.
Re: Colonised Planet 5, Shikasta. [*Canopus in Argos: Archives*]. New York: Knopf, 1979. Print.
Retreat to Innocence. 1956. New York: Prometheus, 1959. Print.
A Ripple from the Storm. [*Children of Violence*, vol. 3]. 1958. New York: Simon and Schuster, 1966. Print.
The Sirian Experiments. [*Canopus in Argos: Archives*]. 1980. New York, Knopf, 1981. Print.
A Small Personal Voice: Essays, Reviews, Interviews. Ed. and intro. Paul Schlueter. New York: Knopf, 1974. Print.

Stories. 1963. New York: Vintage, 1980. Print.
The Sweetest Dream. New York: Flamingo/HarperCollins, 2001. Print.
The Summer Before the Dark. New York: Knopf, 1973. Print.
Under My Skin: Volume One of My Autobiography, to 1949. New York: HarperCollins, 1994. Print.
Walking in the Shade: Volume Two of My Autobiography, 1949–1962. New York: HarperCollins, 1997. Print.

Essays, Interviews, and Other Published Works

"Breaking Down These Forms." Interview with Stephen Gray. *Doris Lessing: Conversations*. Ed. Earl G. Ingersoll. Princeton, NJ: Ontario Review Press, 1994, 109–19. Print.
Interview with Roy Newquist. In *A Small Personal Voice*, ed. Schlueter, 45–60. Print.
Foreword. *The Diaries of Sofia Tolstoy*. By Sofia Tolstoy. Trans. Cathy Porter. New York: Harper Perennial, 2009, vii–x. Print.
"The Habit of Observing." Interview with Francois-Olivier Rousseau. *Doris Lessing: Conversations*, ed. Ingersoll, 146–54.
"Impertinent Daughters." *Granta 14: Autobiography*. Winter 1984: 52–68. Print.
Introduction. *The Mandarins*. By Simone de Beauvoir. 1960. New York: Harper Perennial, 2005, 7–9. Rpt. as "Simone de Beauvoir." *Time Bites*, 206–9. Print.
Interview with Jonah Raskin. *The Progressive* (June 1999). <http://www.dorislessing.org/theprogressive.html>. Web.
"The Need to Tell Stories." Interview with Christopher Bigsby. *Doris Lessing: Conversations*, ed. Ingersoll, 70–85. Print.
"The Older I Get, the Less I Believe." Interview with Tan Gim Ean and Others. *Doris Lessing: Conversations*, ed. Ingersoll, 200–3. Print.
"On the Death of Idries Shah." *The Daily Telegraph* [London] December 7, 1996. Excerpt at <http://www.dorislessing.org/on.html>. Web. Rpt. [slightly revised] as "Summing up: When Idries Shah Died," *Time Bites*, 357–68. Print.
"On Sufism and Idries Shah's *The Commanding Self*." 1994. <http://ishk.net/sufis/lessing_commandingself.html>. Web.
"One Keeps Going." Interview with Joyce Carol Oates (1972). *Doris Lessing: Conversations*, ed. Ingersoll, 33–40. Print.
A Small Personal Voice: Essays, Reviews, Interviews. Ed. and intro. Paul Schlueter. New York: Knopf, 1974. Print.
"A Talk with Doris Lessing." Interview with Florence Howe. *A Small Personal Voice*, ed. Schlueter, 77–82. Print.
Time Bites. London and New York: Fourth Estate, 2004. Print.
"Writing as Time Runs Out." BBC Interview with Michael Dean (May 7, 1980). *Doris Lessing: Conversations*, ed. Ingersoll, 86–93. Print.

Unpublished Materials

The Whitehorn Letters (1944–49). Doris Lessing Archive. University of East Anglia, UK.
Letters to Joan Rodker. TS. Box 2.6. Joan Rodker Archive. Harry Ransom Center, The University of Texas at Austin.
Letter to Clancy Sigal dated June 23, 1959. TS. Box 50.1. Clancy Sigal Archive. Harry Ransom Center, The University of Texas at Austin.

Clancy Sigal

Books

Going Away: A Report, a Memoir. Boston: Houghton Mifflin, 1962. Print.
The Secret Defector. New York: HarperCollins, 1992. Print.
Weekend in Dinlock. London: Readers' Union, 1961. Print.
A Woman of Uncertain Character: The Amorous and Radical Adventures of My Mother Jennie (Who Always Wanted to Be a Respectable Jewish Mom) by her Bastard Son. New York: Carroll and Graf, 2006. Print.
Zone of the Interior. New York: Thomas W. Crowell, 1976. Hebden Bridge, Yorkshire, UK: Pomona Press, 2005. Print.

Published Stories, Articles, Essays, Reviews

"An Abuse of Hospitality." "Rose & Her Friends, 'Three Stories.'" *North American Review* 268.3 (September 1983): 45–50. Print.
"Going Away." *San Francisco Review of Books* Winter 1987–8: 14–15. Print.
"Goodbye Little England." *Weekend Guardian* June 17–18, 1989. Rpt. [slightly revised] *Partisan Review* 59.1 (1992): 129–37. Print.
"Joan Rodker: Left Wing Broadcaster and Campaigner." Obituary. *The Guardian*, February 9, 2011. <http://www.guardian.co.uk/theguardian/2011/feb/09/joan-rodker-obituary>. Web.
Letter. *New York Times Books* December 27, 1998. <http://www.nytimes.com/books/98/12/27/letters/letters.html>. Web.
"Lunch with Rose." "Rose & Her Friends, 'Three Stories.'" *North American Review* 268.3 (September 1983): 41–5. Print.
"Pre-War Tough Guy from Chicago." Rev. of *Nelson Algren: A Life on the Wild Side*, by Bettina Drew. *Los Angeles Times* December 17, 1989. <http://articles.latimes.com/1989-12-17/books/bk-1394_1_nelson-algren>. Web.
"Recalling the Kindness of Algren." *Los Angeles Times* June 7, 1981: L3. Print.
"Rose & Her Friends, 'Three Stories.'" *North American Review* 268.3 (September 1983). Print.
"Short Talk with a Fascist Beast." *New Statesman*. October 4, 1958. Rpt. [abridged] September 8, 2008, vol. 137: 4913, 62. *Academic Search Premier.* EBSCO. Web.

"The Torrid Affair between Nelson Algren and Simone de Beauvoir." Rev. of *A Transatlantic Love Affair: Letters to Nelson Algren*, by Simone de Beauvoir. *Los Angeles Times*. <http://articles.latimes.com/1998/oct/18/books/bk-33545>. Web.
"A Trip to the Far Side of Madness." *The Guardian* December 2, 2005. <http://www.guardian.co.uk/books/2005/dec/03/society>. Web.
"Two Cats on a Mantelpiece." "Rose & Her Friends, 'Three Stories.'" *North American Review* 268.3 (September 1983): 50–2. Print.
Untitled reminiscence of *R. D. Laing. R. D. Laing: Creative Destroyer*. Ed. Bob Mullan. London: Cassell, 1997, 214–6. Print.
"Working with Laing," *New York Review of Books* December 19, 1996. <http://www.nybooks.com/articles/archives/1996/dec/19/working-with-laing/>. Web.
"'You Can't Do It!' I Shouted[.] 'Oh, Can't I?' She Shouted Back." *New York Times Book Review* April 12, 1992: 13–4. Print.

Unpublished Materials from the Clancy Sigal Archive, Harry Ransom Center, The University of Texas at Austin

BBC Contract for Radio Play, "A Visit with Rose." 1983. Box 53.3.
"The Ceiling and the Spike." TS. 1965[?]. Box 34.15.
"Ceiling Spike." TS. N.d. Box 18.9–11.
"The Corpuscle Quartet Rides Again." TS. N.d. Box 34.19.
"C[lancy] S[igal] Writing about D[oris] L[essing]." TS. N.d. Box 50.9: 98–119; Box 50.10: 95–7, 121–5; Box 50.11 : "CS on DL": four unnumbered pages headed "Lily."
Curriculum Vitae. TS. N.d. [1990s]. Box 53.3.
"Dolores." TS. N.d. Box 34.20.
"How to Live with a Lady Writer" and fragments of other drafts. TS. N.d. Box 50.11.
"In England: The Political, Sexual, and Medical History of Sidney Bell" (later titled "Gus Black, Secret Defector"). TS. N.d. Box 19.2.
"In Pursuit of Saul Green." TS. N.d. Box 34.18.
Journal: "Going Away." October 1956–December 1957. MS. Box 51.9.
Journal. January 1958–January 1959. MS. Box 50.8.
Journal. June 1959–March 1960. "Diary and Essay on Leaving England." MS. Box 50.2.
Journal. July–December 1959. MS. Box 51.2.
Journal. September 1959. TS. Box 50.18.
Journal. Late September 1959. TS. Box 50.19.
Journal. June 1959–March 1960. MS. Box 50.2.
Journal. 1962. MS. Box 12.7.
Journal. "Diary: 1968." April 30, 1968–February 20, 1969. MS. Box 12.3.
"Little Big Horn, N.W. 6." TS. Box 35.3.
"The Sexual History of Jake Blue." TS. Box 50.12.
Tribute to Nelson Algren. 1981. TS. Box 32.6.

Untitled autobiographical fragments. TS. Box 50.11.
"A Visit with Rose." TS. BBC radio play. 1983. Box 51.5.

Other Unpublished Materials

Algren, Nelson. Letter to Clancy Sigal dated June 28 [1962]. TS. Box 32.6. Clancy Sigal Archive. Harry Ransom Center, The University of Texas at Austin.
Rodker, Ernest. E-mail message to the author dated July 4, 2012.
Rodker, Joan. Introductory Commentary. 2000. Box 1:1. Joan Rodker Archive. Harry Ransom Center, The University of Texas at Austin.
———. Letter to Carole Klein. April 22, 1996. Box 2.3. Joan Rodker Archive. Harry Ransom Center, The University of Texas at Austin.
———. Notes concerning proof copy of *Walking in the Shade*, by Doris Lessing. TS. n.d. [1996?]. Box 2.6. Joan Rodker Archive. Harry Ransom Center, The University of Texas at Austin.
Sigal, Clancy. E-mail messages to the author dated April 8, 2011; March 10, 2012; April 19, 2012; April 28, 2012; and April 29, 2012.

Other Works Cited

Algren, Nelson. *Who Lost an American?* New York: Macmillan, 1963. Print.
Allardice, Lisa, and Sam Jones. "'It's Me? I've Won After All These Years?'" *The Guardian* October 11, 2007. <http://www.theguardian.com/uk/2007/oct/12/topstories3.books>. Web.
Alterman, Eric. "Inspiring Eggheads." *New York Times Books* July 26, 1998. <http://www.nytimes.com/books/98/07/26/bookend/bookend.html>. Web.
Amos, William. *The Originals: Who's Really Who in Fiction*. London: Jonathan Cape, 1985. Print.
Anonymous. "Sam Jaffe, 98, Hollywood Agent; Represented the Icons of His Day." *New York Times Archive*. January 19, 2000. <http://www.nytimes.com/2000/01/19/arts/sam-jaffe-98-hollywood-agent-represented-the-icons-of-his-day.html>. Web.
Appignanesi, Lisa. "'Our Relationship Was the Greatest Achievement of My Life.'" *The Guardian* June 9, 2005. <http://www.theguardian.com/world/2005/jun/10/gender.politicsphilosophyandsociety>. Web.
Bair, Deirdre. *Simone de Beauvoir: A Biography*. New York: Summit Books, 1990. Print.
Beauvoir, Simone de. *Force of Circumstance*. Trans. Richard Howard. New York: Putnam, 1963. Print.
———. *The Mandarins*. Trans. Leonard M. Friedman. Cleveland and New York: World Publishing, 1956. Print.
———. *A Transatlantic Love Affair: Letters to Nelson Algren*. Compiled and annotated by Sylvie Le Bon de Beauvoir. Trans. Sylvie Le Bon de Beauvoir et al. New York: The New Press, 1997. Print.

Benjamin, Jessica. *Shadow of the Other: Intersubjectivity and Gender in Psychoanalysis*. New York: Routledge, 1998. Print.
Boehm, Beth A. "Reeducating Readers: Creating New Expectations for *The Golden Notebook*." *Narrative* 5.1 (January 1997): 88–98. Print.
Booth, Wayne C. *The Company We Keep: An Ethics of Fiction*. Berkeley: U of California P, 1988. Print.
Carey, John L. "Art and Reality in *The Golden Notebook*." *Contemporary Literature* 14.4 (1973): 437–56. Print.
Cheuse, Allan. "A Comic Quest for Inner Peace: *Zone of the Interior*." *New York Times Book Review* June 27, 1976: 6. Print.
Cohn, Dorrit. *The Distinction of Fiction*. Baltimore, MD: Johns Hopkins UP, 1999. Print.
Donohue, H. E. F. *Conversations with Nelson Algren*. New York: Hill and Wang, 1964. Print.
Draine, Betsy. "Chronotope and Intertext: The Case of Jean Rhys's *Quartet*." *Influence and Intertextuality in Literary History*. Ed. Jay Clayton and Eric Rothstein. Madison: U of Wisconsin P, 1991. Print.
Duffy, Peter. "Character Assassination." *New York Times Book Review* January 16, 2011: 23. Print.
Eakin, Paul John. *Fictions in Autobiography: Studies in the Art of Self-Invention*. Princeton: Princeton UP, 1985. Print.
———. *How Our Lives Become Stories*. Ithaca, NY: Cornell UP, 1999. Print.
Ebert, Roger. "Great Movies": *Shoah* (1985). December 29, 2010. <http://www.rogerebert.com/reviews/great-movie-shoah-1985>. Web.
Edwards, Anne. *Leaving Home: A Hollywood Blacklisted Writer's Years Abroad*. Lanham, MD: Scarecrow Press, 2012. Print.
Ellen, Barbara. "'I Have Nothing in Common with Feminists.'" *Guardian/Observer* September 8, 2001. <www.guardian.co.uk/books/2001/sep/09/fiction.dorislessing>. Web.
Encyclopedia Britannica Online. <http://www.britannica.com>. Web.
Friedan, Betty. *The Feminine Mystique*. 1963. New York: Dell/Laurel, 1984. Print.
Fussell, Paul. *The Great War and Modern Memory*. New York: Oxford UP, 1975. Print.
Galin, Müge. *Between East and West: Sufism in the Novels of Doris Lessing*. Albany, NY: SUNY P, 1997. Print.
Gallagher, Dorothy. "Writers on Writing: Recognizing the Book that Needs to be Written." *New York Times Books* June 17, 2002. <http://www.nytimes.com/2002/06/17/books/writers-on-writing-recognizing-the-book-that-needs-to-be-written.html>. Web.
Gardiner, Judith Kegan. "No Climax: The Rhetoric of Incest and Short Story Form in Lessing's 'Each Other.'" *Doris Lessing Studies* 30.2 (Fall 2012): 9–14. Print.
Hammer, Rhonda, and Douglas Kellner. "Third Wave Feminism, Sexualities, and the Adventures of the Posts." *Women, Feminism, and*

Femininity in the 21st Century: American and French Perspectives. Ed. Beatrice Mousli and Eve-Alice Roustand-Stoller. New York: Palgrave Macmillan, 2009, 219–34. Print.

Hardin, Nancy Shields. "Doris Lessing and the Sufi Way." *Doris Lessing: Critical Essays.* Ed. Annis Pratt and L. S. Dembo. Madison: U of Wisconsin P, 1974, 154–5. Print.

Hazleton, Lesley. "Doris Lessing on Feminism, Communism and 'Space Fiction.'" *New York Times Magazine* July 25, 1982: 20, 21, 26, 27, 29. Print.

Henke, Suzette. "Doris Lessing's *Golden Notebook*: A Paradox of Postmodern Play." *Rereading Modernism: New Directions in Feminist Criticism.* Ed. Lisa Rado. New York: Garland, 1994, 159–87. Print.

Hite, Molly. *The Other Side of the Story: Structures and Strategies of Contemporary Feminist Narratives.* Ithaca, NY: Cornell UP, 1989. Print.

Ingersoll, Earl G., ed. *Doris Lessing: Conversations.* Princeton, NJ: Ontario Review Press, 1994. Print.

Innes, Charlotte. "A Life of Doing It Her Way." Rev. of *Under My Skin,* by Doris Lessing. *Los Angeles Times* December 8, 1994. <http://articles.latimes.com/1994-12-08/news/ls-6665_1_doris-lessing>. Web.

Jelinek, Estelle C., ed. *Women's Autobiography: Essays in Criticism.* Bloomington: Indiana UP, 1980. Print.

Kerridge, Jake. "Doris Lessing and the Honours Pantomime." *Telegraph* [London] October 23, 2008. <http://blogs.telegraph.co.uk/culture/jakekerridge/5522191/Doris_Lessing_and_the_Honours_Pantomime/>. Web.

King, Jeanette. *Discourses of Ageing in Fiction and Feminism: The Invisible Woman.* New York: Palgrave, 2013. Print.

Klein, Carole. *Doris Lessing: A Biography.* London: Duckworth, 2000. Print.

Laing, R. D. *The Politics of Experience* and *The Bird of Paradise.* 1967. Middlesex, England: Penguin Books, 1970. Print.

———. *Wisdom, Madness and Folly.* London: Macmillan, 1985. Print.

Latham, Sean. *The Art of Scandal: Modernism, Libel Law, and the Roman à Clef.* New York: Oxford UP, 2009. Print.

Lejeune, Anthony. "Reluctant Young Louts." Rev. of four books, incl. *Weekend in Dinlock,* by Clancy Sigal. *Times Literary Supplement* January 22, 1960: 45. *TLS Historical Archive.* Web.

Leonard, John. "The Spacing Out of Doris Lessing." *New York Times Books* February 7, 1982. <http://www.nytimes.com/books/99/01/10/specials/lessing-planet8.html>. Web.

Mills, Claudia. "Appropriating Others' Stories: Some Questions about the Ethics of Writing Fiction." *Journal of Social Philosophy* 31.2 (Summer 2000): 195–206. Print.

Mullan, Bob, ed. *R. D. Laing: Creative Destroyer.* London: Cassell, 1997. Print.

———. *Mad to Be Normal: Conversations with R. D. Laing.* London: Free Association Books, 1995. Print.

Parini, Jay. *Essays on Writing and Politics*. New York: Columbia UP, 1997. Print.
Perrakis, Phyllis Sternberg. "Navigating the Spiritual Cycle in *[The] Memoirs of a Survivor* and *Shikasta*." *Adventures of the Spirit: The Older Woman in the Works of Doris Lessing, Margaret Atwood, and Other Contemporary Women Writers*. Ed. Phyllis Sternberg Perrakis. Columbus: Ohio State UP, 2007, 47–82. Print.
Renza, Louis A. "The Veto of the Imagination: A Theory of Autobiography." *Autobiography: Essays Theoretical and Critical*. Ed. James Olney. Princeton: Princeton UP, 1980. Print.
Rev. (unsigned) of *The Secret Defector*, by Clancy Sigal. *Kirkus Reviews* February 15, 1992: 4. *ProQuest*. Web.
Ridout, Alice. "'What Is the Function of the Storyteller?' The Relationship between *Why* and *How* Lessing Writes." *Doris Lessing: Interrogating the Times*. Ed. Debrah Raschke, Phyllis Sternberg Perrrakis, and Sandra Singer. Columbus: Ohio State UP, 2010, 77–91. Print.
Rowley, Hazel. *Tête à Tête: Simone de Beauvoir and Jean Paul Sartre*. New York: HarperCollins, 2005. Print.
Rubenstein, Roberta. "Briefing on Inner Space: Doris Lessing and R. D. Laing." *Psychoanalytic Review* 63.1 (1976): 83–93. Print.
———. *The Novelistic Vision of Doris Lessing: Breaking the Forms of Consciousness*. Urbana: U of Illinois P, 1979. Print.
———. Rev. of *Zone of the Interior*, by Clancy Sigal. *New Republic* 175.12 (September 18, 1976): 12. Print.
Ryan, Marie-Laure. "Fiction and Its Other: How Trespassers Help Define the Border." *Semiotica* 138, 1–4 (2002): 351–69. Print.
Saxton, Ruth. "Sex over Sixty? From *love, again* to *The Sweetest Dream*." *Doris Lessing Studies*. Spec. issue: "Coming to Age" 24.1–2 (2004): 44–7. Print.
Schlueter, Paul, ed. and intro. *A Small Personal Voice: Essays, Reviews, Interviews*. New York: Knopf, 1974. Print.
Seligman, Dee. "Four-faced Novelist." *Modern Fiction Studies* 26 (Spring 1980): 3–16. Print.
Seymour-Jones, Carole. *A Dangerous Liaison: A Revelatory New Biography of Simone de Beauvoir*. New York: Overlook Press, 2008. Print.
Smith, Sidonie. *A Poetics of Women's Autobiography: Marginality and the Fictions of Self-Representation*. Bloomington: Indiana UP, 1987. Print.
Sprague, Clair. *Rereading Doris Lessing: Narrative Patterns of Doubling and Repetition*. Chapel Hill: U of North Carolina P, 1987. Print.
Stern, Daniel. "Surviving the Revolution." Rev. of *The Secret Defector*, by Clancy Sigal. *New York Times Book Review* June 28, 1992: 28. Print.
Stern, Daniel N. *The Present Moment in Psychotherapy and Everyday Life*. New York: Norton, 2004. Print.
Szasz, Thomas. *Anti-Psychiatry: Quackery Squared*. Syracuse: Syracuse UP, 2009. Print.

———. *The Myth of Mental Illness: Foundations of a Theory of Personal Conduct.* 1961. Rev. ed. New York: Harper and Row, 1974. Print.

Tiger, Virginia. "'Sleepers Wake': The Surfacing of Buried Grief in Doris Lessing's *love, again*, Paule Marshall's *Praisesong for the Widow*, and Margaret Drabble's *The Seven Sisters*." *Adventures of the Spirit*, ed. Perrakis, 27–46. Print.

Udovitch, Mim. "Hot and Epistolary." Rev. of *A Transatlantic Love Affair: Letters to Nelson Algren. New York Times Book Review* December 6, 1998. <http://www.nytimes.com/books/98/12/06/reviews/981206.06udovitch.html>. Web.

Ulin, David L. "Reflections in the Fragments." Rev. of *The Secret Defector*, by Clancy Sigal. *Los Angeles Times* June 21, 1992. <http://articles.latimes.com/1992-06-21/books/bk-1083_1_clancy-sigal>. Web.

"Update on *My American Lover* with Johnny Depp and Valerie Paradis." Johnny Depp-Zone.com. Blog post by "Part-Time Poet" (anonymous) February 22, 2011. <http://johnnydepp-zone.com/blog/?s=my+american+lover&x=-1137&y=-108>. Web.

Vlastos, Marion. "Doris Lessing and R. D. Laing: Psychopolitics and Prophecy." *PMLA* 91.2 (1976): 245–58. Print.

Walbridge, Earle. *Literary Characters Drawn from Life*: "Romans à clef," "Drames à Clef," Real People in Poetry. New York: H. W. Wilson, 1936. Print.

Walter, Nicolas. "Frank and False." *Prospect* July 1998: 8. Print.

Watkins, Susan. *Doris Lessing*. Manchester, UK: U of Manchester P, 2010. Print.

———. "'Grande Dame' or 'New Woman': Doris Lessing and the Palimpsest." *LIT: Literature, Interpretation, Theory* 17.3–4 (2006): 243–62. Print.

———. "The 'Jane Somers' Hoax: Aging, Gender and the Literary Marketplace." *Doris Lessing: Border Crossings*. Ed. Alice Ridout and Susan Watkins. New York: Continuum, 2009, 74–91. Print.

Weisenfarth, Joseph. *Ford Madox Ford and the Regiment of Women: Violet Hunt, Jean Rhys, Stella Bowen, Janice Biala*. Madison: U of Wisconsin P, 2005. Print.

Wilson, Elizabeth. "Yesterday's Heroines: On Rereading Lessing and de Beauvoir." *Notebooks/Memoirs/Archives: Reading and Rereading Doris Lessing*. Ed. Jenny Taylor. Boston: Routledge & Kegan Paul, 1982, 57–74. Print.

Woolf, Virginia. *A Room of One's Own*. 1929. San Diego and New York: Harcourt, 1957. Print.

———. "A Sketch of the Past." 1939. *Moments of Being: Unpublished Autobiographical Writings*. Ed. Jeanne Schulkind. New York: Harcourt Brace Jovanovich, 1976. Print.

———. *To the Lighthouse*. 1928. San Diego, New York, London: Harcourt Brace Jovanovich, 1989. Print.

Index

Algren, Nelson, 112–13, 118, 165–75, 177, 197, 202n7, 209n2, 209n5–7
   The Man with the Golden Arm, 165, 174, 209n1
   Who Lost an American?, 169
Alterman, Eric, 6, 209n2
Amos, William, 6, 68
Appignanesi, Lisa, 170
autobiography
   and doubled subjectivity, 57–8
   and ethics, 74
   and gender, 57–8
   historical, 5–6, 55–6, 62, 68, 74, 161, 176, 199
   Lessing on, 2–5, 62, 195–6
   and memory, 199
   theories of, 55–7
   and unreliability, 61
   See also disguised autobiography

Bair, Deirdre, 169–70, 197
Balliett, Whitney, 48
Barnes, Joseph, 71–2
Beauvoir, Simone de, 101, 165–77, 180, 197
   Force of Circumstance, 165, 169–70
   The Mandarins, 112, 166–71, 173–7, 197, 202n7, 209n2
   The Prime of Life, 173
   The Second Sex, 165–6, 174–5
Benjamin, Jessica, 65
Berger, John, 149
Boehm, Beth A., 58–9, 203n12, 203–4n1
Booth, Wayne C., 68
boundaries, psychological, 65–7
Bowen, Stella, 69

Braine, John, 140, 149, 207n4
Briskin, Sid, 111, 207n5

Camus, Albert, 209n2
Carey, John, 203–4n1
Chekhov, Anton, 66
Cheuse, Alan, 138
Cohn, Dorrit, 55–6, 60

de Beauvoir, Simone. *See* Beauvoir, Simone de
diaries and private journals
   and gender, 57
   in *The Golden Notebook*, 14–17, 26, 29–34, 38, 45, 61
   of Leo and Sofia Tolstoy, 34
   of Lessing, 3, 14, 162
   Lessing's reading of Sigal's, 31–6, 44, 51, 80, 103–4, 107–8, 149, 162
   of Sigal, 14, 17–18, 24–5, 30–42, 51, 81, 84–6, 90, 100, 103, 108, 115–16, 120, 133–4, 197
disguised autobiography
   de Beauvoir's use of, 112
   defined, 56
   and ethics, 68, 74, 169
   historical autobiography compared with, 62–3
   Lessing's use of, 13–14, 18–19, 24, 41, 51, 53–6, 62, 68, 70
   as method, 7
   Sigal's use of, 18–25, 32–3, 103, 107, 117, 120–1, 138, 143–4, 147, 158, 198–9
   See also roman à clef
Doherty, Len, 105, 151, 205n3
Donohue, H. E. F., 166, 172

222 ❖ *Index*

Draine, Betsy, 69–70, 204n4
Duffy, Peter, 68–9

Eakin, Paul John, 54–5, 68
Ebert, Roger, 209n4
Edwards, Anne, 202n6
Ellen, Barbara, 95

feminism, 94–7, 112, 124–5, 128, 151–2, 156–7, 160, 164–5, 169
Ford, Ford Madox, 69
Friedan, Betty, 160, 191, 210n2

Galin, Müge, 206n5
Gallagher, Dorothy, 197
Gardiner, Judith Kegan, 206n6
Goldsborough, Fitzhugh Coyle, 69

Hammer, Rhonda, 95
Hardin, Nancy Shields, 135, 206n5
Hazleton, Lesley, 95, 137
Henke, Suzette, 56
Hite, Molly, 61–2
Hobson, Harold, 78
Howe, Florence, 61
Howe, Irving, 126

intersubjectivity, 65–7

Jaffe Agency, 1, 12, 172, 201n1
Jaffe, Sam, 201n1
Jelinek, Estelle C., 57–8
journals. *See* diaries and private journals

Kellner, Douglas, 95
Kerridge, Jake, 206n3
Klein, Carole, 74, 92, 143, 156, 202n6, 206–7n1, 208n4
Klein, Joe, 68–9
Kotcheff, Ted, 78

Laing, R. D., 5, 111–12, 128, 134–44, 146, 156, 198, 206–7n1, 207n2, 207n5, 208n7–8

The Politics of Experience, 134, 136–7, 144
Wisdom, Madness and Folly, 138
Lanzmann, Claude, 101, 171–2, 209n4
Lanzmann, Evelyne, 172
Lanzmann, Jacques, 171, 201–2n4
Lanzmann, Riva Boren, 18, 24, 33, 101, 171–2, 201–2n4
Latham, Sean, 6–7, 143, 205n6
Lejeune, Anthony, 48
Lenglet, Jean, 69
Leonard, John, 125–6
Lessing, Doris
   birth in Persia (Iran), 8, 190
   break-up letter to Sigal by, 131–2
   brother of (Harry Tayler), 8, 190, 201n4, 204n6
   childhood and young adulthood in Southern Rhodesia (Zimbabwe), 8–10, 19, 59, 189–90, 192
   children of, 9, 209n7
   death of, 10
   diaries of, 3, 14, 162
   and drug use, 134–5, 206–7n1
   education of, 8–9
   father of (Alfred Tayler), 3, 8, 179, 186–94, 199
   first meeting with Sigal, 1, 13, 17–18, 20
   and "Jack" (Czech lover), 4, 10, 22–3, 59, 63–4, 70
   and marriage to Frank Wisdom, 8, 21
   and marriage to Gottfried Lessing, 9–10, 20–1, 59
   mother of (Emily Maude Tayler), 3, 8, 179, 186–94, 199, 201n4
   Nobel Prize in Literature awarded to, 1, 124, 158
   parents of, 3, 8, 179, 186–94, 199, 201n4
   and politics, 4, 63–4, 70, 73–4, 108, 122, 153
   and her reading of Sigal's journals, 31–6, 44, 80, 103–4, 107–8, 149, 162

and separation from Sigal, 19, 63, 89, 100, 108, 119, 124, 127, 131–4, 138, 199
and Sufi philosophy, 122–3, 141, 155, 206n4
Lessing, Doris, views and opinions of
on autobiography, 2–5, 62, 176, 195–6
on critics, 203–4n1
on de Beauvoir, 176–7
on her father, 188–90, 192–4
on feminism, 95, 152
on *The Golden Notebook*, 4–5, 53, 64, 134, 168, 197, 199
on her mother, 186–9, 192–4, 201n4, 204n1
on truth, 3, 195–6
on writer's block, 38–9
Lessing, Doris, works of
Alfred and Emily, 3, 179, 186, 189–94, 199
Briefing for a Descent into Hell, 123, 135–8, 144, 207n2
Canopus in Argos: Archives (series), 125–6, 161
Children of Violence (series), 3–4, 10, 123, 141, 186–7
The Diary of a Good Neighbor (writing as Jane Somers), 97, 204n3
Each His Own Wilderness, 72–3, 106
The Fifth Child, 161
Five: Short Novels, 10, 22
The Four-Gated City [*Children of Violence*], 123, 141, 186
Going Home, 10
The Golden Notebook. See Lessing, Doris, works of: *The Golden Notebook*
The Grass Is Singing, 9–10, 192
The Habit of Loving, 10
"Impertinent Daughters," 187, 201n4
Introduction to *The Mandarins*, 176
Landlocked [*Children of Violence*], 123, 208n4
love, again, 97

The Marriages Between Zones Three, Four, and Five [*Canopus in Argos: Archives*], 125
Martha Quest [*Children of Violence*], 3–4, 10
The Memoirs of a Survivor, 123, 187
"My Father," 186, 189–90
"On Sufism and Idries Shah's *The Commanding Self*," 123
"On the Death of Idries Shah" ("Summing Up: When Idries Shah Died"), 206n4
Play with a Tiger, 2, 7, 70, 77–84, 87–9, 92, 99–101, 103–4, 106, 109, 119, 143, 145, 154, 161, 163, 168, 176, 199–200
A Proper Marriage, 10
Re: Colonised Planet 5, Shikasta [*Canopus in Argos: Archives*], 125
Retreat to Innocence, 10
A Ripple from the Storm [*Children of Violence*], 4
The Sirian Experiments [*Canopus in Argos: Archives*], 125
The Summer Before the Dark, 97
The Sweetest Dream, 2, 95
This Was the Old Chief's Country, 10
Under My Skin, 2–4, 9, 21, 134–5, 176, 188, 195–6
Walking in the Shade, 1–2, 4–5, 10, 14, 53, 63–5, 71–4, 108, 131–2, 152, 162–3, 188, 197
"In the World, Not of It," 123
"Writing Autobiography," 62, 136
Lessing, Doris, works of: *The Golden Notebook*, 2, 4–5, 7, 95–6, 103–4, 145, 150, 173–7, 185, 189, 195
Clancy Sigal/Saul Green, 17–25, 32–42, 44, 46–51, 139, 150
Doris Lessing/Anna Wulf, 14–17, 25–31, 42–6
and ethics, 67–75, 197–8
Lessing on, 4–5, 53, 64, 134, 168, 197, 199
and *Play with a Tiger*, 77, 81–5, 87–9

Lessing, Doris—*Continued*
   and psychological boundaries, 65–7
   and "In Pursuit of Saul Green" (Sigal), 112–18
   raw materials for, 53–62, 199
   reception of, 152
   structure of, 14–16
   writing of, 13–14, 132–3, 175
Lessing, Peter (Lessing's son), 9–10, 18, 20, 89, 91, 152, 208n4
libel, 5, 68–70, 137, 143
Lowenstein, Oscar, 78, 85

McCarthy era, 1, 17, 23, 116, 148, 201n1
McKenna, Siobhan, 78
memoir. *See* autobiography
Mills, Claudia, 68, 70, 144, 163, 169
Mortimer, John, 149
Mullan, Bob, 206–7n1, 207n3

Osborne, John, 140, 149, 153
   Look Back in Anger, 106

Parini, Jay, 60
Perrakis, Phyllis Sternberg, 205n3
Persily, Jennie (Sigal's mother), 2, 10–11, 179–85, 188
Phillips, David Graham, 69
poetic license, 70, 145, 149, 161–4

Raskin, Jonah, 3
Renza, Louis A., 55
Rhys, Jean, 69–70
Rodker, Ernest, 72–4
Rodker, Joan, 17, 22–3, 42–3, 46, 70–5, 184
roman à clef
   Alterman on, 6, 209n2
   boundary-straddling nature of, 6–7, 55–6, 58–9, 68–9, 143, 144, 157, 161, 168, 187, 194, 196
   defined, 6–7
   and ethics, 67–70, 74–5, 143, 175
   and *The Golden Notebook* (Lessing), 13–14, 54, 56, 198

Latham on, 6–7, 143
   and *To the Lighthouse* (Woolf), 193
   and *The Mandarins* (de Beauvoir), 112, 166–8, 174–5, 209n2
   "narrative double" in, 205n6
   the novel and, 6–7
   and *Play with a Tiger* (Lessing), 199
   and *The Secret Defector* (Sigal), 70, 120, 157–8, 161, 198
   Sigal's satirizing of, 118, 174
   and *Zone of the Interior* (Sigal), 70, 143–4
   See also disguised autobiography
Rousseau, Francois-Olivier, 38–9
Rubenstein, Roberta, 205n3, 206n5, 207n2–3
Ryan, Marie-Laure, 55, 57

Sartre, Jean-Paul, 165–6, 170–2, 175, 202n7, 209n2
Saxton, Ruth, 205n3
Schlueter, Paul, 203–4n1
Seligman, Dee, 204n6
sexual fidelity, 16, 24, 28, 30–2, 80–1, 96, 104–6, 126, 170, 176
Seymour-Jones, Carole, 166, 169–70
Shah, Idries, 122–3, 155, 206n4
Sigal, Clancy
   birth and childhood of, 10–11, 180–2
   blacklisting of, 1, 12, 148
   at Columbia Pictures (story analyst), 1, 12
   and death of his mother, 183
   and drug use, 134, 138, 156, 206–7n1
   education of, 12
   father of (Leo Sigal), 10–12, 113, 118, 180–1, 184–5
   first meeting with Lessing, 1, 13, 17–18, 20
   first publication of, 12
   Houghton Mifflin Fellowship recipient, 2, 12–13, 24
   at Jaffe Agency (film agent), 1, 12, 148, 172

and Lessing's reading of his
  journals, 31–6, 44, 80, 103–4,
  107–8, 149, 162
and marriage to Janice Tidwell,
  177, 206n6
and marriage to Margaret Walters,
  91, 120, 156–7
mental health of, 12, 24–5, 42–4, 65,
  86, 137–44
military service of, 12, 182
mother of (Jennie Persily), 2, 10–11,
  179–85
musical tastes of, 64
National Book Award finalist
  (1963), 1
parents of, 2, 10–12, 113, 118, 179–85
and politics, 1, 63–4, 122, 146–8, 152–3
and separation from Lessing, 19,
  63, 87, 89, 100, 119, 124, 127, 131,
  133–4, 138, 199
and writer's block, 2, 12, 38–9,
  183–4, 163, 198–9
Sigal, Clancy, views and opinions of
  on de Beauvoir and Algren, 174–5
  on *The Golden Notebook*, 85–6, 145
  on Len Doherty, 105, 205n3
  on literary influences, 202n7
  on *Play with a Tiger*, 85–6, 101
  on Riva Boren Lanzmann, 201–2n4
  on writing, 196
  on writing *Weekend in Dinlock*, 205n3
Sigal, Clancy, works of
  "An Abuse of Hospitality," 127–8
  "The Ceiling and the Spike"
    (unpublished), 110–11, 145
  "Ceiling Spike" (unpublished), 41,
    86, 100–1, 104–7, 109–11
  "The Corpuscle Quartet Rides
    Again" (unpublished), 120–1, 124,
    128, 182, 205n1
  "CS writing about DL"
    (unpublished), 18–25, 32–3, 35–8,
    41, 88, 89, 103
  "Dolores" (unpublished), 108–10
  Frida, 129, 206n6, 209–10n1

"Going Away," 196
Going Away: A Report, a Memoir,
  1–2, 12–14, 18, 24–5, 29–33, 35, 37,
  48, 51, 63, 79–80, 103, 134, 201n2
"Goodbye Little England," 149,
  205n3
"How to Live with a Lady Writer"
  (unpublished), 36, 100–8, 171–2
"Joan Rodker" (obituary), 184
"Little Big Horn, N.W. 6"
  (unpublished), 89–91, 97
"Lunch with Rose," 121–9, 157, 199
"Pre-War Tough Guy from
  Chicago," 172
"In Pursuit of Saul Green"
  (unpublished), 111–18, 174, 200
"Recalling the Kindness of
  Algren," 172
"Rose & Her Friends, 'Three
  Stories,'" 120–30
The Secret Defector, 5, 7, 70, 88, 111,
  120, 145–64, 172–4, 198
"The Sexual History of Jake Blue"
  (unpublished), 18–22, 32, 99,
  103, 147
"Short Talk with a Fascist Beast,"
  116
"The Torrid Affair between
  Nelson Algren and Simone de
  Beauvoir," 174–5
"A Trip to the Far Side of
  Madness," 137, 137, 142
"Two Cats on a Mantelpiece," 127–9
Untitled reminiscence (R. D.
  Laing), 137–8, 140, 142, 207n5
"A Visit with Rose," 7, 89–97, 107,
  120, 129, 157
Weekend in Dinlock, 5, 12, 47–8, 51,
  85, 105, 134, 147, 151, 163, 201n2,
  205n3
A Woman of Uncertain Character, 2,
  11, 91, 142–3, 179–86, 189, 193
"Working with Laing," 138
"'You Can't Do It!'" 161–4, 174, 195,
  200

226 · *Index*

Sigal, Clancy—*Continued*
  Zone of the Interior, 5, 7, 70, 111, 138–46, 156–7, 159, 207–8n6, 208n7–8
Sigal, Leo (Clancy Sigal's father), 10–12, 113, 118, 180–1, 185
Smith, Sidonie, 57–8, 61
Sprague, Claire, 203n12, 205n3
Stalin, Joseph, 64, 73
Stern, Daniel, 198
Stern, Daniel N., 60, 65
Szasz, Thomas, 208n7–8

Tayler, Alfred (Lessing's father), 3, 8, 179, 186–94, 199
Tayler, Emily Maude (Lessing's mother), 3, 8, 179, 186–94, 199, 201n4
Tayler, Harry (Lessing's brother), 8, 190, 201n4, 204n6
Tidwell, Janice, 177, 206n6

Tiger, Virginia, 205n3
Tolstoy, Leo, 34
Tolstoy, Sofia, 34

Udovitch, Mim, 166, 175
Ulin, David L., 6

Viespi, Alex, 78
Vlastos, Marion, 207n2

Wain, John, 140, 149, 207n4
Watkins, Jesse, 136–7, 144, 207n2
Watkins, Susan, 159, 204n3, 210n3
Whitehorn, John R. M., 22
Woolf, Virginia
  To the Lighthouse, 193
  A Room of One's Own, 1, 157–8
World War I (Great War), 21, 189–91, 193
Worth, Irene, 204n2

Printed by Printforce, the Netherlands